Etel Adnan

Etel Adnan

Critical Essays on
the Arab-American Writer
and Artist

Edited by Lisa Suhair Majaj
and Amal Amireh

McFarland & Company, Inc., Publishers
Jefferson, North Carolina, and London

Frontispiece: Etel Adnan. Photograph ©2001 by Simone Fattal.

Library of Congress Cataloguing-in-Publication Data

Etel Adnan : critical essays on the Arab-American writer and artist /
    edited by Lisa Suhair Majaj and Amal Amireh.
        p.   cm.
    Includes bibliographical references and index.

    ISBN 0-7864-1072-8 (softcover : 50# alkaline paper)

    1. Adnan, Etel — Criticism and interpretation.   2. Arab
Americans in literature.   I. Majaj, Lisa Suhair.   II. Amireh,
Amal.
PS3551.D65Z66 2002
811'.54 — dc21   2001044928

British Library cataloguing data are available

Cover art: Etel Adnan oil painting of Mount Tamalpais.

Manufactured in the United States of America

McFarland & Company, Inc., Publishers
  Box 611, Jefferson, North Carolina 28640
    www.mcfarlandpub.com

For Andreas and Nadia
and
for Zaheyeh Ma'rouf Amireh (1926–2000)

Acknowledgments

We offer our sincere thanks to the contributors to this collection for their valuable work, patience and cooperation. Their participation and dedication made this book possible. We would also like to extend thanks and recognition to several artists and writers whose enthusiasm for the project was invaluable to us: in particular, Ammiel Alcalay, Khaled Mattawa, Barbara Lesch McCaffry, Jayce Salloum and Susan Swords.

Special thanks to Simone Fattal, director of Post-Apollo Press, for her generous help in providing information about Etel Adnan's books and art, and for permission to quote Post-Apollo publications of Adnan's work. We are also grateful to Samira Atallah and Nathalie Handal for impromptu research assistance on several continents.

We thank *College Literature* for permission to reprint a version of John Champagne's essay "Among Good Christian Peoples: Teaching Etel Adnan's *Sitt Marie Rose*," which originally appeared in *College Literature* 27, no. 3 (2000). We are grateful to Barbro Lindegren and Jan Lindegren for permission to print Eric Sellin's English translation of the poem "Kosmisk Moder" by Erik Lindegren. We are grateful to Haas Mroue for permission to reprint "Mary Rose" from his poetry collection *Beirut Seizures* (New Earth Publications, Berkeley, California, 1993), and to quote from his unpublished essay on Etel Adnan. And we thank Ammiel Alcalay for permission to quote from the unpublished preface to his essay "weighing the losses, like stones in your hand," which appeared in his *Memories of Our Future: Selected Essays 1982–1999* (San Francisco: City Lights Books, 1999).

Amal Amireh thanks co-editor Lisa Suhair Majaj for her professionalism, determination, and generous spirit; her friends and family for their support; and John and Julian for their love.

For encouragement and inspiration Lisa Suhair Majaj thanks Samira Atallah, Ruth Bayer, Souad Dajani, Nada Elia, Mona Fayad, Elaine Hagopian, Nathalie Handal, Soha Hassoun, Joanna Kadi, Mohja Kahf, Pauline Kaldas, Evelyn Menconi, Julie-Olin Ammentorp, Laura Porter, Therese Saliba, Ranu Samantrai, Stacy Spencer, Michael Suleiman, Paula Sunderman, and David Williams. Lisa is grateful to Amal Amireh for first suggesting that they undertake this collection together. Thanks to Abla Majaj and Marian Johnson for their enthusiasm, and to Nadia Alexandrou-Majaj for bringing so much joy. Most of all, great thanks to Andreas Alexandrou for his unwavering encouragement, support, and love.

Finally, the editors together offer their gratitude to Etel Adnan, who not only gave unrestricted permission to quote her writing and use her artwork, but whose multifaceted creative accomplishments and deep political commitment inspired this collection. We hope this book stands as testimony to her significance as a writer, artist and intellectual of international stature.

Table of Contents

SECTION II. Reading *Sitt Marie Rose*

Preface: Situating Etel Adnan in a Literary Context

Lisa Suhair Majaj and Amal Amireh

This collection brings together essays that reflect upon, analyze and celebrate the work of Etel Adnan. Adnan, who was born in Lebanon and came to the United States in 1955, is known across three continents for her visual artwork and for her writing, especially for her novel *Sitt Marie Rose*, which has been translated into six languages. She is a poet, writer, and public intellectual, author of thirteen books of poetry and prose. Adnan is also an artist whose oils, ceramics and tapestries have been exhibited across the United States, in many European and Arab countries and in Japan.

Adnan occupies a central role for a transnational community of writers and artists. Through her creative work, her regular contributions to journals such as the California-based *Al Jadid: A Review and Record of Arab Culture and Arts*, her role as president of the American organization RAWI: Radius of Arab–American Writers, Inc., and an active speaking schedule on topics ranging from the influence of Ibn Arabi on Dante to the philosophy of Islamic art, Adnan has helped to link Arab and Arab-American artists and writers, and to bring Arab cultural production into the space of American and European literature, philosophy and art.

Paradoxically, however, Adnan's body of work remains understudied, and her own stature as a writer and an artist remains under-recognized in a wider sphere. Although the wide and varied response to our call for papers revealed the extent to which Adnan's work has affected an entire generation of writers, artists, scholars and teachers, on the level of published criticism her work has nonetheless been, with some significant exceptions, in large part overlooked.[1] Despite her growing prominence in the English-speaking context,[2] there is little critical assessment of Adnan's artistic and literary *oeuvre*, and almost no discussion of the role of her work in the context of American and European literature and art. Meanwhile, within the Arab world her work is often overlooked because she writes in English and French, and as a result tends to be excluded from discussions about Arabic literature. This occurs despite the fact that Adnan considers herself an Arab, is attuned to political and cultural events in the Middle East, and writes about topics of crucial importance to the Arab world.[3]

Given the significance of Etel Adnan's work to a growing number of contemporary writers, artists and intellectuals, the increasing inclusion of her books on university curricula, and her stature as a widely exhibited artist, this lack of critical attention is striking. It is to remedy this lack, and to bring attention to a writer and artist whose work, we believe, will only grow in significance in the increasingly diasporan context of the 21st century, that we decided to embark on this collection of critical studies and reflections on Adnan's life and art.

Our initial introduction to Etel Adnan was through her novel, *Sitt Marie Rose*. This novel was first published in French in 1977 and quickly translated to Arabic and published in Beirut in 1979. Published in English translation by Post-Apollo Press in 1982, the novel was for a period of time distributed in the United States by the feminist journal *Sinister Wisdom*. It is through this distribution that the novel first began to reach a general American feminist audience. Meanwhile, the book had begun to gain recognition in Arab-American circles for its powerful depiction of the Lebanese civil war, particularly since this was the first novel to be written on the war. Despite the fact that it was published by a small press with limited distribution, *Sitt Marie Rose* had clearly already started to become what some have since termed "an underground classic." Although we discovered Adnan's novel in different ways and at different times, for each of us the novel provided a powerful encounter with a literary voice that reflected our own experiences and concerns in compelling ways.

As a novel by an Arab woman that addresses gender in the context of politics, and that is formally interesting and challenging, the book proved an effective text for classes on Arab women and on third world and multicultural literature. Moreover, as Adnan is an Arab-American, the book also served to link Arab and Arab-American writing, providing a point of entry to the transnational and postcolonial themes that inform contemporary writing by Arabs and Arab-Americans alike. In addition, the novel provided a useful starting point in our search for other Arab women writers to include on our syllabi.

Teaching *Sitt Marie Rose* in American undergraduate classrooms not only brought the novel into sharper focus, but also made us aware of the array of issues surrounding the reception of Arab women writers and their texts in the United States. Although more and more work by Arab women — and, increasingly, Arab-American women — is being included in literature courses on the undergraduate as well as the graduate level, there is very little critical material available about any of these texts or their authors.[4] In other words, although there is interest in discussing Arab women and reading their texts, such interest is not taken to the level of seriousness accorded other writers whose work is given extended scholarly and critical analysis.

This lack of critical work is particularly dangerous because Arab women writers are often taught in a context rife with stereotypes. Novels by Arab women are used in the classroom as sociological texts, "reflections" of the lived reality of Arab women — a reality assumed to be marked by unmitigated and ahistorical oppression, exploitation, and violation by Arab men. Students come to the classroom with preconceptions about Arab culture and Islam manufactured by Hollywood movies, CNN soundbites and best-selling romances of escapees and converts.[5] This context of reception affects how these works are read. Instead of being considered as works of art emerging from and rooted in specific historical and cultural contexts, they are used, all too often, as examples of how all Arab women are oppressed by their misogynistic societies. Thus, these novels fail to teach students something new, instead simply confirming what they already "know."[6]

We strongly believe that one way in which such stereotypical responses to Arab women's texts can be avoided is by making available critical discussions of their work. Such discussion helps readers unfamiliar with Arab culture to situate these writers, and underscores the necessity of granting Arab women's texts the same level of literary nuance attributed to the work of western authors. Moreover, it shows that there can be different and contradictory ways of looking at a text, a perspective that can help to undermine the reductionism and binarism inherent in stereotyping and "othering."

Although both of us were introduced to Etel Adnan through *Sitt Marie Rose*, we soon realized that her literary and artistic achievements extended far beyond this novel. Adnan is an author, a novelist, a poet, and a cultural critic. She has written documentaries and operas, short stories and plays,[7] and she is a visual artist in different media including pen and ink, oil, watercolor and tapestry design.[8] Moreover her work has inspired other writers and artists in far-reaching ways. We learned, for instance, that her poetry has been set to music and performed in concert halls in different countries;[9] that her words have been incorporated into artists' installations;[10] and that her writing and artwork have inspired the work of other artists and writers.[11] The more we learned about her different areas of creative production, the more impressed we became with her multidimensionality.

We also began to see the extent to which her work reflects, on a formal as well as a thematic level, the many kinds of linkages and mediations in her life — between linguistic and cultural contexts, between artistic genres, and between thematic preoccupations. Adnan is a writer who maintains a fierce engagement with political, social and historical realities, one for whom the experience of dislocation and the mediation of distance and longing are predominant themes. At the same time she is an artist acutely engaged with her immediate surroundings, with nature, with color and light — someone for whom the act of perception is itself the defining moment. Her work, both artistic and literary, builds on myriad junctures between perception, translation, poetic insight, and philosophical paradox; between an interrogation of selfhood and an insistence on being *in the world*. This merging of artistic and philosophical interrogation with political awareness and a postcolonial sensibility informs her cultural production in striking ways.

Our goal in this collection is to provide information about Adnan, to highlight her artistic and literary stature as one of the premier Arab-American writers and artists, and to make available a range of responses to her work. In addition, we wish to situate Adnan's work within the context of other literary and cultural discussions that are so important to the present era, especially those of postcolonialism, exile, and Arab women's feminism. It is our hope that this information and analysis will help readers to go beyond the prevailing generalizations and stereotypes about Arab women. We believe this book will be a useful tool for teachers, students and scholars in areas of study ranging from multicultural and literary studies to Middle Eastern and postcolonial studies. In addition, we hope this book will also provide a resource for Adnan's many readers and viewers outside the university setting.

This book is divided into two sections. Section I, "Beyond Borders: Etel Adnan's Writing and Art," contains critical essays about Adnan's poetry, prose, and art. The section begins with Eric Sellin's appreciative essay,

"Etel Adnan: A Cosmic Poet." Focusing on a reading of Adnan's poetry collection *The Indian Never Had a Horse* (Adnan 1985), this essay provides an overview of Adnan's poetic art, of its "architectonics and optics" — the devices and traits that mark her poetic expression. Significantly, Sellin's essay places Adnan within the context of modern American, European, and particularly French poetry. Emphasizing the element of the "interzone" in Adnan's poetry, a space in which author and reader "collaborate in the aesthetic experience," Sellin describes Adnan as among the most demanding and rewarding of poets.

In the next essay, "*The Arab Apocalypse* as a Critique of Colonialism and Imperialism," Caroline Seymour-Jorn discusses the political themes of this book-length poem, showing how Adnan, through her use of imagery, structure and language, launches a critique of colonial violence and the devastation of war (Adnan 1989). The essay not only delineates the political project of this poem, but also makes clear the inseparability of form and theme in Adnan's work as the poem's surreal images, fractured phrases and hieroglyphic-like drawings come together to reflect Adnan's message visually, structurally, and thematically.

Like Sellin, Michael Sells celebrates Adnan's poetic accomplishments and situates her work within a broad literary context. His essay, "Irremediable Ecstasy: Modes of the Lyric in Etel Adnan's *The Spring Flowers Own & Manifestations of the Voyage*," offers a reading of this volume of poetry that extols Adnan's ability to successfully translate the lyric into a more international poetry (Adnan 1990). In particular, Sells notes the intersection of Adnan's voice with Arabic and French poetic traditions, charting echoes of the Iraqi poet Badr Shaker as-Sayyab as well as Rimbaud in her work. As Sells shows, Adnan's accomplishment in this double collection is to reinvigorate the lyric as a poetic mode, bringing to it a tone that is not only international but also mythic in scope.

Adnan's rootedness in different poetic traditions, highlighted in these discussions of her poetry, is a consequence of her exile. This exile, as Wenchin Ouyang illustrates in her essay "From Beirut to Beirut: Exile, Wandering and Homecoming in the Narratives of Etel Adnan," is "not only political and cultural, but is also geographical, linguistic, literary, familial, and gender related." Ouyang provides a critical reading of Adnan's prose works *Of Cities and Women* and *Paris, When It's Naked* (Adnan 1993a, 1993b), exploring the role of displacement and marginality throughout Adnan's experience of exile as well as in her literary constructs of exile. The essay shows how Adnan's narratives trace a journey away from and back to Beirut, the city that is at once the center of Adnan's displacement and her focal point of longing.

Simone Fattal's essay "On Perception: Etel Adnan's Visual Art" shifts our attention to Adnan the artist, tracing her evolution as a painter and visual artist in multiple media. Fattal is herself a painter and art critic as well as founder of the Post-Apollo Press, publisher of a number of Adnan's literary texts. Her essay provides an overview of Adnan's artistic production and points toward the linkages in Adnan's work between verbal and visual media. Discussing Adnan's folding artist's books, Fattal notes that these books make possible a three-fold interpretation of the poetry text transcribed in them, bringing together the vision of the poet, the transcriber, and the painter. It is a perspective that informs Adnan's literary creations as well. As Fattal notes, "When you read the first lines of Etel's book-length poem *The Arab Apocalypse*—'a yellow sun, a red sun, a blue sun'—you realize how the two realms of her perception, the verbal and the visual, come together. Yellow, blue and red become attributes of the sun the way the names of God in Sufism are linked to our knowledge of God."

The last piece in this section, "Variations on an Andalusian Theme: Undated Letters to Etel," is a series of letters to Adnan by the Lebanese writer and intellectual Fawwaz Traboulsi. Asked to write an essay on feminism for Traboulsi's journal *Zawaya*, Adnan instead wrote a series of letters addressed to Traboulsi. These letters were published in book form as *Of Cities and Women (Letters to Fawwaz)*. Here Traboulsi responds to Adnan's letters, thus continuing an intellectual and literary dialogue with Adnan. In including this piece in the collection, we wish to situate Adnan in her Arab cultural milieu, a positioning that is often ignored. As Traboulsi's response to her makes clear, although Adnan has lived in America and Europe for most of her life, and although she does not write in Arabic, she is still rooted in the Arab world, and is part of a vibrant Arab cultural scene.

The second section of the book, "Reading *Sitt Marie Rose*," is devoted to discussions of Adnan's novel *Sitt Marie Rose* (1977). Because this is Adnan's most discussed and taught book, we felt an extended discussion of the novel would provide a valuable resource. The section begins with a poem by Haas Mroue, "Mary Rose," about the real-life Mary Rose Boulos on whom Adnan based her novel and whom Mroue knew personally.

The success story of Adnan's slim volume is delineated in Annes McAnn-Baker's overview of the novel's foreign-language translations and of its international reception. Translated into English, Arabic, Italian, Dutch, German and Urdu,[12] the novel has reached audiences well beyond Adnan's immediate Lebanese-French-American context, and is now in its fifth printing in English. As McAnn-Baker notes, the novel has won prizes in different contexts and has received favorable reviews in a variety of venues.

In their essay, "Transgressive Subjects: War, Gender, and Colonialism in *Sitt Marie Rose*," Sami Ofeish and Sabah Ghandour concentrate on the historical and political roots of the Lebanese civil war, discussing ways in which the novel "explores the role that patriarchy, sectarianism and colonialism play in the formation of Lebanese identity, and examines the possibilities of resistance to these categories." The historical and theoretical information on the history of colonialism and the workings of neopatriarchy in Lebanon that this essay provides is particularly valuable for readers who may be unfamiliar with the political and social history of the region. Ofeish and Ghandour's reading of the novel against this background provides an examination of the ways in which Adnan's novel acts out this "complex intersection of gender, colonialism and war's violence as these constitute subjectivities through well defined hierarchies."

In his essay "Ever since Gilgamesh: Etel Adnan's Discourse of National Unity in *Sitt Marie Rose*," Mohomodou Houssouba offers a more critical perspective on Adnan's project in *Sitt Marie Rose*. He questions, in particular, the discourse of pan–Arabism, which he believes undermines Marie Rose's rejection of the tribal loyalties of her warring society. Like Ofeish and Ghandour, however, Houssouba emphasizes the need for a historical perspective, especially on the role of political Christianity, in order to avoid the pitfall of reductionism. He warns: "Although the narrative captures the polyphonic diversity of the historical conflict, readers who are unfamiliar with the history of this civil war might construe a clear-cut distinction between the victim and the victimizer categories. In this case, Christians become the embodiment of the cruelty that dehumanizes everyone as the battle intensifies.... [This] constitutes a serious misreading of the allegory at the core of the narrative." Providing an account of the Gilgamesh story invoked in Adnan's novel, Houssouba explores its implications for the contemporary social and political conflicts the novel describes. These essays by Houssouba and Ofeish and Ghandour not only explain the historical and political contexts for *Sitt Marie Rose*, but also are themselves examples of contextualized readings of the work.

However, as John Champagne argues in his essay "Among Good Christian Peoples: Teaching Etel Adnan's *Sitt Marie Rose*," when it comes to reading postcolonial texts like *Sitt Marie Rose* in the American classroom, historicization and contextualization are complex processes. While the historicization that Ofeish, Ghandour, and Houssouba demand is important, it is, Champagne believes, insufficient. According to him: "students must learn to address the way the transaction between subject and text we call reading is necessarily structured by a history always already inscribed in their own subjectivities, as well as in the text. This history inflects not only their interpretation of any given novel, but also any attempts to understand something of the historical context out of which that novel was written and in which it circulates today." He argues for a pedagogy that "requires students to be attentive to their own historical positionings as reading subjects. Such a pedagogy ideally implicates the Western reader in, among other things, the torture and death of Marie Rose."

The final essay, Pauline Homsi Vinson's "Voice, Narrative, and Political Critique: Etel Adnan's *Sitt Marie Rose* and Nawal El Saadawi's *Woman at Point Zero*," places the book in a different context, but one equally important, that of Arab feminist writing. Homsi Vinson compares Adnan's novel to *Woman at Point Zero*, El Saadawi's most well-known novel, and the one that is most often taught in the American classroom. The purpose of the comparison is to show the shared threads between the two works and to situate both within a wider framework of Arab feminist discourse. According to Homsi Vinson, both Adnan and El Saadawi build on and redefine "the Shahrazadian connection between the death of the sexual female figure and the compulsion to speak," and in so doing, they "contribute to a feminist tradition where one woman passes on her story — and her voice — to another who writes it in her own literary creation, a reciprocal act of support and empowerment as well as a hope for meaningful change in the future." The comparative approach Homsi Vinson employs in this essay is particularly valuable in that it reminds us that there is a tradition of Arab feminist writing within which Arab women writers like Adnan and El Saadawi should be situated. This context is especially important in light of the way feminist Arab women writers are usually presented in the West — as either escapees from, or lonely crusaders against, their culture (see, for instance, Kahf 2000).

We hope that the group of essays we have assembled here will provide a valuable resource for those who are already familiar with Adnan's work as well as for those who are just discovering Adnan. We also hope that this book will encourage more scholarship about Arab and Arab-American writers, whose contributions, as Adnan's case illustrates, have yet to be recognized. Through her immensely varied, accomplished and engaged creative work, Etel Adnan has helped to open new spaces for Arab and Arab-American literature and art. For this, both her contemporaries and those writers and artists who come after her will remain in her debt.

Notes

1. Aside from reviews, most published criticism on Etel Adnan focuses on her novel *Sitt Marie Rose*. See, for instance, Harlow (1987), Fernea (1989), Accad

(1990), Cassidy (1995), and Foster (1995). For other discussions of Adnan's work, see Busailah (1986), Cooke (1988), and Alcalay (1993).

2. In addition to her own book-length publications, Adnan's poetry, prose, and drama have been included in a number of anthologies, such as those edited by Lowenfels (1968, 1973, 1975); Boullata (1978, 1982); Banker and Lashgari (1983); Orfalea and Elmusa (1988); Chase (1998); and Mattawa and Akash (1999). Her writing has also appeared in various journals, including *Mundus Artium*, *The Literary Review*, *Middle East Report*, *Resurgent* and others. A videotape of Adnan reading her poetry is available from the American Poetry Archives.

3. Despite this lack of critical recognition, Adnan's importance has nonetheless been noted by many Arab writers. Her poetry and prose have been translated into Arabic by some of the most prominent poets of the Arab world, including Adonis, Yusuf al-khal, Traboulsi, Fawwaz, Sargon Boulos, and Chawki Abdel Amir, and have been published in important Arabic journals such as *Shi'r*, *Mawaqif*, *Zawaya* and *Al Karmel*. Her novel *Sitt Marie Rose* was translated into Arabic by Jerome Chahine in 1978, soon after its original publication in French, and published in Lebanon in 1979.

4. The only noticeable exception to this is the case of the Egyptian feminist writer Nawal El Saadawi, who has been receiving significant critical attention. In addition to the many essays about her in academic and popular publications, there are two monographs about her work: Tarabishi (1988) and Malti-Douglas (1995).

5. The list of movies that stereotype Arabs is too long to include here. But examples of films that were protested by the Arab-American community for their misrepresentations of Arabs and Muslims include Paramount's *Rules of Engagement*, Twentieth Century Fox's *The Siege*, and Disney's *Father of the Bride 2* and *Aladdin*. Popular novels and "true account" narratives are often particularly virulent sources of negative stereotyping of Muslims and Arabs. These seem to have special market appeal when they tell the story of women, whether American or Arab, escaping from the "horrors" of Arab and Muslim culture. See, for instance, Betty Mahmoody's *Not Without My Daughter* (1987) and Jean P. Sasson's *Princess* series (1992, 1994, 1999, 2000). For critical discussions of the representation of Arabs in the American context, see Shaheen (1984), Terry (1985), Suleiman (1988), Kadi (1994), Stockton (1994), and Amireh (1997, 2000).

6. For essays that discuss the politics of reception of third world women writers, including Arab authors, in a transnational context, see Amireh and Majaj (2000).

7. Adnan wrote the scripts for two documentary films on the Lebanese war, and in 1984 collaborated with composer Gavin Bryars on the opera *Civil Wars*, by Robert Wilson, that was due to open the Los Angeles Olympic Games, writing the French section of the opera. That section of the multi-language opera was performed as a complete work in Paris and Lyon, France. Her short stories, published in various journals and anthologies, have been collected and published in Italian under the title *Al Confini della Luna* (The Border of the Moon; 1995). Her one act play "Like a Christmas Tree," set in Baghdad at the beginning of the Gulf war, was published in *Post Gibran: Anthology of New Arab-American Writing* (Mattawa and Akash (1999)).

8. Adnan's artwork is on display at the Tunis Modern Art Museum, the Royal Jordanian Museum, the World Bank, the British Museum, the Musée de l'Institut du Monde Arabe, the International Museum of Women in the Arts in Washington,

D.C., and in many private collections. Her tapestry designs are in a permanent file in The Contemporary Crafts Museums in New York and Los Angeles. She has exhibited her work in over 20 individual shows and 60 group shows.

9. For instance, British composer Gavin Bryars' 1998 CD "Cadman Requiem Hilliard Ensemble" (Fretwork Point Music) includes the "Adnan Songbook," a group of eight settings of love poetry by Etel Adnan, taken from Adnan's *The Indian Never Had a Horse*. This musical composition of Adnan's poetry has been performed in London, Vancouver, Cologne, Bergen, and San Francisco and was broadcast by the BBC. The musical score was published by the German publisher Musik Unserer Zeit in 1995-96. Bryars also set to music sections of Adnan's "Manifestations of the Voyage" from *The Spring Flowers Own and The Manifestations of the Voyage)* (Adnan 1990b). This composition has been performed in Cornwall, England. Another of Adnan's poems was set to music by the American composer Tania Leon and performed in New York in 1990. A two-page section from *The Arab Apocalypse* (Adnan 1989) was set to music by Henry Treadgill and performed in Oakland, California.

10. For instance, an artistic collaboration between writer and filmmaker Trinh Minh-ha and filmmaker Lynn Marie Kirby at the Yerba Buena Center for the Arts in San Francisco in 1999 included "long sheets of acetate [hung] from the ceiling, blazoned with lines of poetry by Audre Lorde, Barbara Guest, Etel Adnan and others" (Baker 1999, screen 4).

11. For instance, Ammiel Alcalay's essay "weighing the losses, like stones in your hand" (1999) bears complex traces of Adnan's writing and Alcalay's own response to her work. In an unpublished preface to this piece, Alcalay writes, "The confrontation with place in Etel Adnan's work, like memory, has allowed me to try and think about ways in which places and memories can be themselves and not at the same time. My experiences as a translator and scholar have shown me that in order for other kinds of sensibilities or works or languages to be absorbed in this culture, they first have to go through poets, to create the vocabulary of their own conditions.... I am quite convinced that because Etel Adnan's work has been absorbed by poets, its deeper influence can only grow." Similarly, artist, photographer and film-maker Jayce Salloum has spoken of the deep impact of Etel Adnan's work on his own. So too have writers Haas Mroue and Khaled Mattawa. In an unpublished essay, Mroue writes of finding *Sitt Marie Rose* in a London bookstore: "I read that book holding my breath, afraid to let go completely and be plunged back into the insanity that was the civil war in Lebanon. Etel captures that descent into hell more urgently than anyone I'd ever read ... I suddenly realized that I was not alone." Khaled Mattawa's prize-winning poem, "For Etel Adnan," published in the journal *Willow Springs*, directly conveys Adnan's influence and impact (Mattawa 1994).

12. See Adnan (1979a; 1979b; 1979c; 1982; 1988; 1997).

References

Accad, Evelyne. 1990. "Etel Adnan: Courage, Engagement and Self-Sacrifice," in *Sexuality and War: Literary Masks of the Middle East*. New York: New York University Press.

Adnan, Etel. 1977. *Sitt Marie-Rose*. Paris: editions des Femmes.

_____. 1979a. *Sitt Marie Rose.* (Arabic). Translated by Gerome Chahine. Beirut: al-Mu'assasa al-'arabiyya lil-dirasat wal-nashr. Reprinted, with an introduction by Ferial Ghazoul, 2000. Cairo: al-Hay'a al-'Amma li-Qusur al-Thaqafa.

_____. 1979b. *Sitt Marie Rose.* (Dutch). The Hague: Novip.

_____. 1979c. *Sitt Marie Rose.* (Italian). Milano: Edizioni Delle Donne.

_____. 1982. *Sitt Marie Rose.* Translated by Georgina Kleege. Sausalito, CA: Post-Apollo.

_____. 1985. *The Indian Never Had a Horse & Other Poems.* Sausalito, CA: Post-Apollo.

_____. 1988. *Sitt Marie Rose.* (German). Frankfurt: Suhrkamp Verlag.

_____. 1989. *The Arab Apocalypse.* Sausalito, CA: Post-Apollo.

_____. 1990. *The Spring Flowers Own & The Manifestations of the Voyage.* Sausalito, CA: Post-Apollo.

_____. 1993a. *Of Cities and Women (Letters to Fawwaz).* Sausalito, CA: Post-Apollo.

_____. 1993b. *Paris, When It's Naked.* Sausalito, CA: Post-Apollo.

_____. 1995. *Al Confini Della Luna (Short Stories)* (The Border of the Moon). Rome: Ed. Jouvenance.

_____. 1997. *Sitt Marie Rose.* (Urdu). Pakistan.

Alcalay, Ammiel. 1993. *After Jews and Arabs: Remaking Levantine Culture.* Minneapolis and London: University of Minnesota Press.

Amireh, Amal. 1997. "Problems and Prospects for Publishing in the West: Arab Women Writers Today." *Against the Current* (March/April): 21–24.

_____. 2000. "Framing Nawal El-Saadawi: Arab Feminism in a Transnational World." *Signs: Journal of Women in Culture and Society.* 26 (1): 215–249.

_____. 1999. "weighing the losses, like stones in your hand." In *Memories of Our Future: Selected Essays 1982–1999,* 3–20. San Francisco: City Lights.

_____, and Lisa Suhair Majaj, eds. 2000. *Going Global: The Transnational Reception of Third World Women Writers.* New York and London: Garland.

Baker, Kenneth. 1999. "Collaborative Ideas at Yerba Buena 'Team Work' Shows Cover All the Bases." *San Francisco Chronicle.* 10 July. Online. 7 July2000.

Banker, Joanne and Deirdre Lashgari, eds. 1983. *Women Poets of the World.* Indianapolis, Indiana: Macmillan.

Boullatta, Kamal, ed. 1978. *Women of the Fertile Crescent: Modern Poetry by Arab Women.* Washington, D.C.: Three Continents.

_____. ed. 1982. *And Not Surrender: American Poets on Lebanon.* Washington, D.C.: Arab-American Cultural Foundation.

Busailah, Reja-e. 1986. "'Unless You Change the World': The Art and Thought of Etel Adnan." *Arab Studies Quarterly* 8 (3): 304–317.

Cassidy, Madeline. 1995. "'Love is a Supreme Violence': The Deconstruction of Gendered Space in Etel Adnan's *Sitt Marie Rose.* In *Violence, Silence, and Anger: Women's Writing as Transgression,* edited by Deirdre Lashgari, 282–290. Charlottesville: University Press of Virginia.

Chase, Clifford, ed. 1998. *Queer 13: Lesbian and Gay Writers Recall Seventh Grade.* New York: Morrow.

Cooke, Miriam. 1988. *War's Other Voices: Women Writers on the Lebanese Civil War.* Cambridge: Cambridge University Press.

Fernea, Elizabeth Warnock. 1989. "The Case of *Sitt Marie Rose*: An Ethnographic

Novel from the Modern Middle East." *Studies in Literature and Anthropology* 20: 153–64.

Foster, Thomas. 1995. "Circles of Oppression, Circles of Repression: Etel Adnan's *Sitt Marie Rose.*" *PMLA* 110.1 (January): 59–74.

Harlow, Barbara. 1987. *Resistance Literature.* New York: Methuen.

Kadi, Joanna, ed. 1994. *Food for Our Grandmothers: Writings by Arab-American and Arab-Canadian Feminists.* Boston, MA: South End.

Kahf, Mohja. 2000. "Packaging 'Huda': Sha'rawi's Memoirs in the U.S. Reception Environment." In *Going Global: The Transnational Reception of Third World Women Writers,* edited by Amal Amireh and Lisa Suhair Majaj, 148–172. New York: Garland.

Lowenfels, Walter, ed. 1968. *Where is Vietnam?* New York: Doubleday.

_____. ed. 1973. *In the Belly of the Shark.* New York: Anchor.

_____. ed. 1975. *For Neruda, for Chile: An International Anthology.* Boston: Beacon.

Mahmoody, Betty. 1987. *Not Without My Daughter.* New York: St. Martins.

Malti-Douglas, Fedwa. 1995. *Men, Women, and God(s): Nawal El Saadawi and Arab Feminist Poetics.* Berkeley, Los Angeles and London: University of California Press.

Mattawa, Khaled. 1994. "For Etel Adnan." *Willow Springs* Issue 33 (Winter).

_____, and Munir Akash, eds. 1999. *Post Gibran: Anthology of New Arab American Writing.* W. Bethesda, Maryland: Jusoor. Distributed by Syracuse University Press.

Orfalea, Gregory and Sharif Elmusa, eds. 1988. *Grape Leaves: A Century of Arab American Poetry.* Salt Lake City: University of Utah Press.

Shaheen, Jack G. 1984. *The TV Arab.* Bowling Green, OH: Bowling Green State University Popular Press.

Sasson, Jean P. 1992. *Princess: A True Story of Life Behind the Veil in Saudi Arabia.* New York: Morrow.

_____. 1994. *Princess Sultana's Daughters.* New York: Doubleday.

_____. 1999. *Desert Royal.* Amherst, MA: Acacia Press.

_____. 2000. *Princess Sultana's Circle.* Woodstock, NY: Windsor-Brooke.

Stockton, Ronald. 1994. "Ethnic Archetypes and the Arab Image." In *The Development of Arab-American Identity,* edited by Ernest McCarus, 119-153. Ann Arbor: University of Michigan Press.

Suleiman, Michael W. 1988. *The Arabs in the Mind of America.* Brattleboro, VT: Amana Books.

Tarabishi, George. 1988. *Woman Against Her Sex: A Critique of Nawal el-Saadawi.* London: Saqi.

Terry, Janice J. 1985. *Mistaken Identity: Arab Stereotypes in Popular Writing.* Washington, D.C.: American-Arab Affairs Council.

Introduction: Biographical and Career Highlights

Lisa Suhair Majaj and Amal Amireh

Etel Adnan was born in Beirut, Lebanon, in 1925. The daughter of a Christian Greek mother and a Muslim Syrian father (an Ottoman officer), she grew up positioned between cultural, religious and linguistic worlds. This anomalous positioning was accentuated by the French education she received at a convent school in Lebanon, which was itself a legacy of Lebanon's colonial history. Describing the effect of this education on a whole generation of Lebanese, Adnan writes:

> We were taught the same books as the French kids in Europe, the capital of the world seemed to be Paris, and we learned the names of all kinds of things we never heard or saw: French rivers, French mountains, the history of blue-eyed people who had built an empire. … Somehow we breathed an air where it seemed that being French was superior to anyone, and as we were obviously not French, the best thing was at least to speak French. Little by little, a whole generation of educated boys and girls felt superior to the poorer kids who did not go to school and spoke only Arabic. Arabic was equated with backwardness and shame [Adnan 1996b, screen 2].

This education alienated Adnan from her Arab context, and produced in her a sense of schism. Although Adnan's parents spoke Turkish at home to each other, and Adnan spent her earliest years speaking Greek and Turkish,

13

by the age of five she was speaking "French and only French" (Adnan 1990a, 7). As the essay by Wen-chin Ouyang in this collection indicates, this had a strong impact on her awareness and sense of self.

Adnan attended the French convent school until the age of fifteen, when she was taken out because of soaring prices during WWII. She then went to work for the French Information Bureau. "It was the beginning of adventure," Adnan recalls (1990a, 15). She earned her baccalaureate while working, and enrolled at the Ecole Supérieure des Lettres de Beyrouth. It was here, while in a class with French essayist and literary critic Gabriel Bounoure, that she came to believe "that poetry was the purpose of life, poetry as a counter-profession, as an expression of personal and mental freedom, as perpetual rebellion" (17). Indeed, she says, "For years I was convinced that the whole human race was created in order to sit on sidewalks and read poetry" (1985c, 116). This view of poetry as "a revolution, and a permanent voyage" (Adnan 1990a, 18) was to continue throughout Adnan's life.

Adnan began writing poetry, in French, in her twenties. Her first work was a long poem called "Le Livre de la Mer" (The Book of the Sea). However, even at this early stage Adnan was made crucially conscious of the problem of writing in a "foreign" language. The poem sought to portray "the interrelation between the sun and the sea as a kind of cosmic eroticism" in which the sea was portrayed as a woman and the sun as a masculine principle (Adnan 1996b, screen 4). Later attempts to translate the poem into Arabic presented difficulties, because the *sea* in French is a feminine noun and the *sun* is masculine, while in Arabic the opposite is true. Indeed, Adnan once commented that the poem "is, in a genuine sense, unthinkable in Arabic" (screen 4).[1] This struggle of how to express herself in a language that was at odds with her Arab identity and yet deeply engrained in her was to become a life-long focus for Adnan.

In November 1949, Adnan left Lebanon for Paris on a scholarship to study philosophy at the Sorbonne. Her choice of subject represented a continuation of her interest in poetry. As she says, "I considered philosophy, after Holderlin and Heidegger, as finding its greatest expression in poetry" (Adnan 1996b, screen 5). She met some American students in Paris and by early 1955 had moved to the United States, stopping first in New York and then continuing to Berkeley, California, for post-graduate studies in philosophy. She also spent a year at Harvard. The shift from the Sorbonne to the University of California was, Adnan says, "like changing planets" (screen 4). However, it was also to prove singularly important for her future literary career, for it was here that Adnan "fell in love with the American language." She was "thrilled by the Californian way of speaking

English, by the style, the lingo, the slang, of American publications, by the 'specialized' languages of American sports; listening to baseball games or football games was like entering secret worlds." But this was not a simple love, for "Speaking in America was like going up the Amazon River, full of dangers, full of wonders" (screen 4). In addition to introducing her to the English language, her move to the United States made possible other discoveries as well: "a whole new world was being opened day after day, and that included the discovery of Nature as a force, a haunting beauty, a matter of daylight dreaming, an obsession. Riding in a car on the American highways was like writing poetry with one's whole body" (screen 5). In 1958 Adnan began to teach humanities and philosophy at Dominican College in San Rafael, California, a position she held until 1972. It was a move, she says, that made her happy (screen 5).

It was during this period that Adnan began writing poetry again. She "still considered [her]self a French-speaking person" even though she was living in the United States and teaching in English (1996b, screen 5). But a war taking place on another continent soon caused her to reject French as a language of poetic expression. As Adnan describes it:

> It was during the Algerian war of independence. The morning paper was regularly bringing news of Algerians being killed in the war, or news of the atrocities that always seem to accompany large scale violence. I became, suddenly, and rather violently, conscious that I had naturally and spontaneously taken sides, that I was emotionally a participant in the war, and I resented having to express myself in French. Today I do not have these violent reactions towards the French language because the problem has long been settled. There is peace between Algeria and France. Then, things were different: Arab destiny as a whole seemed to be dependent on the outcome of that conflict. The dream of Arab unity was very alive then, and Algeria was its symbol.
>
> I realized that I couldn't write freely in a language that faced me with a deep conflict. I was disturbed in one fundamental realm of my life: the domain of meaningful self-expression [screen 5].

Significantly, this dilemma was resolved by a turn toward a different artistic genre, that of painting. The discovery that she could paint was a revelation for Adnan, "as if one morning the sun did not rise where it was expected to rise, but close by, at a different point of the horizon" (screen 5). Painting became, as Adnan puts it, "a new language and a solution to my dilemma: I didn't need to write in French anymore; I was going to paint in Arabic" (screen 5). The shift toward art freed Adnan. "Abstract art was the equivalent of poetic expression," she writes; "I didn't need to use words, but colors and lines. I didn't need to belong to a language-oriented culture but to an open form of expression…I understood that one can move in different directions, that the mind, unlike one's body, can go simultaneously in many dimensions… and that what we consider to be problems can also be tensions, working in more mysterious ways than we understand" (screen 5).

This decision to move toward art was in some ways not unique to Adnan, as she herself has observed. Although it is rare to find a European or American poet who is also a professional painter, Adnan notes, in the Arab world it is not uncommon, partly because of the Arab heritage of calligraphy. At the same time, Adnan stresses the role of the colonial legacy in pushing some people toward visual art. Referring to a discussion she had with the Moroccan poet and painter Muhammad Milihi, she explains "He said that in Morocco the combination of text and visuals may solve the problem of language for many … some of the people speak French only … [but] if you write in French you would also have a part of the population that can read it and another that can't … this may explain unconsciously the dominance of the creative textual writer in the Arab world. Because [writers] may feel that they can surpass the borders through the visual combined with the textual" (Adnan 1999a, 2).

Meanwhile, another faraway war brought Adnan back to poetry, this time in another new language, English. Living in the United States in the 1960s, Adnan was deeply affected by the war in Vietnam, as well as by the American counter-cultural revolution. As she writes, "The cultural revolution that was taking place in America had Vietnam as one of its sources, and one of its consequences was that the war issue became also a literary rallying point, a concern for the poets, and a dynamic subject matter. Poets wrote against the war, or rather, fought against the war through poetry…. I was entering the English language like an explorer: each word came to life, expressions were creations, adverbs were immensely immense, verbs were shooting arrows, a simple preposition like 'in' or 'out' an adventure!" (1996b, screen 6). Not surprisingly, Adnan's first poem in English was an anti-war poem entitled "The Ballad of the Lonely Knight in Present-Day America" (screen 6). Another poem in English, "The Enemy's Testament," was included in Walter Lowenfel's anthology *Where Is Vietnam?*, a collection of anti-war poetry that became an instant classic.

It was not long before Adnan began to establish herself in the field of poetry through book-length publications. Her first poetry volume, *Moonshots*, was published in Beirut, in English, in 1966. Another long poem, *Five Senses for One Death*, was published in New York in 1971. This poem, Adnan has said, was "a kind of funeral oration, something I wrote from deep down in my soul, after the suicide of a friend" (1985c, 119). It was, according to Adnan, "probably the very first poem in Arabic literature, as we know it, where a woman poet writes a love poem about another woman" (see Adnan 2000b), the poem also stood as an indication of Adnan's growing feminist sensibility. A few years after its publication, Adnan was working with a literary editor, Yusuf al-Khal, to translate the poem into Arabic (see Adnan 1973b). "Yusuf ... saw it as a love poem, and wanted to use the masculine form for my friend. I said, no, it wasn't a man but a woman, a young woman, and I wanted it to stay that way. Yusuf said that it was a literary convention. I said, no, women have a right to their own feelings.... For me it [the poem] represents a sort of feminist declaration" (1985c, 119).

Although literary doors were opening for Adnan, this immersion in poetry did not dispel the "old ghosts" of the Arab world and its troubles. One of those ghosts was the Arabic language itself. Although Adnan had not learned Arabic as a child, the language was always part of her consciousness—something neither foreign nor familiar (Adnan 1996b, screen 2). She rediscovered Arabic as an adult through another art form: Japanese folding books (*makimomo*). Adnan learned this art form from a San Francisco painter, Rick Barton. She tells this story: "Once, in China, Barton was drawing a chrysanthemum when a little boy walked by with his father and said, 'Look, look, this man is writing a flower.' It triggered a way of thinking—that handwriting can be a drawing, and on the other hand, that drawing can be writing. That little child bridged the gap: They're the same things" (quoted in Howell 1998, screen 1). Adnan used writing as an art form to construct Arabic poems, copying the Arabic script and combining it with watercolor painting. In the process, she says, "I was discovering, by experiencing it, that writing and drawing were one" (Adnan 1998c, screen 2). As she explains, "Something from my childhood emerged: the pleasure of writing, line after line, Arabic sentences which I understood very imperfectly: I took modern poetry written by the major Arab poets and 'worked' with them. I did not try to have them translated to me, I was satisfied with the strange understanding of them: bits here and there, sentences where I understood but one key word; it was like seeing through a veil.... Year after year I worked on these long papers, like horizontal scrolls, with my imperfect writing, aware that it was the opposite of classical calligraphy that was at stake; it was reading through the art of a poet's work.... These works ... represent to me a coming to terms which I would never have expected until it happened, with the many threads that make up the tapestry of my life" (Adnan 1996b, screens 6-7).

In 1972 Adnan returned to Lebanon to work as cultural editor of the newly founded French-language newspaper *Al-Safa*. In the French-speaking environment of Beirut, she returned to writing in French. In 1973 she published a volume containing two long, impassioned poems on the Palestine conflict and on the growing crisis in Lebanon and the Arab world, "Jebu" and "L'express Beyrouth—➤ Enfer" (The Beirut-Hell Express). These were poems of fierce political, cultural and social critique. In "Jebu" (which Adnan had first published in 1970, in her own English translation, in the Washington journal *The Arab World*) Adnan wrote, "we are conquered by / falsifiers of History   thieves of / undergrounds   and we have in our own / councils a rottenness more dangerous / than the sea serpents surrounding Sinbad" (1978b, 50). Similarly, in "The Beirut-Hell Express" she exhorted, "take your vertebrae and squeeze out / colonialism like pus" (1978a, 83).

Adnan continued this vein of political critique, bringing together political concerns, artistic explorations and literary experimentation with strikingly original results. In 1975 she wrote "Pablo Neruda is a Banana Tree" for the anthology *For Neruda, For Chile* (Lowenfels 1968). The poem was later translated into Arabic by Yusuf al-Khal and published in the Lebanese newspaper *Al Nahar*, and was published in book form in Lisbon (see Adnan 1982b). In 1975 she also began the long poem *L'Apocalypse Arabe* (The Arab Apocalypse), published in Paris in 1980 by Editions Papyrus, and subsequently published in her own English version in 1989 by the Post-Apollo Press, and in Arabic in 1990 by Al Saqqar Editions (Paris) (see Adnan 1980, 1989, 1990c). The poem began, Adnan says, as "an abstract poem on the sun." However, while she was writing it the Lebanese civil war began and "the war took it over. I don't know what it [the poem] would have been if the war hadn't happened" (Adnan 1987 n.p.). Through both imagery and form the poem brings together Adnan's growing interest in the realm of color and perception, her political commitment, and her view of art as another "language." The poem begins with a series of descriptive phrases: "A yellow sun   A green sun   A yellow sun   A red sun   a blue sun" (1989, 17). However, visual symbols quickly enter the poem —first a rough drawing of a sun, then hieroglyphic-like markings that stand in for words. As the poem progresses, these drawings and signs begin to signal the breakdown of language under extreme conditions, as well as making clear the inseparability of word and image in conveying emotion. Adnan herself describes the poem as written "out of the type of tension that brought about the war. The sense of explosion, of catastrophe. An apocalyptic sense.... I was so inhabited by that ominous sense of disaster, of madness, that only that way could I express it.... I was writing on explosion per se, on apocalypse per se and I saw it in color" (Adnan 1987).

Two years after the Lebanese war began, Adnan left Beirut for Paris. While there, she heard an account of the kidnapping, torture and murder in Beirut by Phalangist militiamen of a woman named Marie Rose Boulos, an acquaintance whose political commitment she respected. Out of that incident came the novel *Sitt Marie Rose*, written and published in French. This novel, a fiercely feminist portrayal of the Lebanese civil war, brought to the forefront Adnan's increasing emphasis on linking political and social critique. Winner of the France-Pays Arabes Award in 1978, the novel, which was to become the best-known and most widely translated and discussed of Adnan's books, also makes evident her ongoing interest in the relationship between formal and thematic elements (see Adnan 1977b, 1979a, 1979b, 1979c, 1982c, 1988, 1997a).

In 1979 Adnan moved back to California to write and paint. While her focus on social and political commitment has never wavered, she has continued to experiment with poetic and artistic form. In 1982 she published *From A to Z*, a poem about everyday life in New York during the Three Mile Island nuclear accident (Adnan 1982a). Like much of her work, this poem turns upon compressed, often surrealistic images that accumulate in power over the course of the work. This was followed in 1985 by the poetry collection *The Indian Never Had a Horse*, published in California by the Post-Apollo Press (1985b). This book, which takes as its central theme and metaphor the genocide perpetrated against native American people, was described in the *San Francisco Chronicle* as "an ingenious synthesis of the best elements of the surrealist, cut-up and Language schools of writing," a volume through which Adnan had "attained a unique poetic voice" (Volpendesta 1986). She also published, in 1985, *L'Artisanat créateur au Maroc* (The Creative Crafts of Morocco). Meanwhile, Adnan had increasingly begun to explore the boundary separating poetry and prose. While *Sitt Marie Rose* had infused narrative fiction with the lyricism, symbolism and intensity of poetry, Adnan's 1986 publication *Journey To Mount Tamalpais* expanded poetic moments of insight into the more narrative medium of prose. A contemplative meditation on perception, art, nature and place, this book intersperses Adnan's reflections on California's Mount Tamalpais and on the philosophical questions these reflections engender with Adnan's own black and white drawings and paintings of the mountain. Moving between poetry, philosophy and visual art, *Journey*, which has been translated into Italian and French (see Adnan 1993d, 1995b), brings to the foreground the linkage of different genres.

In 1990 Adnan returned to poetry with the publication of *The Spring Flowers Own & The Manifestations of the Voyage* (1990b), a two-part collection of "haiku-like epiphanies" (Sellin, this volume) parts of which have been set to music. Of this book, literary critic Michael Beard writes, "The determining sensibility combines the vistas of an insistently decentered consciousness, defining the poetic self through a contemplation

of mortality [in a] voice which combines visionary intensity with a distinctive, gentle, controlled and even pace" (Beard 1992). The year 1993 saw
the publication of *Paris, When It's Naked* (Adnan 1993c), a prose meditation on Paris—the city that, in its various roles as emblem of colonial
power and locus of beauty and art, has long inhabited Adnan's imagination and shaped her life. The same year also saw the publication of *Of
Cities and Women (Letters to Fawwaz)* (1993b) , a collection of letters from
Adnan to Fawwaz Traboulsi, the Arab writer and intellectual living, like
Adnan, in exile from Lebanon. As noted previously, Traboulsi had asked
Adnan for an essay on feminism to publish in his journal *Zawaya*. Adnan
never wrote the essay, but instead wrote him, from various European cities
and from Beirut, a series of letters exploring issues of gender and feminism. These letters are infused with what Barbara Harlow, in a blurb on
the back cover of *Cities*, calls the "provocative combination of meditation,
mediation — and immediacy — that has so distinguished [Adnan's] international writing." Like *Paris, When It's Naked*, this volume makes evident
Adnan's ongoing attunement to feminist issues, dislocation as a state of
consciousness, and the reverberations of historical and discursive forces.

Adnan's most recent English-language book is *There: In the Light and
the Darkness of the Self and the Other* (1997b), a prose poem that explores
issues of love and enmity and continues her preoccupation with poetic and
philosophical questions within a politically informed postcolonial consciousness. The book continues, too, Adnan's probing of the boundaries
between genres, in this case between philosophy, poetry and prose. As
Michael Beard describes it, "A smooth surface conceals a universe of sudden shifts and transitions from one level to another — a philosophical level
which pursues the mysteries of consciousness and place, a second level
which asks the same questions ('do I have to have a nationality in order
to be human?') in a committed social and political vision, a passionate and
engaged post-modernism" (back cover blurb). In *There*, Adnan poses a
series of questions that push her explorations of identity and power to new
levels. "Where are we?" she asks. "Out of History, of his or her story, and
back into it…. Who are we, a race, a tribe, a herd, a passing phenomenon,
or a traveler still traveling in order to find out who we are, and who we
shall be?" (1997b, 1). The answers she finds are, finally, grounded not only
in awareness of self, but in historical consciousness and in the global
dimension of human experience linking nations and cultures. As Adnan
writes near the end of the book, "On my American screen I saw the Viet-
namese peasant who was running and on whose skin napalm on fire was
closer than his wife: war, which liberates and kills those it liberated, joined
us forever" (69).

Meanwhile, Adnan has begun to move publicly into another new space, that of lesbian and gay writing. While her early work gave only slight indications of this dimension, in a recent essay, "First Passion," published in the anthology *Queer 13: Lesbian and Gay Writers Recall Seventh Grade*, Adnan writes of a friendship that was "somewhere between friendship and something else which we were too young to name" (1998b, 242). Linking, in characteristic fashion, recollections of her friend and memories of Beirut in the 1930s with questions about selfhood and the nature of love, Adnan describes this "first passion" as opening a door not only to the mysteries of relationships, but also into self-awareness. "Love is the most important matter we have to deal with," she writes, "but it is always the hardest. It comes about like a wave of infinite strength and creates the fear of drowning.... It creates a desperate need, the need to arrest in space and time the person beloved; it has to do with the absolute" (245).

Adnan continues to be published in English and French, as well as in other languages. In 1993 her "Growing up to Be a Woman Writer in Lebanon" (Adnan 1990a) was published, in Italian translation, as *Crescere Per Essere Scritrice In Libano* (1993a). In 1995 a collection of Adnan's short stories originally published in various journals in English, French and Arabic was compiled and published in Italian translation under the title *Al Confini della Luna* (The Border of the Moon; see Adnan 1995a. In 1998 she published in her own French translation the poetry volume *Ce Ciel Qui N'est Pas*. This collection was originally written in English and published, in part, in the New York magazine *Bomb* as untitled poems. It was then published in Arabic translation in 1996 under the title *Sama' Bila Sama'* (see Adnan 1994b, 1996a, 1998a). The collection is forthcoming in English under the title *Disappearance*.[4]

Adnan now lives part of the year in California and part of the year in Paris. She continues to visit Beirut, her birthplace and focal point of her exile. As she explains, the sense of exile that she carries with her "goes back so far [and] ... lasted so long, that it became my own nature.... I am both a stranger and a native to the same land, to the same mother tongue" (1996b, screen 7-8). This sense of exile and yet rootedness, presence and distance, of constant motion and simultaneous immersion into the present moment, informs all of her work. In an essay about her artist's folding books she comments, "Working for years in this direction led me to the suspicion that our mental world is an ongoing 'translation,' that perception is a translating of the object of that perception, and that any thought that we may think to be primordial, spontaneous, is already an interpretation of something which precedes it and may even be of another nature" (screen 3). It is this tension between perception and translation, a tension

heightened by a historical and political immersion in postcolonial realities, that grounds Adnan's work, making her writing and art reflections
of the dilemmas facing us all. As she writes in *Of Cities and Women*, "We
are the scribes of a scattered self, living fragments, as if the parts of the
self were writing down the bits and ends of a perception never complete"
(1993b, 54).

Notes

1. However, this poem has since been translated into Arabic by Abed Azrie
and published in Beirut as *Kitab Al Bahr* (see Adnan, 1994a).
2. The Italian translation, *Viaggio al Monte Tamalpais*, was published in 1993
(Salerno: Multimedia). The French translation, *Voyage au Mont Temalpais*, was
published in 1995 (Tarabuste).
3. *Paris, When It's Naked* was translated into German (as *Paris, Paris*) in 1999
(Frankfurt: Suhrkamp Verlag).
4. Other editions of Adnan's work include a Greek translation of *Cities and
Women* (2000c), translations of *The Arab Apocalypse* in Arabic (1990c) and in Italian (Adnan 2001b), and Arabic translations of *There* (2000a) and of "The Linden
Tree Cycle" (Adnan 2001a).

References

Accad, Evelyne. 1990. "Etel Adnan: Courage, Engagement and Self-Sacrifice." In
    Sexuality and War: Literary Masks of the Middle East, 64-77. New York: New
    York University Press.
Adnan, Etel. 1966. *Moonshots*. Beirut: Reveil.
_____. 1971. *Five Senses for One Death*. New York: The Smith.
_____. 1973a. "*Jebu*" suivi de "*L'Express Beyrouth* ⟶*Enfer.*" Paris: P. J. Oswald.
_____. 1973b. *Khams Hawas Li Mouten Wahed*. Translated from the English by
    Yusuf al-Khal. Beirut: Gallery One.
_____. 1977a. "In the Heart of the Heart of Another Country." *Mundus Artium: A
    Journal of International Literature and the Arts* 10 (1): 20–34.
_____. 1977b. *Sitt Marie-Rose*. Paris: Femmes.
_____. 1978a. "The Beirut-Hell Express." Translated from French by the author.
    In *Women of the Fertile Crescent: Modern Poetry by Arab Women*, ed. Kamal
    Boullatta, 72–83. Washington, D.C.: Three Continents.
_____. 1978b. "Jebu." Translated from French by the author. In *Women of the Fer-
    tile Crescent: Modern Poetry by Arab Women*, ed. Kamal Boullatta, 47–
    61. Washington, D.C.: Three Continents.
_____. 1979a. *Sitt Marie-Rose*. (Arabic.) Jerome Chahine, trans. Beirut: al-Mu'as-
    sasa al-'arabiyya lil-dirasat wal-nashr. Reprinted, with an introduction
    by Ferial Ghazoul, 2000. Cairo: al-Hay'a al-'Amma Li-Qusur al-Thaqafa.
_____. 1979b. *Sitt Marie Rose*. (Dutch.) The Hague: Novip.
_____. 1979c. *Sitt Marie Rose*. (Italian.) Milano: Delle le Donne.

_____. 1980. *L'Apocalypse Arabe*. Paris: Papyrus.

_____. 1982a. *From A to Z*. Sausalito, CA: Post Apollo.

_____. 1982b. *Pablo Neruda Is a Banana Tree*. Lisbon: Da Almeda.

_____. 1982c. *Sitt Marie-Rose*. Georgina Kleege, trans. Sausalito, CA: Post Apollo.

_____. 1985a. *L'Artisanat Créateur au Maroc*. Paris: Dessain et Tolrat.

_____. 1985b. *The Indian Never Had a Horse & Other Poems*. Sausalito, CA: Post Apollo.

_____. 1985c. Interview with Etel Adnan. By Hilary Kilpatrick. In *Unheard Words: Women and Literature in Africa, the Arab World, Asia, the Caribbean and Latin America*, ed. Mineke Schipper, trans. from the Dutch by Barbara Potter Fasting, 114–120. London and New York: Allison and Busby.

_____. 1986. *Journey to Mount Tamalpais*. Sausalito, CA: Post Apollo.

_____. 1987. Woman Between Cultures: Interview with Etel Adnan. By Allen Douglas and Fedwa Malti-Douglas. Jan. 8, 1987. Forthcoming in a volume co-authored by Fedwa Malti-Douglas and Allan Douglas.

_____. 1988. *Sitt Marie-Rose*. (German.) Frankfurt: Suhrkamp.

_____. 1989. *The Arab Apocalypse*. Sausalito, CA: Post Apollo.

_____. 1990a. "Growing Up to Be a Woman Writer in Lebanon." In *Opening the Gates: A Century of Arab Feminist Writing*, eds. Margot Badran and Miriam Cooke, 5–20. Bloomington and Indianapolis: Indiana University Press.

_____. 1990b. *The Spring Flowers Own & The Manifestations of the Voyage*. Sausalito, CA: Post Apollo.

_____. 1990c. *Yaoum Al Kiyama Al 'Arabi*. Translated from the French by Chawki Abdel Amir. Paris: Al Saqqar.

_____. 1993a. *Crescere Per Essere Scritrice in Libano*. Salerno: Multimedia.

_____. 1993b. *Of Cities and Women (Letters to Fawwaz)*. Sausalito, CA: Post Apollo.

_____. 1993c. *Paris, When It's Naked*. Sausalito, CA: Post Apollo.

_____. 1993d. *Viaggo al Monte Tamalpais*. Salerno, Italy: Multimedia.

_____. 1994a. *Kitab Al Bahr*. Trans. from the French by Abed Azrie. Beirut: Amaouaj.

_____. 1994b. *Untitled Poems*. Bomb Magazine. Winter 1994–95.

_____. 1995a. *Al Confini della Luna*. Rome: Ed. Jouvence.

_____. 1995b. *Voyage au Mont Tamalpais*. Translated from the English by the author. Saint Benoit du Sault, France: Tarabuste.

_____. 1996a. *Sama' Bila Sama'*. Translated from the French by E. Malas. Beirut: Amouage.

_____. 1996b. "To Write in a Foreign Language." *Electronic Poetry Review*. Online. Internet. 23 June 2000.

_____. 1997a. *Sitt Marie-Rose*. (Urdu). Pakistan.

_____. 1997b. *There: In the Light and the Darkness of the Self and the Other*. Sausalito, CA: Post Apollo.

_____. 1998a. *Ce Ciel Qui N'est Pas*. Paris: Ed. L'Harmattan.

_____. 1998b. "First Passion." *Queer 13: Lesbian and Gay Writers Recall Seventh Grade*. Clifford Chase, ed. 237–245. New York: Morrow.

_____. 1998c. "Notes on Unfolding Writing: The Mystic Transfer. Excerpts from The Unfolding of an Artist's Book." *Discourse*. 20 (1 & 2). Online. Internet. How2. 1, 1 (1999). 23 June 2000.

_____. 1999a. "Hiwar with Etel Adnan." Interview by Ali Alwan 'Ubad, Nasri Zacharia and Mohammad Jamil Dagman. March 10, 1999. New York University. Café Arabica.com. Internet 6 July 2000.

_____. 1999b. *Paris, Paris*. Frankfurt: Suhrkamp.

_____. 2000a. *Hunaka*. Translated by Sargon Boules. Cologne, Germany: Dar Al Jamal.

_____. 2000b. Interview with Etel Adnan by Nathalie Handal. Paris, March 10.

_____. 2000c. *Peri Poleon ke Yinekon*. Thessaloniki, Greese: Nissides.

_____. 2001a. *Kassa 'ed al Zaysafoun*. Arabic translations of Adnan's "Linden Tree Cycle," comprised of portions of *The Indian Never Had a Horse*, and all of *The Spring Flowers Own & The Manifestations of the Voyage*. Translated by Fayez Malas. Beirut: Dar an-Nahar.

_____. 2001b. *L'Apokalisse Araba*. Translated with a preface by Toni Maraini. Rome: Semar.

Beard, Michael. 1992. Review of *The Spring Flowers Own & The Manifestations of the Voyage*, by Etel Adnan. *World Literature Today*. World Literature Today (Winter 1992): 199.

Howell, Daedalus. 1998. "Writer-painter Etal Adnan." *San Francisco Chronicle*. Online. Internet. *Scam Magazine*. 23 June 2000.

Lowenfels, Walter, ed. 1968. *Where Is Vietnam?* New York: Doubleday.

Volpendesta, David. 1986. Review of *The Indian Never Had a Horse, and Other Poems*, by Etal Adnan. *San Francisco Chronicle*, March 23.

SECTION I

Beyond Borders:
Etel Adnan's Writing and Art

1

Etel Adnan: A Cosmic Poet
Eric Sellin

There is a ludic quality that characterizes Etel Adnan's approach to the architectonics of poetry. This is not to say that her work is not serious, at times even charged with tragic impulses, but that she, as an artist, is aware that she is "playing" with the toys and fire of nature; that she has an intimate interaction with things, people, and elements in the palpable world; that she brings to the contemplation of this world a cosmic vision.

I have long admired Etel Adnan's work and yet I have never taken a moment, as it were, to try to put my finger on what it is about her work that I find enchanting. No doubt the enchantment comes in part from the poet and in part from the predilections of the reader. Indeed, there seem to be two major itineraries that an artist can follow: on the one hand, an existential assault on the unknown by which the writer carves out a realistic entity admitting of no prior essence and which the reader is offered *en bloc*; on the other, a mystical approach that indicates the figurative synapses of an essentialist artistic experience and requires that the reader take part in the establishment of the overall network of the experience. What I consider to be Etel Adnan's most important work falls in the latter category. Her imagery is often concrete, even mundane, and yet there is a marvelous cosmic sense or vision behind the various elements she provides for our consideration in a given text.

Robert Bly once spoke of the Swedish poet Tomas Tranströmer's talent for knowing just when to stop writing in order to let an image resonate in the margins of the poem, like musical notes in an instrument's sound box (letter to author dated 6 March 1965). Etel Adnan has this talent. Unlike some poems by La Fontaine, Verhaeren, and numerous sonneteers, where the last stanza or *envoi* of the text condescendingly translates into life experience the moral or political-social message of the poem, texts by poets like Tranströmer, Adnan, Bly, Yves Bonnefoy, Cesar Vallejo, J. C. Renard, René Char, James Wright, Giuseppe Ungaretti, Louis Simpson, Sandro Penna, Gary Snyder, René Ménard, Jack Gilbert, and others pay the reader the courtesy — a demanding courtesy — of letting him or her collaborate in the composition of the invisible *envoi*.

Etel Adnan is totally aware of this covenant with the reader — and I should add art appreciator, for Adnan's *ars poetica* functions in symbiosis with her co-vocation as a painter, words and art interact on several levels in her opus, most notably in *L'Apocalypse arabe* (1980), in which dingbat-like figures are interspersed with the words of the text. She has spoken of this covenant in an interesting interview with Kathleen Weaver, from which I would like to quote at some length:

> I was educated with words. What I discovered about painting is that it is a language that can go as far as any other language. It is not a surface thing. We are used to communicating with words.... Painting, I suppose, later influenced my poetry, in the sense that I started as an abstract artist, very close to Nicolas De Stael's approach, painting with a palette knife, which dictates flat broad surfaces of color.... A certain method of painting led me to write the same way.
> *What do you mean?*
> I didn't paint as a person who comes from literature. If I did I would have been more realistic. I was not. But I am writing as a person who comes from painting. By that I mean what you do is make your composition. You trust your colors and your shapes, your gestures. You trust that something beyond that will come through even if you don't know exactly what. You know that you are not just decorating a surface. You know that you are saying more than meets the eye. In a way this is what we call a collage, but instead of using bits of paper you abstract shapes or planes of color. This is the way I proceed in poetry. I have the need to say something very precise, but I don't need to say it in a precise way. And I trust that whatever I want to say will come through. That I don't need to be sequential. I don't even need to be clear. I have to be clear in my intentions, not in my words [Weaver 1986, 15].

Whatever Etel Adnan's intentions are, they work marvelously! It seems to me an absolute given that poetry can say something precise in an imprecise way and that such a procedure is worthy of our attention. The fact of the matter is that very few people have the gift to do just that; however, Etel Adnan is a master of this procedure.

The reader must permit me a generalized moment of reverence, after which I shall try to consider some of the architectonics and optics of Etel Adnan's poetry; or some of the principal elements upon which I suspect I base much of my appreciation of her work.

There is a poem by another Swedish poet, Erik Lindegren, that has haunted me for years. It is titled "Kosmisk Moder" (Cosmic Mother) and in the anthology I have before me the poem is illustrated by a painting which would seem to be the source of inspiration of the poem (Hassler 1990, 124–5). The language is simple, the rhythm authentic, the imagery — even without privilege of the painting I have just mentioned — suggestive of Böcklin's famous allegorical painting of the final voyage to the Isle of Death. The painting beside Lindegren's poem superimposes a Maillot-esque woman upon an eerie seascape with clouds and cliffs and looming shapes suggestive of elongated icebergs or ships with sails a-luff drifting forth from the horizon towards a lighthouse. In the eye of the Cosmic Mother there is a star-like gleam. Lindegren calls it a "stjärnbild," literally a "star picture" or "star image," but I would prefer to translate it as "stargram," "starglyph," or "stargraph," all compromises.

I only recently, after rereading Adnan's poems, had what I would like to call the "serenity" and the proper frame of mind to translate this poem. In her poems I found the power and the tenderness, the humility and the nobility, and — above all — the holy handclasp of celestial angels and earth-bound cliffs necessary to convey Lindegren's threnody. I mention Lindegren's text and the picture because Etel Adnan is, in her poetry, a cosmic mother. Here is Erik Lindegren's poem:

Cosmic Mother

let there be within me the breath of your winter streets
let there be within me that which you already are and have always been
a dream beyond the cliff of dreams and beyond all secrecy
something realer than reality
something that I can neither remember nor forget
something like dark ships sailing slowly up toward beacons
something like clouds like light cliffs and something like cliffs like dark clouds
something that transforms incredible chill to incredible warmth
something that was within me and transformed me
oh transform me
turn me into a haven for my ship of grief
wait for me under the earth
look for me in my urn

transform me and be within me
just as I imperceptibly rest in you
dreaming the unconscious dream of the stargraph of your gaze

[1990, 124-25]

Let us now consider some of the devices or traits that mark Etel Adnan's poetry — traits that indeed permit her to say something precise in an apparently imprecise manner. Her poetry runs the gamut from rhythmic prose (*Sitt Marie Rose* [French version, 1977; English version, 1982]; *Journey to Mount Tamalpais* [1986]; and passages in *Of Cities and Women* [1993a]) and prose poems (*Paris, When It's Naked* [1993b]) to haiku-like epiphanies, even theophanies (*The Indian Never Had a Horse* [1985] and *The Spring Flowers Own & The Manifestations of the Voyage* [1990]).

Adnan demonstrates innovation and intensity in all of the above-mentioned sub-genres, but I find particularly inspiring the texts of the last variety... and particularly impressive is the collection titled *The Indian Never Had a Horse & Other Poems* in many of whose poems we can pinpoint areas in which there is a clue to what Adnan means when she speaks of conveying the precise in an imprecise manner. Indeed, the essential message, as happens with the successful haiku or the surrealist's polar image, is conveyed not by metaphor or paraphrase but by the silent sparks emanating from the ineffable contact point of two precise realities, the truth residing in the precise silence in which the similitudes and distinctions of the realities interact.

Valéry's masterpiece, "Le Cimetière marin," charts the celestial geometry of pure meditation (there is no loftier poetry) that occurs at a moment whose chronology exists only in terms of the point of juncture of two measurable time definitions, namely "midi le juste," which has no actual duration and is more properly the timeless moment between ante- and post-meridian duration. Thus the poetry evolves in a moment (ironically like Zeno's intellectual diddling so maligned by Valéry) that has movement without change, philosophical development without forward chronological movement.

In this context, I am also reminded of the somewhat more facile and not utterly uncommon exploitation of this device by cinéastes like Jean Cocteau who, in his film *Orphée*, has much of the action take place in a neutral Purgatory-like zone between daily life and the oblivion of death, a zone from which the characters return upon the precise stroke of the clock that accompanied their entry into the zone, a zone now eradicated from memory and preserved only in the work of art *per se*. The particular action that absorbs and enlightens us, that occurs in a no man's land of the imagination, is especially tantalizing in poetry; for unlike the cinéaste who concretizes the "interzone," the poet of print or the spoken word forges for us an interzone in which the author and the reader collaborate. The poet provides the framework for the interzone and may orient us toward presupposed verities (the composer of a haiku, for example, subtly steers the reader by means of a pivot image in the second line toward a nuanced connection of the imagery of the first and third lines), but ultimately the reader must collaborate in the aesthetic experience. It is the cooperation of the reader requisite to this sort of appreciation that makes poetry written by Etel Adnan and the other poets mentioned above inaccessible to some readers, while to others it may be an acquired taste, like that for caviar, beer, or olives. At the same time, when one *does* grasp the connection in the imagery, as with the surrealist polar image, there can be no more genuine poetic experience. For this reason, I feel that *The Indian* collection is Etel Adnan's most successful and inspiring work and that it belongs, as well, on the shelf of the most inspiring poetry written today.

Let us now examine the interzone effect in some of Adnan's poems. Whether we are dealing with the minimalism of the juxtaposed realities of a poetic image that reveal an implied third reality or the susurrus of an ungraspable but genuine emotion left unstated between realities — respectively a reality toward which we are steered or a mythic silence which we can acknowledge but barely explain — the interzone is the sounding box in which Adnan's poetics resonate. In either instance, suggested reality or implied resonance, the strength of many of what I consider to be Adnan's most successful poems lies in their ability to create a kind of *mytheme* in the interzone — a mini-epic narrative that is neither metaphor nor symbol. As I once wrote in a review of *The Indian Never Had a Horse*, "Adnan has the rare and wonderful ability to transcend metaphor and to turn image into myth" (Sellin 1985, 26).

The abrupt and apparently transitionless linking of imagery characteristic of the haiku is ever at play in Adnan's poems. The ellipsis in such poems is the muscle of their poetics. Generally the haiku provides us, be it ever so subtly, in the imagery of the text itself, clues to the dynamics of the ellipsis. For instance, in the three lines of a haiku, an image of snow in the second line might link, on the basis of several paradigmatic similitudes (color, motion, the marriage of two of the elements — the frozen and melted states of H^2O — the two domains frequented by aquatic fowl, topographical probabilities), an image in the first line of billowing clouds o'er mountain peaks and an image in the third line of a swan gliding on a pond. I should add that the more subtle (and yet present) the connections in its imagery, the more estimable the haiku. In some of Etel Adnan's imagery we can readily intuit a connection:

There are no boats on the
River and the world's beauty
is blinding. Three astronauts
are on their way back. In the
garden a single leaf is shaking

[Adnan 1985, 7]

Although the substantive propositions of this text are limited to boats (not there), to the world (beautiful and blinding), to three astronauts (returning) and to a garden with leaves (a single one of which is shaking), as well as to a river (made abstract and/or mythic by use of the capital R), the dynamics among the elements provide for interesting lines of force. Boats on the River parallel the spacecraft's heavenly path and reentry, both areas of bright reflection and dazzling light. The cosmic force (River) is given its parallel in the no less dazzling minutiae of the world in the single leaf's movement that reminds us of the vitality and regenerative power of nature, functioning somewhat like the single leaf on a tree in the otherwise bleak world of a play by Samuel Beckett.

Sometimes in a group activity the haiku is linked to others in a kind of open *cadavre exquis*, the second haiku pursuing its own imagistic tenets but also subtly linking its key imagery to that of the preceding haiku, and so on. Etel Adnan's poems often seem to follow such a linking pattern. The opening poem of *The Indian Never Had a Horse* may serve as an example. Two texts appear on the page and as we start to read her book we do not know (as is true with a number of Adnan's texts) if they are meant to be taken as two discrete poems or as a single poem or, indeed, as the first two stanzas of a longer poem. This characteristic of many of Adnan's poems causes the reader to concentrate on the crystalline nature of her texts, weighing each image in and out of several contexts:

The certitude of Space is brought
to me by a flight of birds. It
is grey outside and there is a trembling:
fog is too heavy a word

The zookeeper sends his love
letters to the female mayor of

San Diego
The lioness in her den fainted
on April Fool's day
the man hanged himself in
her cage

[Adnan 1985, 3]

The two "paragraphs" function well individually or, read together, as contrasting/reinforcing haiku-like images, each one subdividing into link-ings of images. The first section spins its dynamics around the linking of elements like "Space" / "flight of birds," "grey" / "fog," etc.; and the sec-ond text — even as it, itself, provides enough imagery to create two sepa-rate haiku — is linked to the first text by animal imagery and such subtle connections as "trembling" / "love" and "too heavy" / "hanged himself." Each stanza in Adnan's poetic sequences (yes, let us call them "sequences") contains its particular mytheme. Sometimes the linkages within and among stanzas are traceable, as in the above examples. At other times the link-ages are ones of absence, the interzone functioning in symbiosis with rather than an elaboration of the realities, like a checkerboard or crossword puz-zle in which voids are a vital part of the overall design. For example:

The world is smaller than the center
of your eye. Banners are floating
over San Francisco announcing Spring's
end. A young man came running down
from the top of Mount Rainier. We
received him with orange peels.

one day even the stars
became soldiers
Isis wept over the empty
sky

[Adnan 1985, 11]

A glossing of Isis, the age-old goddess of nature and an object of wide-spread worship in the ancient Middle East and Mediterranean world, pro-vides a self-sufficing urgency to the last four lines, but the linkages within the preceding text and between the two texts remain enigmatic. That is precisely my premise: Etel Adnan creates linked enigmas as often as she does linked images.

Any poet who traffics in reality- or ideo-images without providing supplementary information risks an accusation of obscurity; however one should remember to distinguish obscurity (involving lack of clarity or unintentionally ambiguous syntax or semantics) from difficulty. For example, Ezra Pound's *Cantos*, though difficult, could not be more explicit; it is simply that many of the concrete references are very personal and therefore tend to escape us if we try to read too much into them. A team of scholars and biographers has been able to explain most of the "references" in the *Cantos*. Similarly, in Adnan's sometimes difficult imagery, there must be, I believe, a concrete referent behind the images, such as that, say, of the young man running down from Mount Rainier or in the references in a stanza like the following one.

> Hills are better than elephants
> and the Mountain is the last
> bluejay. Rimbaud went too far
> into Abyssinia. There were too
> many volcanoes in Aden
>
> *[Adnan 1985, 7]*

In this stanza/poem, the reference to the French poet Rimbaud's abandonment of poetry at an early age for the life of a desperate adventurer in Abyssinia is clear enough; and, if I am not mistaken, the first line is a ludic intertextual wink at Hemingway and his story "Hills Like White Elephants," although another image in the same book offers us the possibility of a visual comparison: "I flew over an elephant / thinking the Himalayas were / far below" (p. 34). But the reference to the bluejay escapes me and I do not know if there are volcanoes in Yemen, much less in Aden, unless we are dealing with political upheavals. I must provisionally assume that these lines are grounded in some sort of reality and that with patience and more research, I might draw out their secrets. In the meantime, I make do with the levels of linkage I am able to grasp ... and there are enough gems to constitute a treasure while I search for others in the poems.

André Breton, Pierre Reverdy, and the surrealists deemed that poets should exclude from their arsenal of tropes any simile (notably the word "comme") and even metaphor in favor of the polar image in which we have the *rapprochement* or "bringing together" of two remote "realities." Yet there is the sense of an attenuated likening or an abstract "comme" between the terms of many of their images. The connector is, as it were, the very adhesive between the two juxtaposed realities. Such concrete realities are, to be sure, abutted in Etel Adnan's work, but frequently the connector between images is modal, both explicitly and implicitly. The idea of "like" (and the actual word) is less frequently encountered than the idea and the actual utterance of "because," "for," and "since" as connectors between ideo-images.

The manipulation of the natural imagery in a cosmic framework — and the sense of vital force that one finds in poems such as those by Adnan and Lindegren mentioned here — are hallmarks of the mystic. In addition, one senses that Adnan's version of feminism is inclusive rather than exclusive. In *Of Cities & Women (Letters to Fawwaz)*, Adnan reflects: "The women have kept contact with the earth, if I may say, in the ancient roles of witnesses and memory keepers. They have surpassed themselves: their strength has overcome their habits and their prejudices" (Adnan 1993a, 72). Her sensitivity to people and objects may, in a sense, emanate from her feminism, but it reaches out to embrace all humankind. She writes, in another letter to Fawwaz:

> As I move from the city center to Ras-Beirut, where my heart beats and where the sun sets, trying to think about women's condition, I meet the male inhabitants instead, and I feel as though I share their lives and understand them much better: mechanics, pushcart vendors, bums, beggars, and hustlers ... they all have eyes, wrinkles, worries, and miseries, that I contemplate the way I contemplate the sea. I am overcome by a profound sense of a homecoming, of a coming to terms in this luminous month of August.
>
> It is impossible to conclude. Every theory is a burial. There is nothing to say. In this place, all banalities die [Adnan 1993a, 81].

To contemplate the sea! This place where all banalities die! And, for the fortunate reader who knows how to approach poetry, to envision an eerie seascape with clouds and cliffs and looming shapes suggestive of elongated icebergs or ships with sails a-luff drifting forth from the horizon towards a lighthouse and a sovereign siren, Erato, the Cosmic Mother with the glint of a stargraph in her eye.

References

Adnan, Etel. 1977. *Sitt Marie Rose.* Paris: Des Femmes.
_____. 1980. *L'Apocalypse arabe.* Paris: Papyrus.
_____. 1982. *Sitt Marie Rose.* Sausalito, CA: Post-Apollo.
_____. 1985. *The Indian Never Had a Horse & Other Poems.* Sausalito, CA: Post-Apollo.
_____. 1986. *Journey to Mount Tamalpais.* Sausalito, CA: Post-Apollo.
_____. 1990. *The Spring Flowers Own & The Manifestations of the Voyage.* Sausalito, CA: Post-Apollo.

_____. 1993a. *Of Cities & Women (Letters to Fawwaz)*. Sausalito, CA: Post-Apollo.

_____. 1993b. *Paris, When It's Naked*. Sausalito, CA: Post-Apollo.

Hassler, Göran, ed. 1990. *Århundrets Ordmusik, från Anders Österling till Lars Forsell*. Avesta: Litteraturfrämjandet.

Lindegren, Erik, 1990. "Kosmisk Moder." In *Århundrets ordmusik, från Anders Österling till Lars Forsell*, edited by Göran Hassler, 124–125. Avesta: Litteraturfrämjandet.

Sellin, Eric, 1985. Review of *The Indian Never Had a Horse & Other Poems*, by Etel Adnan. *CELFAN Review* 1 (November): 25–26.

Weaver, Kathleen. 1986. "The Non-Worldly World: A Conversation with Etel Adnan." *Poetry Flash* 158 (May): 1, 14–16.

2

The Arab Apocalypse as a Critique of Colonialism and Imperialism

Caroline Seymour-Jorn

Etel Adnan's *The Arab Apocalypse* (1989) is a series of fifty-nine poems that both critiques colonial and neo-colonial violence on a global scale and provides a warning of the tragic future that awaits humankind if it continues on its present course. Adnan carries out her critique of the colonial process by making use of two poetic techniques, one having to do with imagery and the second with structure. First, Adnan employs unusual and violent natural imagery to describe colonial, neo-colonial, and imperialist powers and their effect on subjugated peoples. She describes a universe in which various natural entities such as the sun, moon, and sea engage in an adversarial relationship, one similar to that which exists between the colonized and the colonizer. Second, Adnan manipulates the language and the form of her poems in such a way as to suggest that language cannot express the suffering of individuals who have experienced the physical violence, displacement, or emotional trauma brought on either directly or indirectly by colonization. Adnan inserts hieroglyphic-like sketches into the text of her poems as if to suggest that words have become inadequate to express her intended meaning. She also makes ironic use of the language of the telegram, once an important method for communicating the results of war, to describe the terrible destruction of war and to call for its termination.

37

It is important to point out that Adnan's poetic style in *The Arab Apocalypse* resists analysis to a great extent. Adnan works largely by evocation; her lines of poetry consist of groups of nouns and adjectives or verbal phrases that often have little or no syntactic logic. Each line embodies a thought that is struggling to be expressed, and that brings with it a mass of multivalent symbols and connected ideas. Many of the poems in the collection hurl images at the reader just as bullets fly from the Kalachnikov, and in doing so express a situation of frightening confusion, a reflection, perhaps, of a warring world. The fractured structure of the poems reflects their topic: the chaos of war and the incomprehensible death and destruction that are its inevitable result.

O Celestial Comrade! The Imagery of the Sun in The Arab Apocalypse

As noted above, Adnan employs violent natural imagery to describe colonial and neo-colonial powers and to critique their effect on the people whom they subjugate. Sometimes her poems allude to the displacement and genocide of populations who were colonized by various European powers, such as the indigenous people of America. At other times, Adnan refers to the psychic damage done to the Lebanese and other Arab peoples by colonial regimes that asserted the superiority of their own languages and cultural traditions over those of the Arabs. At still other moments she refers to the ravages inflicted on the Palestinian population by the occupying Israelis with the support of the American government. The figure of the sun plays a prominent role in the imagery Adnan uses to describe these colonial processes. She describes this entity as an extremely powerful one, one that inflicts considerable suffering on other entities in the universe, including human beings. In many poems, the sun appears to represent the brutal power of the colonizer. However, the sun, like many of the images that Adnan uses in this poem, is a multivalent symbol, and it is difficult to pin a specific and consistent meaning to it as it is used throughout the poem. But the very slippage between symbols and meaning in Adnan's poetry is itself significant. It seems to reflect the chaotic nature of her subject, a world constantly at war with itself — one in which meaningless suffering and death figure prominently.

Many of the poems in *The Arab Apocalypse* pit the ruthless power of the sun against that of the sea, the moon, and the earth and its inhabitants.[1] In these cases Adnan clearly uses the strength and intensity of the sun as a metaphor for colonial powers that, in their determination to control the earth, decimate much of what stands in their way. The sea, moon, earth and various specific groups of people, such as the Hopi and the Palestinians, variously represent the brutalized, colonial subject (Adnan 1989, 10, 15, 54). At other times, the sun seems to be a more general symbol for the violent potential of human beings as it manifests itself, for example, in civil wars (19, 50). However, Adnan's sun also appears at several points in the poems as wounded, or deteriorating or even dead (19, 23, 24). These descriptions of the sun suggest that while the human capacity for cruelty and violence seems enormous, it is not necessarily a permanent feature of the universe. Finally, Adnan's sun sometimes seems merely to be an element of a larger universe that follows its own cycles and is completely indifferent to the travails of human beings on earth.

The Arrows of the Sun vs. the Tubes of the Sea: Adnan's Depiction of Colonial Violence

Originally published in 1980, *The Arab Apocalypse* appears to make reference to the tumultuous period of the 1970s in Lebanon which saw not only civil war but also invasion by the Israelis, clashes between the PLO and the Israelis on Lebanese soil, and the suffering of Palestinians in refugee camps located in the southern part of the country. In poem VII, Adnan describes a sun hovering in the sky over a scene of butchery on the earth:

[Adnan 1989, 19]

Like many of the poems of the *The Arab Apocalypse*, the lines of this poem consist of individual phrases whose meanings are opaque. Some of these phrases evoke vivid images of war and the frightening aftermath of a battle, while others ("cool breeze on the ships" and "meanderings in PARIS") seem to refer to another world that is connected with and yet strangely removed from the chaos in Lebanon and Palestine. The sun in this poem may represent the Israeli government, which has not only waged war against the Palestinians but whose forces also raided southern Lebanon in the 1970s. Or it may be a more general symbol for the forces of colonialism and imperialism that have contributed to political conflict in both Lebanon and Palestine. The poem describes the violence of the "warring sun" as a total violence; one that injures every aspect of its victim. Indeed, later the poem describes the sun, the colonizer, as "cannibal anthropophagus sun — an entity that not only wages war, but completely consumes its victim, the Arab.

In poem XXXV, Adnan develops this idea of the all-consuming nature of colonial violence. She refers once again to the Palestinians, who have experienced a continuous assault on their national identity, land, homes, and lives by the Israeli occupation:

> the besieged Palestinians walk on all four
> the Great solar Circle has encircled them in its iron ring
> And tired of words they begin to bark
> *[Adnan 1989, 54]*

The poem suggests that the colonizer, the great solar circle, has committed the ultimate act of violence by actually breaking the human spirit. By oppressing the Palestinians so completely and convincing them of the futility of their words, the colonizer has deprived them of dignity and, therefore, of something of their humanity. Elsewhere, the verse is suggestive of how the colonizer justifies its acts. In poem XL, the sun seems to represent the Israeli authorities, and is described as a camera that takes only black and white photos. After having captured its subject, the sun (camera) leaves nothing behind:

> the sun is a camera which operates only in black and white
> white white white is the color of Terror
> from their eyes nothing remains but egg-white and trees! blackness
> in the underground blackroom always black is   experience
>
> *[59]*

The poem suggests that, at some level, the colonizer is incapable of acknowledging or is unwilling to acknowledge, the value and complexity of the culture of the people that it seeks to dominate, seeing it only "in black and white." The poem goes on to describe the manner in which the sun — the colonizer, observes the earth — the colonized: "the sun is counting the earth's rotations." It then specifically names the Palestinian as the colonized subject that suffers the results of the colonial gaze and its subsequent violence:

> the sun is counting the earth's rotations   automobile wheel
> and on the Palestinian's head rolls a truck
> a concrete roof collapsed on 500 bodies
> and the sun took the picture for the C.I.A.'s archives
> *[Adnan 1989, 59]*

Here the colonizer's calculating gaze, and its simplified vision of its subject, facilitates the violence that it later uses to subdue that subject. The last line quoted alludes to the relationship between the Israeli regime and the United States government. The line again makes reference to the camera, and is suggestive of the recording aspect of the colonial project, an aspect that allows the colonizer to measure and report its success to allies.

While many of the poems of *The Arab Apocalypse* focus on the violence of the colonial encounter, others treat more ambiguous aspects of this relationship. Adnan describes the sun as not only violent towards the other natural entities such as the moon, rivers, and the ocean, but also as being both fearful of and attracted to these entities. She describes the sun as tremendously powerful and bellicose and yet also jealous, vain, romantic, amorous, sorrowful and haunted (Adnan 1989, 7). The sun emits solar arrows that creatures below dread, and yet it is, itself, not immune to fear. The sun is frightened of the sea, "terrified by Blue horizontal" (7) and also of the world's great rivers: "between the Tigris and Euphrates the sun is quivering" (43). While the sun emits fearful rays, the ocean possesses powerful waves, "the tubes of the sea" (7), that haunt the sun.

The cosmic struggle between the sun and the sea in particular appears and reappears throughout the poems of *The Arab Apocalypse*. In the first poem of the book, Adnan refers to this relationship of love, fear and violence:

Another sun jealous of Yellow enamoured of Red terrified by Blue horizontal
A sun romantic as Yellow jealous as Blue amorous as a cloud
A frail sun a timid sun   ⬤▶   vain sorrowful and bellicose sun
A Pharaonic 🚣 boat an Egyptian sun a solar universe and a universal sun

A solar arrow crosses the sky An eye dreads the sun the sun is an eye
A tubular sun haunted by the tubes of the sea 🔄 a sun pernicious and vain
A ⊕ Hopi a Red Indian sun an Arab Black Sun a sun yellow and blue

[Adnan 1989, 7]

In the second poem of the series Adnan describes the sun's "union" with the sea during the sunset, when it appears to sink into the vast blue of the ocean, as a moment of reckless and passionate abandon.

A yellow sun a sun ➤ toward the sea a sun reckless and in love with the sea

[9]

While Adnan's sun is in love with the sea, it is also terrified of it as the only other natural element that is its equal and to which it must succumb at the end of every day. This is the perpetual struggle of their cosmic union.

This struggle seems to be a metaphor for the struggle between the colonizer and the colonized, in which, as Edward Said argues, the dominant force is attracted to, repulsed by, and determined to control its subject. In the case of the European colonizer of the Middle East, the colonizing power is attracted to its subject as the source of its own history, languages and mythologies; and in this sense its attraction is a very romantic and deeply emotional one. The colonizer justifies its power over the colonized through its view of itself as part of a civilizing mission, determined to tame and order the uncivilized, corrupt East. Yet it also fears its subject because of the latter's own history, because of its previous political might as a powerful Islamic Empire, and also because of the extent to which it is, despite colonization and intensive study, still an unknown quantity (Said 1978).

While the poems detail the complex and ambivalent attitude of the sun/colonizer toward its subject, they describe in no uncertain terms the suffering of individuals whose bodies and souls have been crushed by the force that seeks to control them. The poems describe the colonizer's physical assault on the colonized in graphic terms, but they also treat the issue of the psychic damage endured by those who have experienced oppression and dispossession. Many of the poems make reference to the profound psychological damage suffered by people in colonial contexts where the language and culture of the colonizer are valorized and considered superior to those of the colonized. Poem LVI refers to scenes of destruction where people have been killed and bodies brutally mutilated. The poem suggests, however, that violence has been directed not only at the bodies of the subjugated peoples (here, the Arabs), but also at their culture, as represented by the Arabic language:

> I said that this tongue smoking like roast-lamb will disappear
> make tomorrow's men speak in signs collectively
> They threw the Arabic language to the garbage toads took it up
>
> [Adnan 1989, 75]

Here men are deprived of their ability to communicate both through physical mutilation and through a cultural violence that degrades the Arabic language itself. We might understand the poem to refer to the fact that many of the European governments that colonized Arab countries (including the French in Lebanon) not only assumed the superiority of their languages, but also attempted to institutionalize them by creating systems of education in the colonies that focused instruction upon European languages, history and geography. The schools established and influenced by European colonial authorities and missionary groups often neglected to educate children adequately in Arabic and thus ensured that many children gained more formal training in the foreign tongue than in their own. In so doing, these schools forced the children of the colonized to exist, in Fanon's terms, in a situation wherein their very speech emphasized the marginalization of their own language and culture. Thus "tomorrow's men" would be at some level linguistically, and perhaps emotionally, alienated from their own culture; unable either to fully relate to their tradition or communicate with their elders, and thus forced to "speak in signs."

Adnan and the Limitations of Language

In *The Arab Apocalypse*, Adnan very effectively uses the imagery of the natural world to describe and critique the horror of war as it exists as part of the colonial process. However, I argue that she also suggests in these poems that language, even poetic language, is inadequate to describe the human experience of occupation and war. Indeed, throughout the poems of *The Arab Apocalypse*, Adnan sometimes seems to abandon language altogether as a method for communicating her ideas, and instead inserts sketches to complete the lines of poetry.

Many of Adnan's sketches look like hieroglyphics that might be seen in an ancient Egyptian tomb. Although she places these sketches into the text at places where words seem to have become inadequate, the sketches themselves offer little more than ambiguity. They are truly hieroglyphic in the sense of being enigmatic symbols that make reference to some hidden meaning. For example, in the first poem of *The Arab Apocalypse*, Adnan begins to describe the sun, her symbol for the colonial power, with a series of adjective-noun phrases. However, by the second line of the poem, adjectives seem to have become inadequate to describe the intensity and complexity of this phenomenon, and so Adnan begins to insert small sketches into the text itself, in the place of adjectives:

[Adnan 1989, 7]

It is difficult to interpret the individual sketches here. They seem to represent different qualities of the sun that words cannot capture, or they may represent different images of the sun or its rays at different moments. They do, nevertheless, convey the general meaning that language is incapable of capturing the essence of the sun or of describing its various aspects.

In poem XL, which, as mentioned above, refers to the colonization of Palestine, the sketches seem to serve a similar function. Adnan places a series of sketches at the end of the first four lines of a poem that alludes to the simplifying view of the colonizer's gaze and its implication for justifying colonial violence:

the sun is a camera which operates only in black and white
white white white is the color of Terror
from their eyes nothing remains but egg-white and trees! blackness
in the underground blackroom always black is   experience

[59]

At some level the black lines and spots seem to refer to the blackness of experience that Adnan refers to, a state of hopelessness and depression that words cannot begin to describe. Perhaps they refer to the devastation that the Palestinians may feel as a result of their dispossession and the violence inflicted on them. At another level, they seem to represent the poet's own frustration or even anger in attempting to deal with this topic. At yet another level, the box-like figure may represent a camera, Adnan's symbol for the colonial gaze. Black arrows and lines lead from there to a black circle — devastation for the object of that gaze.

This black circle appears throughout the poems of *The Arab Apocalypse* and has a variety of meanings. In poem L, it seems to represent the Arabian moon, sitting off in the margin, almost as if it is observing the nightmare described in the poem:

There have been pounds and pounds of decomposed flesh   tons of suffering

Millions of dollars of pain   tons of crushed flesh
There have been mountains of corpses and rivers of blood
Bags filled with bones   baskets filled with eyes   bowls filled with lymph
There have been meadows covered with human skin under the Arabian moon

[Adnan 1989, 69]

In this poem, Adnan describes the destruction of war in terms of the millions of dollars spent on military equipment and the tons of bombs dropped on the besieged population. As in poem XL, Adnan inserts black lines where words seem to have become inadequate to describe the human suffering caused by war. The black circle in the margin appears to be the

"Arabian moon" mentioned, here presiding over this moment of darkness on the human landscape.

In poem IX, the black circle represents at least two things simultaneously. It evokes the image of a black sun overlooking a scene run through with bullets, guns, ambulances and rotting bodies. At the same time, it seems to signify a meteor hurtling through space, whose path of destruction Adnan compares in the last line to that of a bullet emanating from a Kalachnikov:

a militant sky aims its Kalachnikov at the earth   ●   BANG !

[Adnan 1989, 24]

In poem XLV the black circle also appears, once again representing the sun, but here it is depicted as a setting sun, falling down behind the horizon. The poem begins:

We all are future corpses the sun like you is covered with flowers

Eye of Baudelaire haunted by violence   Divine eye haunted by matter
we are future astronauts gone to lunar funerals
the last assault is broken on the Tell the smell of thyme portends evil !
continents broke away from their moorings   1.2.3.4.5.   A horse swallows its teeth

[Adnan 1989, 64]

This poem seems to allude to Baudelaire's poem "Romantic Sunset,"[12] which evokes the experience of watching the bright sun sink below the horizon, its glorious rays overcome by the oppressive dark of night. Adnan's poem also refers to the sunset by describing the sun as "covered with flowers," i. e., prepared for burial. In this first line, which is also punctuated by a sketch of a setting sun, Adnan describes the sun's demise as just as inevitable as that of the warring humans below it. The verse suggests that the influence of the sun, which represents colonial power, is as finite as the lives of those fragile human beings whom it seeks to control. The finite nature of colonial power or imperialism is a subject that Adnan alludes to again at the end of the collection, when she describes the Apocalypse.

The second line of poem XLV also makes reference to a point of vulnerability on the part of the colonizer, its capacity for being haunted by its violent deeds. "Eye of Baudelaire" refers to the setting sun, as Baudelaire describes it in his poem (1989, 208). In this line, Adnan uses the figure of the sun to represent both the colonizer, haunted by its own acts, and also the majestic, if not divine aspect of nature that is sometimes overcome by its own darker aspects. Indeed, the poem goes on to describe a scene in which the order of nature is overcome by chaos: the continents break loose from their earthly moorings, the horse swallows its teeth, and the sun is described in unnatural terms, as both yellow and green and then as extinguished altogether.

In a sense, this cataclysmic event seems to be a result of the violence of human beings. The poem goes on to refer to the carnage that remains at the end of a battle, and alludes to a cycle of violence, wherein everything is motivated by revenge and returning acts of cruelty. At the end of the poem the black lines reappear, as if to represent the blackness of the moment when the fighting is done and death is left to be reckoned with:

on the wires travelling doves read messages
the radio gave the numbers and television the colors
[Adnan 1989, 64]

The colors mentioned here are not the colors of the setting sun in the first line of the poem, but the awful colors of war; the images of the wounded and the dead. These lines also seem to reflect Adnan's view that while human beings are capable of causing tremendous suffering and death, they are at some level incapable of processing the results of this violence. She seems to suggest that their very language is inadequate to describe the results of their behavior. Adnan addresses this issue elsewhere in the poem by making ironic use of the style of the telegram, a technique which is discussed below.

O Disaster STOP

In *The Arab Apocalypse*, Adnan attempts to bridge the gap between the hideous reality of war as it is experienced by colonized people or those in the midst of civil war, and the imagination of her reader. But, as mentioned above, she also seems to be making the point that language is unable to convey the sheer brutality of war and the resulting human suffering. Throughout the poems, Adnan also adopts the language of the telegram, to make an ironic point about the way in which human beings have communicated about this suffering. In many poems she writes lines as though they were a part of a telegram: a missive that, during wartime, was dreaded because it often brought news of the death or serious injury of a loved one in the battlefield. For example, a number of poems that describe the terrible destruction of war are written in an elliptical fashion and include the word STOP as it was used in telegrams to indicate the end of a sentence. However, Adnan frequently places the punctuating word STOP within a line, highlighting the inadequacy of the words to convey their intended meaning:

> 7 thousand Arabs under siege thirsty blinded STOP extinct suns
> There are tumors on the moon's craters and Mars' dunes
> 7 thousand Arabs in the belly of vultures STOP a yellow sun   in their eyes

[Adnan 1989, 31]

While the style of the language is reminiscent of the information-bearing telegram, the poetry itself offers little clear meaning to the reader, suggesting the difficulty of describing or comprehending the situation of the Arabs. Elsewhere, Adnan uses the punctuating word STOP as an imperative, demanding that the violence described in the poem come to an end:

> A clear morning of cold rocks lost on an oceanic trail . . .
> a lighthouse calls the tide of Palestinians branded with red
> their guts protrude as umbilical cords
>
> savage is the enemy who settles in their eyes STOP O sorrow!

[57]

Here, Adnan describes the violence suffered by the Palestinians while simultaneously evoking the image of rocks brought in by the high tide and stranded on the beach as the water recedes. She characterizes the violence inflicted by human beings as being on so great a scale as to be comparable with the larger forces of nature, whose processes continue unceasingly without regard to the fate of individual entities within it. The fate of the Palestinians is like that of the cold, stranded rocks which are tossed and moved about as the eternal cycles of an indifferent universe run their course. The Palestinians' protruding guts—the mark of their impending death—look like, and indeed, emanate from umbilical cords, the very organs that allowed their growth within their mothers' wombs. Here, they are nothing but tragic reminders of human potential, a potential drowned in the red tide of blood brought about by human savagery. In the last line Adnan uses the word STOP as an injunction, calling for an end to this violence and sorrow.

Adnan uses this injunction again in one of several poems that describe the weakness and ultimate decline of the sun/colonizer. In poem XXI,

Adnan describes the frightening fury of the sun and then writes STOP as though commanding the sun to cease its endless violence. The poem then goes on to describe the sun as experiencing the sort of physical and mental decline that characterizes old age in human beings, thereby alluding to the very temporary nature of colonial power:

> the sun is ferocious its black center turns ceaselessly   STOP
> the sun is ill its hair is falling in black space
> the sun disoriented cosmonaut cuts the contact with Earth
> the sun is losing its teeth ◀━━   It lost its gum
>
> [Adnan 1989, 40]

Adnan returns to the theme of the ultimately temporary nature of colonial power in the final poem of the collection. This closing poem describes an apocalyptic event during which the all-powerful sun seems to have burned itself out and all creation is destroyed by fire:

> When the sun will run its ultimate road
> fire will devour beasts plants and stones
> fire will devour the fire and its perfect circle
> when the perfect circle will catch fire no angel will manifest itself STOP
> the sun will extinguish the gods the angels and men
> and it will extinguish itself in the midst of its daughters
> Matter-Spirit will become the NIGHT
> in the night in the night we shall find knowledge love and peace
>
> [78]

Interestingly, this final poem is reminiscent of the Qur'anic verses that describe judgment day, when the world will come to an end and each person will achieve true knowledge of his or her own deeds and will be held accountable for them. Consider the following verses:

> When the sun is folded up, The stars turn dim and scatter, The mountains made to move
> When Hell is set ablaze, and Paradise brought near, Then every soul will know what it had prepared for itself. So I call the receding stars to witness, The planets withdrawing into themselves, The closing night, The rising dawn, That this is indeed the word of an honored Messenger.
>
> [Suratu Takwir 1-3; 12-19; Ali 1994, 524]

While the Qur'an describes judgment day as a dawn when the message of the Prophet is verified and only those who have done good in the world will reap their rewards, Adnan describes this final moment as a night, when the evil and destructive force of the sun has consumed itself. However, the apocalypse that Adnan describes is not that brought about by a patriarchal god. In her apocalypse, the sun actually devours the gods, along with the angels and the men. Perhaps she is suggesting that human society and all its evils, including colonialism, neo-colonialism, and imperialism, will culminate in a moment of terrible destruction, in which even human constructs such as religion will be destroyed. In the same way that the Qur'an says that a cataclysm is needed to jolt people away from their self-deception and evil preoccupations, Adnan suggests that only a cataclysm will allow humans to reach a new level of rationality that will help to free them of the suffering that they inflict upon each other.

The Arab Apocalypse provides a sweeping critique of colonial, neo-colonial and imperialist violence, warning of the ultimately cataclysmic results of this violence. This is a collection of poems shot through with despair; despair over the long and repeated incidence of violence by governments on peoples over whom they are able to wield political and military dominance. However, the final lines of the poem provide a glimmer of hope, manifested in the moment following the Apocalypse. Adnan leaves open the question of what the nature of this event might be, but describes its culmination as a night, in which the fury and violence of the warring world will be replaced with the calm and rationality of a human race that has, perhaps, gained some knowledge from witnessing the results of its own brutality.

Notes

1. Adnan's imagery of the sun, moon, and ocean is reminiscent of that which is found in Charles Baudelaire's *The Flowers of Evil* (1989). Baudelaire was among the nineteenth century poets that Adnan studied intensively as a young student of literature in Beirut (Adnan 1990; 17–18).
2. From the collection *The Flowers of Evil*, p. 208.

References

Adnan, Etel. 1989. *The Arab Apocalypse*. Sausalito, CA: Post-Apollo.
_____. 1990. "Growing Up to be a Woman Writer in Lebanon," in *Opening the Gates: A Century of Arab Feminist Writing*, edited by Margot Badran and Miriam, 5–20. Bloomington: Indiana University Press.
Ali, Ahmed, trans. 1994. *Al-Qur'an: A Contemporary Translation*. Princeton: Princeton University Press.
1984. *Al-Qur'an: A Contemporary Translation*. Princeton: Princeton University Press.
Baudelaire, Charles. 1989. *The Flowers of Evil*. New York: New Directions.
Fanon, Frantz. 1967. *Black Skin, White Masks*. New York: Grove.
Said, Edward. 1978. *Orientalism*. New York: Pantheon.

3

Irremediable Ecstasy: Modes of the Lyric in Etel Adnan's *The Spring Flowers Own & Manifestations of the Voyage*

Michael Sells

During a discussion of modern American poetry focusing upon William Carlos Williams and Wallace Stevens, Denise Levertov was asked if a particular poem under discussion was about death. Her response was that all poems are about death in some way.[1] In a mordant essay on contemporary trends in American poetry, Sam Hamill suggested that the strong lyric we had known in Levertov and Kenneth Rexroth had subsequently declined when poets were taught to write as they speak, and they took the injunction literally (Hamill 1975). While Hamill's point concerned sound, sound not only as meter but as cadence, diction, assonance, and all the other sound figures that the lyric can contain, his point could be expanded to the area of subject. Much contemporary lyric seems focused on what might be called the "banal I," the persona of small thoughts and feelings. Both cases, lyric without sound and the poetry of banal occasion, might be considered a literalizing and thus a betrayal of the American lyric diction introduced by William Carlos Williams—a more idiomatic and realistic diction in which Levertov had found liberation from the sentimentalized voice of late Victorian verse. Indeed, in a series of incisive essays collected in the volume *American Poetry: Wildness and Domes-*

ticity, Robert Bly casts a polemical and questing glance over the landscape of contemporary American lyric and, like Hamill, finds a smallness—a lack of the vitality and vision offered by a poet like Rexroth (Bly 1990).

There is nothing small about Etel Adnan's double collection of poems, *The Spring Flowers Own & The Manifestations of the Voyage*. The poetic persona is a realistic subject in an unromanticized world, yet she is also a subject that takes on the depth and grandeur of the mythic persona and the mythic sense of time. She speaks about death and evokes life in unexpected places and unexpected ways. She mourns the dead — the wasted dead in Iraq and Beirut, and the living dead in Paris—with mordancy, without spite. Yet in the midst of such mourning, she evokes beauty with a searing ambivalence. She brings to American verse a voice that intersects with Arabic and French poetic tradition; indeed, that echoes two of the poets evoked by name in the volume — the Iraqi Badr Shaker as-Sayyab and Rimbaud, whose voices can be heard within the poems of this collection.

It is not easy to write about Adnan's latest volume. The two collections of poetry in one volume, *The Spring Flowers Own & The Manifestations of the Voyage*, offer a double reading. Each collection is more than a chapter or section of a book and can be read as a separate work; but each collection also calls for a reading in conversation with the other. The moods and modalities of thought are subtle and shifting. The range of emotion is wide. The perspective shifts from the personal, to the everyday, to the stars on the other side of reality. The tone shifts from lament, to satire, to surprising moments of purely delicious individualism. The essay below offers an appreciation and commentary without attempting to fit the shifting and allusive nature of the poetry into a schematic framework. My remarks relate Adnan's poetry and its elegiac suppleness to the contemporary world of the lyric in North America, Europe, and the Middle East — three of the sanctuaries of her muse or *jinni*.

The Spring Flowers Own

The speaker in *The Spring Flowers Own* begins by contemplating her future, post-mortem self:

> The morning after
> my death
> we will sit in cafes
> but I will not
> be there
> I will not be.
>
> [Adnan 1990, 15]

The speaker includes herself among those sitting in the cafe, even as she announces that she will not be. This post-mortem existence without being haunts the poems of this latest collection of Etel Adnan, from that dream place where the self can observe its life from the other side of being.

The paradoxical use of the poetic "we" in which one of the parties is absent is found throughout much of Middle Eastern literature. In the *Qur'an*, the "we" is the voice of the absolute one God, a first singular plural that has generated fascination and speculation among commentators for centuries. In the *Nūniyya* of Ibn Zaydun, perhaps the most famous love poem of classical Andalus, the "we" can refer to the poet and all poets, or to the poet and the beloved. In the latter case the abandoned lover/poet uses a reputed "we" in an effort to conjure a community whose very brokenness is at the heart of the poem.[2] In the master *ghazal* of the Ottoman lyricist Na'ili, the "we" undergoes multiple shifts: it is the Qur'anic voice of the deity at Sinai, the voice of all poets, the paradoxical voice of lover and beloved (again lost), the voice of the poet and his audience.[3] Without suggesting that Adnan makes allusions to these examples of the paradoxical "we," it is possible to savor her use of it through comparison with some of its classical manifestations.

The flowers within *The Spring Flowers Own* take on the pale glow of flowers under moonlight, or under the light reflected from the split of a persona that watches and speaks from the other side of night. With an inversion of the more accustomed associations of flowers with evanescent beauty, the poems make flowers into the perdurable. It is the flowers that mark death and surpass death, mock mortals, eat ruins, and poison. *Fleurs du mal,* perhaps, but with their own distinct realm — as in Adnan's dirge to the soldiers dying in the Tigris.[4]

In the following verses, Adnan offers, through an evocation of the flowers of dying that are distinctive of the volume, a lyrical condensation of beauty and mourning:

> I see   heading East   the pearl-colored
>   march of clouds
>   roses lend their blood to young
>   soldiers drowning in the Tigris
>   flowers triumph
>   over the human race
>   their tragedies are
>   short-lived
>   their agonies exude incense and myrrh

at the entrance of
temples they are the
ones to be eternally eternal.
[Adnan 1990, 22]

In these verses, one takes notice of the stanzas beginning with a single-lined triplet, as above. As the poems in *The Spring Flowers Own* unfold, the triplet opening phrase becomes a marker, modulating the flow of stanzas and foreboding a particular intensity. The meditation on war and death moves from the elegiac evocation of the flowers at the entrance to the temple, to a more impersonal, sardonic voice:

a young man among us a hero
tried to straddle one of the
sea creatures
his body emerged as a muddy pool
as mud
[22]

Also modulating *The Spring Flowers Own* are repeated references to the sky darkening or the hour of the darkening. At times the darkening leads to a moment of lyricism and connection:

The sun darkened for one
hour
that day
we were on the beach
playing with fireflies
light filtered through your eyelashes
your eyes darkened with the sun
[Adnan 1990, 23]

In this moment of close lyrical observation, the darkening of the sunlight allows a moment of intimacy within a modulation of color and light. At other times the sky darkens to reveal stars as brilliant as flowers.

Indeed, throughout *The Spring Flowers Own*, references to the mournful or fatal beauty of flowers are interspersed with references to the night sky. The second poem of the collection speaks of the moon being consumed with fire and stars visible until noon (Adnan 1990, 15). The poems begin in succession with the moon, the sun, and then the moon again darkening (16). Flowers are said to shine more brightly than the sun and to go into eclipse (19). By interweaving the references to the lights of the night sky and the references to the flowers, the poems create an implied isomorphism between sky and earth, stars and flowers— an isomorphism that becomes explicit in a later poem:

> The sun went into total darkness
> the stars took over
> the sky became a garden with
> billions of flowers
> Spring seemed to be
> with us forever.
>
> *[26]*

Earlier references to the night sky vary in mood from funereal, to ironic, to elegiac. Here the mood becomes that of the idyll, but given the associations of flowers in this collection, a rather haunting idyll.

Both the connection of flowers and stars and the ability of that connection to mediate a rich set of emotions are vital to classical Arabic poetry, which exploits the double meaning of words like *najm* (star/flower) and the isomorphism between the garden on earth and the garden of the spheres. One example from this long tradition can be found in a poem by the Cordovan Ibn Hazm (d. 1063 C.E.). Ibn Hazm integrates the star/flower reflection within a play on the classical motif of the "pasturing of the stars," in which the poet tends the stars as a pastor would tend his flock:

> I pasture the stars as though entrusted
> To tend all fixed constellations
>   and planets that incline to set.
>
> For, when the night's ablaze
>   with passion's flames, they seem
> To have ignited out of the darkness of my mind,
>
> And I become like a green meadow's keeper,
> Its grasses cross-garlanded with narcissus.[5]

The eternity of the stars, their immutability, and their imperviousness make the star-flower connection particularly acute in *The Spring Flowers Own*. That night sky returns in the second collection, *Manifestations of the Voyage*, at a key moment that ties the two collections together and brings their movement to a culmination.

At times the realms of the pale brilliance of the flowers is personified. Spring appears as both mortal and fatal. She dies. Who is she? We know the voice of the poem speaks from the other side — of oneness, of being. Later in the volume we hear of a mother who has died. We hear of a lover; of death herself; of Theodora, the queen of ecstasy — all referred to as *she*. For Spring personified, the flowers are both celebration and funeral.

The flowers are not limited to the funereal. At times the poems open onto a sense of wonderment beyond the opposition of life and death itself — as in the following verses which combine, in Adnan's special way, specific references to the everyday and the depths that can be found within it:

> We got drunk in a barroom
> the small town of Fairfax
> had just gone to bed
> cherry trees were bending under the
> weight of their flowers:
> they were involved in a ceremonial
> dance to which no one
> had ever come
>
> *[Adnan 1990, 18]*

Here the local has shifted to Fairfax and the cherry trees. And once again Adnan's voice is one step further into the world of impossibility: no one has ever come to these revels, and yet the poetic persona presents them as if she had been there.

For years, Adnan has been an astute reader of the writings of Ibn 'Arabi (1165-1240), the Sufi poet and philosopher who was born in Murcia, Andalus, and whose tomb and shrine are in Adnan's native Syria in Damascus. Ibn 'Arabi is fond of offering a creation myth that is at once comic and profound. The divine names really cannot exist without a world and a human consciousness of which and in which they are refractions. Before the creation of the world, the divine names complain to one another that they do not exist and thus feel tense. They send a delegation of seven gatekeeper names (including the Hearer, the Seer, and the Merciful) to Allah (the comprehensive divine name) to complain of their tension. Allah orders the Compassionate to breathe the world into existence. The world acts as a mirror and prism of the names, and human consciousness is the polishing of that mirror, allowing the divine to see itself in its multiple manifestations in the polished mirror of the human heart.[6]

In her poems Adnan offers a metaphysical mythology that is as deeply paradoxical as that of Ibn 'Arabi, but one which begins not with the deity and creation, but with the human speaking after her own death. Toward the end of *The Spring Flowers Own*, we hear again the persona speaking post-mortem. The irony reflects the pre-creative tension of the Ibn 'Arabi story, but with a contemporary and more elegiac perspective: "We the dead have conversations / in our gardens / about our lack of / existence" (Adnan 1990, 34). The post-mortem conversation about lack of existence in *The Spring Flowers Own* offers a retrospective ontological irony that seems to mirror and invert Ibn 'Arabi's pre-creative ontological irony. In an earlier volume, *Of Cities and Women (Letters to Fawwaz)*, Adnan recounted a visit to Murcia, Ibn 'Arabi's natal city in Andalusia, and offered the following meditation:

> These last few days we have spoken of Ibn 'Arabi as if we were deal-ing with a ghost or shadow. Where is his house? Where are the places he frequented, the libraries of his parents, the gardens in which he played?
> Hearing the Arabic words behind the Spanish ones, I tell myself that Andalusia is the first loss, the death of the Mother, and of the orchards of which Lorca was the last tree.
> Ibn 'Arabi pursued the Whole when all the details were falling one after the other around him. He had foreseen the fall. (Adnan 1993, 55-56)

This earlier meditation on the loss of Andalusia and on Ibn 'Arabi as a figure of that loss— a meditation made on the 500th anniversary of the fall of Granada and the destruction of Andalusian multireligious culture — allows a glimpse into the cultural dimensions of loss in her latest poems, the loss that occurs especially in Beirut and Damascus.

In Adnan's recent work, these cultural dimensions of loss are fre-quently embodied in the linden tree. The linden trees appear toward the conclusion of an earlier volume of Adnan poems, *The Indian Never Had a Horse* (1985). The first appearance of the linden trees in *The Spring Flow-ers Own & Manifestations of the Voyage* is a personification that is at once regal and earthy, cosmic and cosmopolitan, theatrical and lyric. It brings together into one tableau the various modes and perspectives of *The Spring Flowers Own*— a personification that recalls the walking cypress trees of Rumi within a range of associations both contemporary and classic:

> linden trees wear crowns of blossoms
> they circle   move on   and
> gather moss on their limbs
> they belong to a Theatre-Universe
> cities are their stage
> they perform under balconies

and undress
to the winter when a curtain
of fog
has fallen.
            [Adnan 1990, 31]

These linden trees are urban. They perform their dressings and undress-
ings on stage. By contrast, the trees of classical Arabic poetry — the
tamarisk, the lote, the acacia, and the moringa — are more often desert
trees. The stations of the journey are recounted in Adnan's poems but they
are marked by the city tree, the linden, which takes on the various shades
of tone, feeling, and ambiance experienced by the urban journeyer.

As the sequence comes to an end, we ask about the word "own" in
the title, *The Spring Flowers Own*. The flowers are the proprietors in this
poem. They own the life and the death perhaps. They own the cycles of
time and nature over which they appear, despite their more common associations with evanescence, and they are the perduring being. Their beauty
is placed in unsentimental juxtaposition to an infinite longing or longing
for the infinite (*gout de l'infini*), but a juxtaposition that seems to have a
deeper core of gentleness, perhaps, than the *fleurs du mal* of Baudelaire.

Manifestations of the Voyage

In the prelude to the second set of poems in the volume, *Manifestations of the Voyage*, the linden trees take over, in part, the role of the flowers.
They have a different persona, however. Like the flowers, they are at the
center of a meditation on death, desire, and time. As with Rumi's cypress
trees, these linden trees can walk and journey, but they are also rooted and
rooted in the most immutable realities. Like the lote tree (*sidr*) in Muhammad's journey (a journey evoked powerfully within this sequence), they
can be seen at the furthest boundary.[7] And like the lote tree *(dal)* in classical Arabic love poetry, they are the haunting sign of a *locus amoenus* after
the loss of the beloved.[8] They dance, hurry, and talk "of love and madness"
(Adnan 1990, 41). The linden tree prelude is a landscape marked as well
by stairways and ladders, ascents and descents, with a Borgesian twist:

with a crown of birds circling
him
a child is running in an abandoned
house

> the stairway takes the measure of
> its own emptiness
>
> I myself am the stairway that
>   Time has used in its
>   funereal course.
> *[Adnan 1990, 43]*

Then, after one of the longer stanzas in the volume, dedicated to the prophet Muhammad's dual voyages (horizontal to the "furthest site of prayer," vertical to the divine throne, and, in later versions, down through the levels of hell), the staircases recur in the realm of the observatory (Adnan 1990, 47). The author/persona observes stars and black holes and then goes on to "take mechanized stairs / which advance with no advance."

Beirut and Damascus are mentioned, the first great city reduced to ruins by recent civil war, and the second now being threatened by environmental and demographic pressures. Are these staircases the ruins of the cities, of buildings whose outer walls and roofs have been blasted apart by shelling or dynamite? The ruins are evoked in the center of the linden tree prelude in a manner that unmistakably evokes the Arabic *atlāl*, the abandoned ruins of the beloved's campsite (which in later times becomes the abandoned ruins of the great cities) and the halts (stations) of the pilgrimage, of the beloved away from the lover, of the lover toward the shrine, of both around each other. Unlike the classical *atlāl*, however, the flowers that overtake the ruins are not evocative of a pre-separation garden of fullness, but carry with them their own thorns:

> exile   emigration   the voyage
> are the halts of Knowledge
> but roses overtook
> the bombed out quarters
> the desert is inhabited with thorns
> *[Adnan 1990, 42]*

Manifestations of the Voyage is a longer sequence of poems than *The Spring Flowers Own*. It is divided into sections by numbers, by "crossings," by "returns," and occasional other categories, with some breaks and idiosyncrasies in the divisions that keep them from freezing into a set list. It takes the modes of *The Spring Flowers Own* — dirge, elegy, satire, dance, *ghazal*, theatre — and refracts them into a wider arc. Throughout *Manifestations of the Voyage*, the linden trees appear and reappear, refracted differently, as

Monet's cathedral was refracted differently in different lights. In "VIII: Return and Effusion of the Linden Tree," (Adnan 1990, 64), after a sustained and wrenching meditation on violence and violation, the linden is depicted stretching "its limbs from one side of the / horizon to the other / carrying along the space which / defines our world." On page 65, there follows the first of several prose poems, a nightmare version of the curse of photography with its "mechanical brain." But again we return to the linden, in an elegiac light:

> Absence of the linden, the laurel's absence
>
> Absence of green and dilated water
>   of fire, of flames
>
> Absence of a woman's passage from one room
>   to another
>   of the encounter in the road's
>   middle
>
> Absence of the body's dust
>   according to rituals
>
> Absence of the atom
>   of the heart
>
>   *[Adnan 1990, 72]*

Here the ontological irony is played out within a hymn-like structure, with each item conjured for presentation by the evocation of its absence. Just as the beloved of the classical Arabic poem is conjured by the *atlal* (the signs of her departure and absence), or by the *khayāl* (the shade or phantom of the beloved), so here absence, in an even more insistent manner with full syntactical parallelism, becomes evocation.

In "Crossing No. 17," the elegiac gives way to a dirge that is at once apocalyptic and intimate. Once again the garden and the sky are brought together. At one point in the Crossing, the evocation of the stars becomes particularly urgent:

> messenger stars were falling through
>   the night
>   in a conflagration of light
>   clashing with others...
>   The tranquillity of the university
>   was shattered.
>
>   *[Adnan 1990, 81]*

This tearing of the sky combines awe and intimacy in a manner not unlike that of early Qur'anic suras such as Sura 82, The Tearing (*al-infitar*), and with the lyricism of verses from Sura 81, The Overturning (*at-takwīr*):

> When the sky is torn
> When the stars are scattered
> When the seas boil over
> When the tombs burst open
> Then a soul will know what it has given
> and what it has held back
>
> *[Qur'an 82:1-5]*

> I swear by the stars that slide,
> stars streaming, stars that sweep along the sky
> By the night as it slips away
> By the morning when the fragrant air breathes
>
> *[Qur'an 81: 15-18]*[9]

While the Qur'anic passages evoke the stars as signs, gateways to reality, or in a final, irrevocable day of reckoning in which every destiny will be revealed, Adnan's stars are less immediately present — on the "reverse side of Space":

> the stars are on the reverse side
> of Space
> their droning to and fro tears
> the sky apart
> and keeps it broken
> as well as me and everyone I know.
>
> *[Adnan 1990, 82]*

Like the flowers, linden trees, and stars, the staircases and mazes take on varying refractions of tone and mood. In "XIX Parenthesis and Visitation" another prose poem brings the labyrinth into a world resembling Rimbaud's *Illuminations*:

> Yet there are fountains in the Luxembourg
> Gardens on which the sky pours itself; these are
> magical geometries, referential marks in the forest
> of our shredded senses and in the Disorder
> Labyrinth, focal spot, strangely akin to the real
> Paradise: city where death is always put off until
> tomorrow.[10]

Rimbaud suggested that the poet makes himself a seer through rational disordering of the senses. In his late collection of prose-poems, *Illuminations,* Rimbaud seems to have reached a point, similar to that described by the poet in the Luxembourg Gardens, where the senses are shredded without any further need for active disordering on the part of the poet. Nature turns mystic, alive with beauty but haunted with absence, even as culture turns to ruins and mechanisms symbolized, as in *Manifestations of the Voyage,* by staircases. In the first case we might compare the intense lyrical glow of the flowers, the linden trees, and the stars in Adnan's poems with a similar lyricism in *Illuminations.* At the end of Rimbaud's poem "L'Aube" (Dawn), a personification of the dawn as goddess and the derangement of the poetic persona occur simultaneously:

> Je ris au wasserfall blond qui s'échevela à travers les sapins: à la cime argentée je reconnus la deésse.
> Alors je levai un à un les voiles. Dans l'allée, en agitant les bras. Par la plaine, où je l'ai dénoncée au coq. A la grand'ville, elle fuyait parmi les clochers et les dômes, et, courant comme un mendiant sur les quais de marbre, je la chassais.
> [I laughed at the blond waterfall, disheveled between the fir trees: in the silvery peak I recognized the goddess.
> Then I lifted the veils, one by one. In the avenue, waving my arms. On the plain, where I declared her to the cock. In the city, she fled among the belfries and domes, and I, running like a beggar across marble quays, chased after her.] [Rimbaud 1962, 268]

In Rimbaud, here and throughout *Illuminations,* a feature of nature, the dawn, takes on a lyrical and symbolic shape, and ultimately a shape of absence. The poetic persona in *Manifestations of the Voyage* seems less likely to be drawn into the illusion as a madman chasing a phantom goddess on quays of marble, but more likely to comment from the perspective of after-the-chase.

In *Illuminations,* also, the spells and hypnotisms of nature can give way suddenly to the mechanical staircase in a manner that both contrasts and compares with the staircases in *Manifestations*:

> Les révoltes anciennes grouillent dans le centre du Céleste Empire; par les escaliers et les fauteuils de rocs un petit monde bléme et plat, Afrique et Occidents, va s'édifier. [Ancient revolts ferment in the heart of the Celestial Empire; across the stairways and armchairs of rocks, a little world, pale and flat, Africa and Occidents, is to be built.] [Rimbaud 1962, 280]

In the cities of Damascus and Beirut within *Manifestations of the Voyage,* one senses that the stairways are parts of a large world (though no less intimate, and perhaps large in its intimacy), partially demolished, or at least on the verge of demolition.

Yet, the potential relationship to Rimbaud's *Illuminations* is always one that contains the surprise, the turn, and the ironic twist. Thus "The Sunrise of the Sun" builds an intensity of imagism toward a climax:

> Somnolence envelops my bones and I shiver not because of the cold but from impatience. The waves of the Bay undulate their music and the sun is gentle with the boats. A flame is surging through my throat tearing apart my reason. My divagations are on the same wavelength as that reflection in the tree which is staring at me for days now with no end in sight [Adnan 1990, 92].

Into these "divagations" there breaks the following:

> Trains were fast   then
> people stopped   at an
> intersection   and went
> catatonic
>
> *[Adnan 1990, 92]*

The divagations have suddenly been interrupted by a song in an up-tempo key, fast-paced, where, even so, people at the intersection stop and go catatonic. The mad humor of the antimony within the expression "went catatonic" leads back toward a more personal voice, the voice of a poet caught in a reality of cosmic intensity and, at times, most whimsical circumstance.

This Side of the Oneness of Reality

The volume closes with a series of hymns to Theodora, the Byzantine empress known for regal and unmatched sexual performances. At one point she may be conflated with the goddess of love, or perhaps she achieved apotheosis:

> There is in Her and around Her
> irremediable ecstasy
>
> *[Adnan 1990, 98]*

She is also a heretic hero of the language of orgasm (p. 101) who "broke apart the trinity / of Matter, Mind and Divine Will." The empress of love achieves a mosaic monumentality and luminescence, with an exquisitely timed reference to the "tolling" of her jewels:

> The Empress   with her hands
>   drained of their blood
> stands in absolute darkness
> Her jewels toll...
>
> *[101]*

And in a poem that helps open the Theodora epilogue, entitled "The Venus of Milo," a truly magnificent set of love lyrics cascade:

> there has been the taking over of one
> body by the other body's love, by that
> love, by the furor of being, by the mad
> and tender need to exist within and without,
> simultaneously, and in duration, and within
> two fused spaces, existences abolished
> and transfigured,
> and mainly,
> forgotten
>
> *[Adnan 1990, 95]*

This poetry touches the intensity of Rimbaud in its madness, its willingness to reach those emotions that reason hides, its evocations of a beauty that perdures and haunts a life that can never possess it. Indeed, this world is a kind of death in life. At one point the poetic persona asks, rephrasing graffiti written in Arabic, "Is there life before death?" Yet perhaps life is in the unlimited longing and the moment — sought, and perhaps momentarily attained — of irremediable ecstasy. Adnan's is an international poetry, not tied down to one particular provenance, but moving among and through the shattered worlds of Beirut and Iraq; the loss of the linden trees of Damascus; a Paris "dreading a future / hurled at it like a / lightning-bolt" (Adnan 1990, 79); the gardens of Andalusia "standing ready to die" (45). The irremediable ecstasy is in a somewhat different key than in Rimbaud's *Illuminations*. In *Manifestations of the Voyage*, we do not find the poet persona running after the goddess like a beggar along quays of marble. In speaking post-mortem, she speaks, in part, from outside the ecstasy; or, given that ecstasy means a "standing outside" in the sense of being taken outside of oneself, perhaps at a reduplicated ecstatic perspective outside, herself and outside the outside of herself — another irony Ibn 'Arabi would have no doubt savored.

We have been waiting for such translations of the lyric into a more international poetry. One meaning of the term "translation" is the ritual movement of relics from one shrine to another, a movement that is essential for the growth of certain religious traditions. In a poetic sense the "crossings" and "returns," these "halts of Knowledge," are bringing to us a lyric of the intensity that existed within specific traditions, including the American tradition, but that has seemed, in American verse, to be increasingly marginalized by a stubborn parochialism.

At once grounded, yet eluding parochial definition, Adnan's poetry manages to maintain the distilled intensity of symbol and feeling that is the essence of the lyric:

> Often at night camellias glow their
> phosphorus whiteness in the
> garden's hushed silence
> my reason falters
> losing its
> steps
> and tumbles into some
> somber music
> this side of the oneness of Reality
>
> *[Adnan 1990, 27]*

Notes

1. Personal recollection. Stanford University, 1984.
2. See Ibn Zaydun (1975, 9–13). The tension over the "we" haunts the entire poem. The last verse offers a strong example: "God bless you / as long as our love for you still burns, / the love we hide, / the love that gives us away" (translated by Michael Sells).
3. See the exquisite translation in Walter Andrews, et al. 1997, 122–123).
4. This poem was published in 1990, after the catastrophic Iran-Iraq war and, presciently, before the Gulf War, during which several hundred thousand Iraqis were sacrificed by leaders in both Baghdad and Washington. The person ostensibly being attacked, Saddam Hussein, was one of the few Iraqis not harmed. In a betrayal still not fully comprehended, the Bush administration, after defeating Saddam militarily, addressed Arabic pleas to the Iraqi people to revolt. When they did revolt, the Bush administration decided they did not want a popular revolution in Iraq after all, and authorized the Iraqi military to use helicopter gunships to annihilate Saddam's opposition — an opposition that exposed itself by

responding to the Bush administration's urgings to revolt. Since that time, the regime of Saddam Hussein has systematically annihilated not only those who took part in the revolt personally, but their families and villages, and in the case of the Marsh Arabs, their entire land and culture.

5. Translation by Stetkevych (1994, 157). For the Arabic text, see p. 235, selection 135, in the same work. Chapters 4 and 5 of Stetkevych (1994) offer a sustained exploration of astral and flower imagery in classical Arabic lyric.

6. For a detailed discussion, see Michael Sells (1994, chapters 3–4) and (1993) . Etel Adnan has been an important presence at the annual symposia of the Muhyiddin Ibn 'Arabi Society in Berkeley.

7. Sura 53: 13-18 (translation by Michael Sells):

> Another time he saw it descending
> at the lote tree of the furthest limit
> There was the garden of sanctuary
> when the lote tree was enveloped in something enveloping
> His gaze did not turn aside nor did it exceed its bounds
> He had seen the signs of his lord, great signs

8. "Locus amoenus," Latin for "beautiful place," has become a technical term in literature for "the place in which the lover and beloved consummated a love union, the place of fulfilled longing, when seen or imagined in retrospect by a lover who is separated from the beloved." For a discussion of the classical Arabic *locus amoenus*, see Stetkevych (1994, 50–201).

9. Translated by Michael Sells. (See Sells, 1999).

10. See Rimbaud (1962, 233–96) and (1985).

11. Another work that offers a rich conversation with Rimbaud's *Illuminations* is Etel Adnan's *There: In the Light and Darkness of the Self and the Other* (1997). In *There*, Adnan uses a condensed prose-poem format that mirrors and plays against, in theme, tone, and genre, *Illuminations*.

References

Adnan, Etel. 1985. *The Indian Never Had a Horse*. Sausalito, CA: Post-Apollo.
_____. 1990. *The Spring Flowers Own & The Manifestations of the Voyage*. Sausalito, CA: Post-Apollo.
_____. 1993. *Of Cities and Women (Letters to Fawwaz)*. Sausalito, CA: Post-Apollo.
_____. 1997. *There: In the Light and Darkenss of the Self and the Other*. Sausalito, CA: Post-Apollo.
Andrews, Walter, Najaat Black, and Mehmet Kalpakli, eds. 1997. *Ottoman Lyric Poetry: An Anthology*. Austin: University of Texas Press.
Bly, Robert. 1990. *American Poetry: Wildness and Domesticity*. New York: Harper & Row.
Hamill, Sam. 1975. "Lyric, Miserable Lyric (Or: Whose Dog Are You?)." *The American Poetry Review* (September/November): 31–34.
Ibn Zaydun. 1975. *Diwan ibn Zaydun*. Beirut: Dar Sadir.
Rimbaud, Arthur. 1962. *Collected Poems*. Translated by Oliver Bernard. London: Penguin Classics.

_____. 1985. *Illuminations.* Edited by Andre Guyaux. Neuchatel: A la Bacco-
niere.
Sells, Michael. 1993. "Towards a Poetic Translation of Fusus al-Hikam," in
Muhyiddin Ibn 'Arabi: A Commemorative Volume, edited by S. Hirtenstein and
M. Tiernan, 124–140. Longmead: Element.
_____. 1994. *Mystical Languages of Unsaying.* Chicago: University of Chicago Press.
_____. 1999. *Approaching the Qur'an: The Early Revelations.* Ashland, OR:White
Cloud.
Stetkevych, Jaroslav. 1994. *The Zephyrs of Najd: The Poetics of Nostalgia in the Clas-
sical Arabic Nasib.* Chicago: University of Chicago Press.

4

From Beirut to Beirut: Exile, Wandering and Homecoming in the Narratives of Etel Adnan

Wen-chin Ouyang

> *... I feel that I haven't settled anywhere, really, that I'm rather living the world, all over, in newspapers, in railway stations, cafes, airports... The books that I'm writing are houses that I build for myself.*
> [Adnan 1993a, 111]

Exile has been a major creative and critical concern of modernism and postmodernism. While most critics and writers tend to focus on exile as a consequence of political oppression, a new generation of writers, especially those concerned with feminism(s) and postcolonialism(s), are beginning to look upon exile as a complex, dynamic phenomenon that goes beyond political alienation. Etel Adnan is one such writer. In books such as *Paris, When It's Naked* and *Of Cities and Women*, exile emerges as a multi-layered experience, one located in her reality as a postcolonial subject living in the postmodern era, and in her own understanding and expression of her exile.

Displacement and marginality are central to Adnan's exile, both as a reality and as a mental construct of this reality. In recent studies on cultural identities in the postmodern era, displacement, as both a point of departure and site of inquiry, is probed as a theoretical signifier, a textual strategy, and a lived experience. As a term used by critics such as Angelika Bammer, displacement carries resonances of both Freud and Derrida; it is a form of "pushing aside," a process in the course of which uncomfortable feelings and thoughts are repressed (Freud), and meanings are infinitely dispersed, indefinitely deferred (Derrida). In both cases, what is displaced — dispersed, deferred, repressed — is, significantly, still there: displaced but not replaced, it remains a source of trouble, the shifting ground of signification that makes meaning tremble (Bammer 1994, xiii). Thus defined, displacement in postmodern experience is intricately related to modernism, whether the latter is viewed as a historical precursor or as a trend setter, as Fredric Jameson argues in his seminal work on postmodernism.

Modernism, which took shape in Western Europe between the two world wars, was predicated, according to Jameson, upon the structural displacement of significant parts of the western world and the western sense of self into parts "located elsewhere ... in colonies over the water whose own life experience and life world ... remain unknown and unimaginable for the subjects of the imperial power" (1991, 51). This simultaneously split and doubled existence — stretched across the multiple ruptures between "here" and "there"—constitutes the "new and historically original problem" of modernism: "the inability to grasp the way the system functions as a whole" (51). Whether viewed from the perspective of the colonizer or the colonized — those displaced from their place of origin as a result of the expansion of their own imperial power, or those displaced by the presence of power "located elsewhere"— the experience of displacement is much the same as that charted by Jameson: the individual is "forced by cultural displacement to accept the provisional nature of all truths, all certainties" (51).

This sense of uncertainty, Bammer observes, is becoming even more acute now:

> In the present, so-called postmodern time, this sense of palpable, yet "unknown and unimaginable" contingencies, has become, if anything, even more foregrounded. As the "post-" designations proliferate, defining us in terms of what we supposedly no longer are (post-modern, post-colonial, post-feminist, etc., and as we ever more obsessively attempt to specify our precise locations (the familiar "I am [fill in the blanks]" recitation), our sense of identity is ineluctably, it seems, marked by the peculiarly postmodern geography of identity: both here *and* there and neither here *nor* there at one and the same time. It is in this sense and for this reason that marginality and otherness increasingly figure as

the predominant affirmative signifiers of (postmodern) identity. Indeed, it would appear, almost by definition, that to "be" in the postmodern sense is somehow to be an Other: displaced [1994, xii].

Adnan's narratives indeed reveal symptoms of such universalized postmodern experience of displacement and of fragmented identity. Geographically she spreads herself across three continents—North America, Europe, and Asia. Feeling at home yet not home in Sausalito, Paris and Beirut, she is here, there and elsewhere, but not really here, there nor elsewhere. She can be both insider and outsider, the self and the other, or neither insider nor outsider, neither the self nor the other; her narrative voice unpredictably oscillates between "we," "I" and "you." Indeed, her very hybridity, which is a phenomenon of postmodernism, is at the heart of her exile. "There is unity in some people's lives," she writes. "A Frenchman in Paris watches French variety shows. To my life there is no such center. I borrowed the French language (it was decided for me, I should say), borrow their city, buy Yugoslav shoes, Scottish cashmere sweaters, Italian socks (like all of you). I'm not going to carry this any further lest I discover that my cells are made of Argentinean meat and Dutch milk" (Adnan 1993b, 33). This hybridity is an obvious characteristic in her narratives. Narratives of exile, they hardly fall into traditional categorization of literary genres; for even though *Paris* is categorized as fiction and *Cities* as women's studies and literature, one can easily argue that they are essays or novels, depending on one's definition of each category.

However, to locate Adnan's displacement only as part of the postmodern phenomenon is problematic. "The problem with this notion of displacement," Bammer writes, arguing for the necessity to look at exile beyond the generalized post modern condition, "is that differences, thus universalized, disappear. What is more, the historical experience of difference on the basis of such socially constructed categories of discrimination as race, class, gender, sexuality, or religious, ethnic or cultural affiliation is appropriated for the purposes of elaborating a new, postmodernistically hip version of the universal subject" (1994, xii–xiii). What makes Adnan's, or anyone's exile unique, are the lived experiences that resist generalization. As Adnan tells us, "knowledge acquired by experience goes directly to the heart, to the truth of the matter more carefully than any theory" (1993a, 98).

In a review of *Cities* and *Paris*, Ammiel Alcalay says of Adnan: "She now writes in English, after having composed in French for many years (she also divides her time between California and Paris). At the same time, she is unquestionably an Arab writer. How, then, can one come to an easy definition of Adnan? Is she a Lebanese writer, a French writer, an American writer, a woman writer?" (1994, 311). Adnan's exile is the result of complex, multiple and intricately-related marginalizations born of her personal circumstances, of the conditions of Lebanon in particular and the Arab countries in general as they emerged from the ashes of colonialism, and of the processes of decolonization.

Marginalism, as a term used by David C. Gordon in a study on ethnicity in Lebanon, "refers to the situation or condition of a person or a group living within a society with which the individual or group feels only partial identification, while nourished and sustained by a culture that differs from that of the majority" (1980, 17). According to Gordon, "The group may be either an ethnic minority ... or it may be a class of modernizing individuals who have rejected or transcended the conventions and traditions of their society" (17). Marginalization results in the diminished possibility, if not complete absence, of free and full participation in the political and cultural life of the perceived homelands — in Adnan's case, Lebanon, France and the United States. The marginal person is stripped of the power to inform, change and shape the political and cultural discourses. "What powers do I have?" Adnan wonders, contemplating the situation of the Iraqis during "Desert Storm" and of the Algerians in Paris. "Let's take a breather and answer this fundamental question. None, is the reply. Almost none. Absolutely no power" (1993b, 32).

Adnan's marginalization is not only political and cultural, but is also geographical, linguistic, literary, familial and gender related, all of which are intricately connected. Born in 1925 in Lebanon, at that time under the French Mandate, to a Muslim Syrian-Arab father and a Christian Greek mother, Adnan was thrown into exile at birth: she began her life by straddling two cultures, the Syrian Islamic one of her father and the Christian Greek one of her mother. She portrays this schism as a tension between two poles, Damascus and Beirut. "In Beirut it was puzzlement and everyday life, in Damascus it was magic and recreation. In Beirut I was a little Christian. In Damascus I was at the door of the Islamic world" (1990, 11). Adnan moved from Beirut to Paris in 1950 to study at the Sorbonne, and in 1955 she moved to the United States, where she studied at Berkeley and Harvard and taught philosophy at Dominican College in San Rafael, California. In 1972 she returned to Beirut, where she worked as the literary editor to the daily *L'Orient le Jour* until the outbreak of the Lebanese civil war in 1975. She left Beirut, then, and moved first to Paris and then to Sausalito, California. But her decision to adopt an Arab-American identity did not help to alleviate her sense of exile, for Adnan is Lebanese, Arab, and Mediterranean at heart. The fragmentation of the Arab world as it emerged from the ashes of colonialism, and the subsequent social, political, and cultural volatility manifest in its many crises, especially the civil war in Lebanon and the loss of Palestine, remain a constant preoccupation in all her works. Her choice to reside in the West and her inability to write in Arabic exasperates her displacement, her feeling of "standing between situations," of "being a bit marginal and still a native," whether in the United States or the Arab world (11).

Speaking of her linguistic exile, Adnan acknowledges she was not given a choice with regard to language: "I borrowed the French language (it was decided for me, I should say)" (1993b, 33). As a colonized subject living under the French colonial rule, which pervaded all aspects of life, she had to learn French. The French, she writes, "expanded the already existing French schools in the country and favored the establishment of new ones. They created in Lebanon, and imposed on it, a system of education totally conforming to their schools in France, an education which had nothing to do with the history and the geography of the children involved." Under this educational system, Adnan "started speaking French and then only French" at the age of five. Since "Arabic was forbidden in these French schools" French quickly became her first language, and even dominated her familial background. "The Lebanese children spoke it [Arabic] at home. My mother not knowing Arabic, French took over as the language at home; we spoke less and less Turkish or Greek and more and more French" (1990, 7). For a self-defined "Arab"[1] to be deprived of her "native" language was not only to have her medium of expression taken away, but to be severed from her own history, alienated from her culture, and lost to her family.

Language is everything, Adnan readily admits (1993a, 111). It is not merely a medium of expression, but a construct of self, for self is given content, and is delineated and embodied primarily in narrative constructions of stories (Kerby 1991, 1). Without words life comes to a standstill:

> I was trying this morning to figure out how one could think without out words. A noble desire, I thought. I wanted to get close to what I presume could be forms of animal thinking: what happens in a cat's brain when a cat decides between jumping and not jumping?... I tried to stop this inner language that keeps rolling like a reel, and something else stopped, too. I faced blank space. I stared intently at the windows across the courtyard, moved my eyes north, south, sideways. I found myself stroking walls with my glances and establishing no connections. I became a pure vision of surfaces.... I stopped recognizing objects as such. Started to fight somnolence. My ears felt heavy. No animal ever experienced such a state, I'm sure.... But when I tried to put words aside, for good, I ended

in a painful state of being: surfaces hypnotized me, and, in front of an orange, I did not know how to behave [Adnan, 1993b, 53].

Having the French language, and the psychological, literary, and cultural baggage that comes with it, forced upon her, Adnan was deprived of the literary and cultural identity stemming from the heritage of the Arabs, and placed in an intellectually restricted world. Her dilemma is similar to that of V. S. Naipaul, who, Judith Levy observes, "by accepting the language and education of the colonizing British Empire ... was taking on a usurper Father with his own law" (1995, xiii). The colonized subject is severed from his/her past, a necessary component in the construction of identity. As Levy comments, "the accession into the alien symbolic order and language inevitably involves a severance from both personal and collective. The acquired usurping language cannot instill a past in the subject, and the past is barred from constituting a sense of self" (xiii). Unlike Naipaul, who, despite his problematic relations with the culture of his colonizers, identifies with the West and accepts the intellectual restrictions imposed on him by the language of the colonizers (Naipaul 1984, 18–19), Adnan remains true to her Arabness and is resentful of her own colonization by the French. For Adnan, to be unable to write in Arabic is to be denied her role in the decolonization process.

However, her decision to stop writing in French, and to write instead in English, did not help bring her from the periphery to the center; she remains marginalized in both Arabic and English speaking worlds. In the Arab world, English, the official language of the United Kingdom and the United States, continues to be regarded as the language of the colonizers, and the Americans are considered heir to the colonizers. In an age of raging orientalist and counter-orientalist discourses, works written in English may be accused of orientalism and of complicity with colonialism, and are often excluded from Arab discourses on cultural and literary modernity and on the fate of the newly "imagined" Arab nation. The insistence on using Arabic as the language of modernization by the Arabs is understandable. Concerns for cultural and literary continuity aside, notions of national revival are ineluctably bound by the definition of the Arab nation, of which language is one of the most important components. However, as a result, even though Adnan's positions are genuinely pro-Arab and her observations insightful, her works have been marginalized in the Arab world. *Sitt Marie Rose* (1977), for which she won the France-Pays-Arabes Award, is perhaps the first novel written on the Lebanese civil war, but it is often not included in the corpus of war novels on the Lebanese civil war, except by critics outside the Arab world, because it was written in

French. Writing in English, Adnan faces no fewer obstacles. "Although she has lived in America for more than thirty years," Alcalay observes, "the pleasure and power of Etel Adnan's writing remain the privilege of far too few readers in this country" (1994, 311). A member of the Arab-American minority, writing in a culture that is at worst hostile and at best indifferent to Arabs, Adnan expresses sensibilities that, unfortunately, fall outside the concerns of the majority.

Linguistic exile in Adnan's case is, moreover, gender dependent, linked to the difficulties faced by women writing in a language traditionally shaped by men. In an essay on the writer Judith Grossmann, Susan Canty Quinlan observes that the woman writer "is exiled by the language she must use in order to name the 'thinking' that characterizes her ability to understand and interpret the world around her." She writes, "Women are exiled from symbolic language that structures law and social conventions, among which perhaps the most significant are parental and marital relationships." In other words, linguistic exile is tantamount to the lack of "ability to structure or restructure words in order to connote the real experience" (Quinlan 1995, 118).

"Women and exile" are inextricably linked, Adnan observes in her meditations on the Picasso's paintings" (1993a, 24). To Adnan, Picasso's *Vauvenargues Buffet* is a metaphor of exile, for it is

> a woman. A feminine object as container, a domestic object. Picasso paints the buffet, his mountain, a Spanish buffet, which is to say Spain itself, a country spelled in the feminine in French as well as in Spanish. In other words, he paints the woman/earth that he has lost.... The young Picasso, in Spain, painted portraits of men: his friend Sabartes, his self-portrait, fishermen, acrobats, children, and also women, which is to say that he painted a complete world, a kind of universe leaning against the sea or landscape. Picasso in exile paints nothing but still-lives and women, a succession of women who surrounded him.... After his departure from Spain, Picasso painted nothing but his exile.... He made paintings, drawings and engravings of women, especially during his later years. Could he have seen in women prisoners like himself, prisoners of their own sexuality, prisoners caught in their own condition? ... Picasso becomes voyeur, therefore witness, therefore woman.... He can be but the voyeur, even, if necessary, as participant.... This is why he portrays himself as an artist painting the scene. Pleasure feminizes. Picasso looked too closely and he found himself in the bodies of women.... One paints only oneself. Picasso, a bull enamored with doves, paints only the feminine. In his exile he identifies with women, they who are exiled from Power, the place of origin [1993a , 24–27].

This metaphor works on multiple levels of association. At the outset, the Spanish buffet serves as a symbol of Spain, the country Picasso lost in his exile. Since Spain, both in name and concept, is defined as feminine in the Spanish language, "woman" easily replaces the objects found in this painting as metaphor for homeland. The shift in Picasso's paintings to women instead of men as objects of meditation confirms to Adnan the association between woman and home, therefore woman and the loss of home — exile. Pushed into the margin where choice is absent, subject becomes object imprisoned in its own condition of marginality. The painter-author becomes a voyeur looking in from outside, yet what he/she sees is the very prison of his/her exilic condition. Voyeurism becomes synonymous with marginalism and the exiled subject with the object of the exilic condition. When Picasso paints in exile, he paints his exile and turns himself into the object of his art — woman. Woman is therefore exile and powerlessness, a notion that rings true to Adnan, the Arab woman writer and artist deprived of her language and denied her voice. Women's role in writing, as Adnan sees it, is similar to their place in paintings: they are the "object," not the "subject."

Adnan is all too familiar with the difficulty of being female in the Arab world. From childhood she was made aware that "a little girl was a daughter, a school girl, and a future wife," not "an autonomous being whose life could turn out to be something other than what was considered to be the social norm" (Adnan 1990, 12). When she defied the social norm, she was accused of being "adventurous and irresponsible," as well as "in danger of losing her mind" (18). In a culture where women have been historically discouraged from participating in public life, the difficulties Adnan faces as a member of the first generation of professional Arab women writers and artists are many. (Adnan details many of these difficulties, including marginalization and persecution, in her novel *Sitt Marie Rose*).[2]

Adnan's exile is not merely cultural, intellectual, political and linguistic; it is familial and personal as well. "By the time I was fourteen," Adnan confesses, "a new problem faced me at home; studying in a language basically foreign to my parents created a distance between us: I was engaging myself in territories alien to them and I was being estranged.... I was becoming a foreigner in my own house" (1990, 14). Her relationship with her mother deteriorated to such an extent that the latter was openly hostile, taking steps to prevent her from continuing her education. Though Adnan did complete her education, both her mother and her father were lost to her. "Dear parents...," she laments, "Neither of you ever saw Paris, or intended to. Your trains never ended at Gare de Lyons. You thought of Paris as an intruder into the order of things as you knew them. Paris was a place of perdition, you said. Be reassured: I did not lose my soul in it. I only lost my illusions. And you" (1993b, 101). This loss was irrecoverable. Years later, she tells us, "I went to Greece ... partly, or perhaps even mainly, because I was looking for (and am still looking for) the voice of my mother. I have lost the memory of the voice of my parents. ...I was unable to find the voice I am seeking" (1993a, 45).

This is not to say that Adnan's exile is not a physical one as well. It was that and more. Her marginalization and the civil war forced her to leave Beirut. "Separation from one's country," however, "means more than a lack of physical contact with land and houses," as Paul Ilie observes about the post WWII Spanish exiles; "It is also a set of feelings and beliefs that isolate the expelled group from the majority" (1980, 2). For Adnan to be exiled from her beloved country and family was to be thrown into chaos (see, for instance, Adnan 1993a, 27), to lose her center, and to be forced to wander, to be homeless; for "home suggests close emotional belonging and the gnarled roots of one's identity" (Seidel 1986, 218). Paradoxically, her exile became the new center around which she wandered. As an exiled Arab woman writer and artist, she was imprisoned in her multifarious exiles, unable to write about or paint anything but her exile. What Adnan sees in Picasso's *Vauvenargues Buffet* is precisely her own exilic condition and practice. She too has turned her exiled self into the object of her works. She writes mainly in English about her wandering and homelessness both as an Arab and a woman, and makes the Arabic language, the script of which she has learned to reproduce but the workings of which have remained elusive to her, the object of her art. As she has said to me more than once, she "painted in Arabic." She took poems by modern Arab poets and copied, in color, on Japanese folded papers, line after line of the Arabic sentences of which she understood little. Even as she continues to stay "outside" the Arabic language, she turns this language — a forbidden paradise and another symbol of her exile — into the object of her meditation. Her loss, her exile, is paradoxically a gain. Working outside the confines of tradition, whether social, cultural or literary, Adnan is freer to roam, both physically and intellectually; to find a definition for herself as a woman; to find her own literary expression; and to find a home of her own, as her paintings and, above all, her writings tell us.

Homelessness: Textualization of Wandering

Adnan's narratives, starting with her novel *Sitt Marie Rose* and ending with *Paris* and *Cities*, are both a consequence and manifestation of her exile. Her textual nomadism — "a boat wandering for long" (Adnan, 1986, 18) —

stands in relation to real changes in her geographical locations. In *Sitt Marie Rose*, she documents her exit from Beirut, suggesting how the civil war as well as the binarisms of colonial domination, the reemerging pre-colonial order,[3] and the oppressive patriarchal structure forced her to leave her homeland and wander. In *Paris* and *Cities*, she meditates on her exilic experience as she roams across three continents, always yearning for the lost world — Beirut, the Arab world, and the Mediterranean basin — and always searching for an alternative center.

Like other narratives of exile, Adnan's narratives are, perhaps by necessity, autobiographical: the experience of exile is so overwhelming that writing about it becomes the only resistance to the abyss created by the state of placelessness. "Third world writers of the diaspora," Trinh T. Minh-ha observes, "are condemned to write only autobiographical works" (1994, 10). In all of Adnan's narratives the subject is one and the same: her fragmented, exiled self. This is especially true of *Paris* and *Cities*. These two works not only complete the journey begun by *Sitt Marie Rose*, but complement each other, detailing two parallel, simultaneous journeys: decolonization of the self in *Paris* and coming to terms with exile in *Cities*. Taken together, these works comprise one journey: the homecoming of an exile, and the loss and retrieval of both place and self.

After the initial departure recounted in *Sitt Marie Rose*, Adnan embarks in *Paris* and *Cities* on a long journey in search of a place she can call home. These narratives, which function as parts of the same exilic journey, differ in their objectives and strategies. While *Paris* deconstructs the old illusory notions of home — a geographic space with memorable associations — *Cities*, by decolonizing the self and by deterritorializing Paris, the capital of the colonial empire, redefines the meaning of home. The two processes of deconstruction and redefinition come hand in hand. In *Paris* and *Cities* they are presented in the form of travel: inside Paris itself, out-side Paris, and in Europe, with the journey ending in Beirut. Narrative structure, write Barry Curtis and Claire Pajaczkowska, can be "regarded as an intro-subjective journey. Through narrative the subject self is allowed a regressive splitting — into fragment component selves — and is offered forms of identification for subsequent reintegration" (1994, 212). By recounting her journeys in and between Beirut, Paris and Sausalito, each city representing a fragment of her divided identity, Adnan willfully cre-ates coherence for her self through her narratives, and arrives "home" after a long sojourn in exile.

Adnan's departure and "homecoming" take place concomitantly on the landscape of Paris, the ultimate symbol of her exile and a source of both significance and trouble for her. As a place, Paris serves as an important component of her sense of identity. "There is for virtually everyone," argues E. Relph, "a deep association with and consciousness of the places where we were born and grew up, where we live now, or where we have had particularly moving experiences. This association seems to constitute a vital source of both individual and cultural identity and security, a point of departure from which we orient ourselves in the world" (1976, 8). Adnan, who had been colonized by the French language, culture and sensibility, as an adolescent thought Paris was "the center of the world" (Adnan 1990, 19). During her first stay, between 1949 and 1955, she fell in love with Paris. Even almost half a century later, when Paris has become a source of anguish to her, she realizes that it remains "the crucible of our [colonized subjects'] identities" (1993b, 8). "Why do I love this somber city," she asks, "give my life to its streets, spend it in its restaurants, break it under its melancholy — why? Should I get to know myself in order to know why Paris is so central to my life, or should I know this city even more than I do to find out at least a few essential things about myself?" (76). Adnan experiences Paris through what Yi-Fu Tuan describes as "experiential associations," the "assimilation of experience in the unconscious — the processing of everyday life" (1977, 7). Paris invades her, takes over her being: "I opened the windows ... and Paris slid in, filled all the spaces" (Adnan 1993b, 7). She is "possessed by the city" (90) — "ensnared by [its] geometry, architecture, and a river which gives life to all these stones" (104).

Adnan's experiences in Paris intensify her consciousness of the importance of Beirut to her, thus fragmenting her self. "[Immersion] in a foreign culture," Gerald Kennedy argues in his book on literary constructs of Paris in the writings of American expatriots, "...reveals the considerable extent to which we are creatures of place, deriving our most basic sense of self from the relation which we have formed with the place or chora in which we have our being. The experience of expatriation often discloses an alternate self, responsive to the differences which constitute the foreignness of another place" (1993, 28). By immersing herself in Paris, Adnan willy-nilly creates another identity that is different from, even conflicting with, her Beirut one. Paris and Beirut are locked in the binarism created by colonialism, of the colonizer and the colonized. Paris is a paradox; it takes her away, as well as provides her with refuge from the turmoil at home.

Having escaped from Beirut in some of the worst moments of the civil war, including the siege of Tel Zaatar (Adnan 1993b, 63–64), Adnan finds refuge in Paris. However, her mind is preoccupied with the perils of war and the fate of her people. Unable to sleep, she roams Paris, walking down Boulevard Saint Germain. The direction she takes—

East — takes her towards Beirut, and the distance she feels she must cover (Boulevard Saint Germain being an epic road) reminds her of how far she has gone as well as implying how arduous her return journey will be. The magnificence and magnanimity of this boulevard, paradoxically, throw her into conflict. She is torn between her "colonial desire" for Paris as the place of romantic fantasy and refuge, and her recognition of it as the symbol of her exile; between her love for the city and the near-misery of being in it: "Paris is beautiful. It aches to say so, one's arms are never big enough to hug such an immensity. Claude can say it innocently. It's harder for me to say, it's more poignant. It tears me apart. Paris is the heart of a lingering colonial power, and that knowledge goes to bed with me every night. When I walk in this city I plunge into an abyss, I lose myself in contemplation, I experience ecstasy, an ecstasy which I know to be also a defeat (1993b, 7).

Paris is troublesome because it makes one forget the harsh realities of the Arab world: one "can go on living like a fish in the huge aquarium of Paris, and feel safe..." (1993b, 10). However, the false sense of security cannot blind Adnan to the cruel conditions in which the Arabs live, nor can it resolve the conflict between her desire and anguish. "How can I let myself go into an oceanic happiness, face an incantatory bliss in front of the sea," she wonders, "when I know that so many immigrant workers face deportation?" (42). In Paris she is always caught between her admiration for the French culture and the pain of witnessing, powerlessly, the French policies towards the Arab world and the conditions of the Arabs (43). Her Paris is haunted by her Damascus (104). Adnan cannot call Paris home because, for her, it is not the "calm center of established values"; rather, it is a place of conflict — there is too much that is against everything Arab. From its past colonial history to its anti-immigrant (mainly anti-Algerian) sentiments and its support for the war against Iraq, Paris is at war with Beirut, the symbol of Adnan's Arab identity. She remains an outsider in Paris, feeling "not here," "not existing at all" (67) and "totally elsewhere" (7). Paris is, for Adnan, a "dead center," and living in Paris is like experiencing slow death: it is "daily poison, minute drops of arsenic, distilled evil, a passionate addiction" (27). When she is in Paris she is seized by a need to run away from it: her "mind furiously runs towards distant places. *Anywhere out of this world*" (43). Having "no guts" to move back to the Arab world (10), she chooses to reside elsewhere, in Sausalito.

But running away from Paris and Beirut does not and cannot solve the problem of her split self. In fact, it exasperates it, fragmenting her further. It is only by coming to terms with her life that Adnan is able to reintegrate her self. *Paris* is the documentation of her journey towards this reintegration. By deterritorializing and then reterritorializing Paris, Adnan achieves first her own decolonization and later the reintegration of her self. Deleuze and Guattari (1986, 16-27) use the term deterritorialization to speak of how Kafka's use of the German language changed its land-scape. I borrow their term here and apply it to the change of landscape, but in this case the historical landscape of Paris, the symbol of coloniza-tion. Adnan's narrative reterritorializes this landscape. She rewrites the history of colonialism as she documents the physical beauty of Paris, and she decolonizes her self as she strips Paris and her colonial desire naked of their power over her.

Adnan's textual construct of Paris is also the textual construct of her self, where "the inside and the outside look more alike than one knows" (Adnan 1993b, 27). While her narrative of her journey in Paris is both spa-tial and temporal, her deterritorialization of Paris is both geographical and historical. Hers is a counter narrative to the colonial narratives of travel in the Arab world. As Dissanayake and Wickramagamage argue in their study of Naipaul's travel narratives,

> Narratives of travel, understandably enough, are often seen as con-quest of space. However, it is important to bear in mind the fact that there is, in travel writing, a vital interplay between geography and history; the production of space is deeply implicated in the production of history. What we often find in these works is the discursive opening up of new space; while the history of the writer and his culture is valorized, the history of the colonized, the cultural Other, is devalorized. There is a constant pol-itics and poetics of displacement taking place. The writer, displaced from his home, is seeking meaning in alien cultural geographies, while the "natives" are displaced from their natural habitat through the power of the constraining and distorting Western discourse. What we see in this dual displacement process is the initial interaction between history and geog-raphy. Newer cultural geographies are created by the systematic dehistor-izing of the indigenous peoples and their spaces [1993, 18].

Set in the contemporary Paris, the Paris at a crossroad, Paris is about shifting geographical boundaries and changing historical tides. Antici-pating changes in Europe, Adnan compares the potential realization of the European Union with the fragmentation and humiliation — what she calls national disasters (1993b, 113)— occurring in the former European colonies of the Arab world. The geographical movements of Paris—"receding North as do its sister-cities of Berlin and Warsaw," looking East towards Moscow, and keeping the "[S]outh at bay" (49)— are historical reorganizations of world powers: the former colonial empire is gaining new power through the European Union as well as the new alliance with Russia, former ally of the colonized world, while the previously colonized territories still suffer from the effects of colonization. France maintains its influence on Algerian politics while Algerians, especially those immigrants who live in Paris, are abandoned, with no protection against discrimination; Iraq suffers from the consequences of "international" sanctions in the aftermath of "Desert Storm"; the Palestinian issue remains unresolved; and Lebanon, a country torn by civil war (thanks in part to its colonial legacy), is in shambles. The contrast is sharp; despite the "Arab Apocalypse," a vision of the disintegration of the Arab world she articulates in a collection of poetry of the same title, no apocalyptic wind blows over Paris (Adnan 1993b, 39). Here, geography and history are intricately intertwined: movements occur "on the surface of continents, or back and forth, from the past to the future" (24).

Adnan's wandering in Paris is both physical and mental; she walks its streets while her mind wanders (Adnan 1993b, 28), contemplating the future of Europe, the fate of the Arab world now and in history, and her own relationship to Paris. The textual constructs of her wanderings, however, help her to decolonize both the Arab collective she belongs to and herself. Adnan juxtaposes almost every landmark in the various *arrondissments* of Paris — viewed quarter by quarter, street by street, fountain by fountain, garden by garden, church by church, restaurant by restaurant, cafe by cafe, bookstore by bookstore — to unpleasant realities of the Arab world and the Arab experience in France, and to ugly episodes in the Arab world's colonial history. The beauty of the city, for example, is contrasted to the ugliness of its Arab Quarter. "Look, look how ugly are the Arab Quarter's pimps, how dehumanized the Algerians who squat in it, how destroyed their women, how degrading their prostitution to the very ones who vote for their expulsion" (1993b, 7-8). The beauty of Marie de Medicis is juxtaposed to "that movie ... of Iraqi children dying from the effects of the continuing blockade imposed on their country" (15). The ramifications of the actual occupation of countries like Algeria and Lebanon, the destruction of the Middle East, and the reconfiguration of its geography are never far from her mind when she marvels at the beauty of Paris. While Paris is thriving, the Middle East has fallen into ruin. Adnan quotes Hölderlin:

> You cities of the Euphrates!
> and you, streets of Palmyra!
> you forests of pillars on the desert's face,
> what became of you!

[1993b, 62]

While "Paris is open to the round earth" (59) and traveling from it to, say Russia, is easy, the Middle East is closed upon itself: "It is to Teheran that one can't go easily nowadays, a place I could have reached by bus from some market place in Damascus" (51).

The process of decolonization is disorienting — "The trouble is, that I don't know where I come from, and even less, where I'm heading" (Adnan 1993b, 100) — but necessary. The process begins with the reexamination of the place of Paris in her heart: "Look at Paris, do it in your imagination if your eyes can't find it" (4). Paris may be the labyrinth where she misplaced her soul temporarily (47), but to recover a soul that is not lost (101) is not impossible; it involves redefining the meaning of Paris. In other words, "Paris has to be reduced to energy points, has to be obliterated, and then rebuilt by one's mind, to be livable" (105).

Adnan begins by acknowledging that "Paris weighs on [her] with all its mass," and that its meaning to her is complex; "[t]he different threads which make it up can hardly be sorted out..." (Adnan 1993b, 43). She then proceeds to examine the various aspects of the issue as she explored Paris, whose "avenues [are] made for the soul to expand and meander within its own thoughts and desires" (66). She recognizes that "Paris is no solid ground," but is "a fairground for illusions," and that despite its reputation as a home of exiles it is in fact a "degenerous place" where exiles' hope "to find a freedom and security ... has lived and died at [its] walls' feet" (58). She lets "the walls ... come down" (67) and comes to the realization that she could love Paris and choose to live far away from it, for "[t]here is no use living in Paris when all one cares for is the sea" (57), the sea here being a symbol of Lebanon. "I have been inhabited for a while by such revelation of cosmic beauty," she writes, "that I felt — at last — that I would be able not to spend all my life (i.e., what's left of my life) in this city" (46). Coming to terms with Paris, or with her love for it, she realizes that to love Paris does not mean she is possessed by it but that she possesses it in her mind (107), that to love her enemy does not mean she is her enemy's prey (106).

This revelation works wonders for her: the mist that has enveloped Paris, as well as her state of mind (Adnan 1993b, 66) finally lifts, "letting a dying sun send myriads of lit particles into the air," giving her "a new freedom" to enjoy Paris (103), and her spirit "lands anew" (115). As she comes to terms with Paris she also comes to terms with living in California, even though it is also a site of exile; she sees the beauty of Yosemite (67) and the paradisiacal quality of Baja (43). And she comes to terms with living away from Paris, the home of her colonized self, and with the loss of Beirut, the original home.

Homecoming: (Re)-Construction of the Self

In the segment on Arabic literature she wrote and narrated for the 1983 BBC documentary series, "The Arabs: A Living History," Arab critic Khalida Sa'id says that "The Power of the Word" lies in that it gives something a name. And to name something is to bring it into existence, to make it tangible, to make it real. Adnan, like other postcolonial writers, writes to articulate the painfully disorienting experiences of postcolonial subjectivity, to bring to the fore the exile's inner turmoil that would otherwise have been denied, obscured, obliterated. To narrate is to bring cohesion, coherence, and structure to fragmented memories; it is not only to write history but to take control of one's destiny, and more importantly, to seek justice. Justice, to a colonial subject, is, among other things, recognition of personal history, both as such and as part of the collective history of displacement and exile; it is an act that brings the exile from the margin to the center, a process of empowerment. Writing is, therefore, a willful journey toward the center, ending in some sort of homecoming. Home ceases to be the physical space from which one is initially exiled, but is the world the writer creates for herself in her writing.

Cities, one narrative written in the form of nine letters dating from 1990 to 1992, details Adnan's journey of homecoming, her redefinition of the self. Even though she seems at first to descend "into the unknowing," she eventually "emerge[s] from the tunnel that life in California or Paris can become" (Adnan 1993a, 38) and finds the "right geography for [her] revelations" (93). Even as Adnan complains that "we are the scribes of a scattered self, living fragments, as if the parts of the self were writing down the bits and ends of a perception never complete" (54), her "temporal expanses," as Kerby observes of narratives of exile in general, "are given meaning through the unifying action of narration" (1991, 3). In *Cities*, her narrative journey, which, like other narratives, is "a structure of development, growth and change, the acquisition of knowledge and solution of problems," is "conceived as a physical process of movement, of disruption, negotiation and return" (Curtis and Pajaczkowska 1994, 199). With her movement from one city to another as she meditates and mediates the meanings of femininity, both for her identity as a woman and as a symbol of her exile, she has embarked on a journey in search of the meanings of her exile. Her journey ends in Beirut, the city that "clings to [her] like hot wax, even in slumber" (Adnan 1993a, 73).

In *Invisible Cities*, Italo Calvino depicts the situation of the wandering expatriate in paradoxical terms: "Arriving at each new city, the traveler finds again a past of his that he did not know he had: the foreignness of what you no longer are or no longer possess lies in wait for you in foreign, unpossessed places" (1974, 27-28). Adnan's travels in each European city — Barcelona, Aix-En-Provence, Skopelos, Murcia, Amsterdam, Berlin, Rome — reveal to her meanings of womanhood, its definitions, manifestations and practices, and its relationship to manhood and humanhood historically and geographically. As she acknowledges that she has become a stranger to certain definitions of womanhood, she also admits to being a stranger to the places she lives in. Her experiences in various cities call into question her identity and force her to reexamine the relationship between these places and her self. Following her reevaluation of her relationship with Paris in *Paris*, in *Cities* she now reexamines her ties with Beirut, with Sausalito in the background.

Adnan's textual strategies in *Cities* are similar to those she employs in *Paris*, but her objectives are different. Here, she deterritorializes and reterritorializes Europe and Beirut to (re)-construct her self. In *Cities* Adnan reclaims and asserts her identity as Lebanese, Arab and Mediterranean by creating a discursive narrative that places her squarely in those three imaginary constructs. Her narrative creates a unity, both geographically and historically: she rewrites the landscape of her self by giving an integral and integrating history to the divergent places of her wandering. The threads that hold these places together are Adnan's meditations on notions of femininity in the past and present, the arts and society, and Islam and Christianity, and the re-delineating personal and collective history she writes for the region. Freedom for women in Barcelona invites comparison with how women carry themselves in Marrakesh and Beirut; freedom for women in Skopelos reminds her of lack of freedom for women in Saudi Arabia; in Aix-en-Provence exile is linked to womanhood through the paintings of Cezanne and Picasso; the role of woman in Ibn 'Arabi's thought is explored in Murcia; patience as women's virtue is reconsidered in Amsterdam; in Rome the place of woman in Christianity is scrutinized through Michaelangelo's paintings; the absence of women in post war Beirut's public arena and its role in redefining this city is discussed; and in Beirut the notion that woman equals death is refuted.

The historical ties between Spain and the Arab-Islamic world are remembered, though not without some sad notes about the Arabs. For instance, Adnan writes, "Spain descends toward the South, and in the landscape, Arab castles follow one after the other (chimerical castles), ochre, in ruins, tenacious and crumbling, like everything that is Arabic. The plain shrinks, the high peaks stand on each side with miradors still standing guard. These witnesses to the civil wars of Arabic Spain make me think that nothing can destroy an Arab better than another Arab" (1993a, 49).

Even in Berlin, her narrative is of the Gulf War in Iraq, by which she links the contemporary history of Iraq to world events. Roman ruins in turn remind her of Baalbek and Syria: in Rome "I lived again my childhood's visiting sites like Baalbek and the Crusaders' fortresses of Syria" (93). In fact, Rome reminds her of the entire Mediterranean culture to which she was first exposed to in Beirut: "It was as though I am haunted with Beirut and the entire Mediterranean culture based on the adoration of the son" (90).

The journey that began in *Sitt Marie Rose* comes to a full circle in *Cities*. Between the two texts is a journey of self-discovery that begins with departure and ends with arrival. Every letter/chapter in *Cities* is a step towards her homecoming — not a permanent physical return, even though the physical journey is part and parcel of the process, but a coming to terms with exile, with leaving Beirut. Beirut is recognized for what it is, and more importantly, its proper place in her life is determined. Her question in the very first pages of her narrative, "Beirut? But which Beirut?" (1993a, 3) is a curious one. Is the question geographical-social, about the multiplicity of Beirut societies, or is it historical, about the difference between Beirut in the past and Beirut now, or is it rhetorical, about the Beirut in her heart and the real Beirut? As the narrative unfolds, however, we realize that Beirut is the "lost paradise" (33) that now embodies all the ugliness of the Arab world (10), as well as the potential for its destruction (42). More importantly, we realize that the Beirut that she longs for is the city in its days of glory, between 1925 and 1975 (45). The "ideal" country it symbolizes no longer exists (106). As a matter of fact, Beirut can no longer be home to her. For one thing, the city "which is by excellence a woman's place, has become the exclusive domain of men" (80). In other words, the reasons that made her leave are still there, only more omnipresent.

Adnan's narrative ends with an "unplanned" letter from Beirut in which she recounts her experience attending the funeral of her close friend, Janine Rubeiz. Here, she bids farewell to the Beirut she remembers as she says goodbye to her friend: Beirut and Janine become one. She ends a paragraph on Beirut with the sentence, "One cries over the 'ideal' country" (1993a, 106) and moves immediately to, "The tears I'm having over my friend's death make a screen of light which hides her image as well as the city and its problems" (106). Her grief over her friend's death is also her grief over the entire Arab world: "On my dead friend's frail shoulders, encroached upon by disintegration, I place the Arab world's destiny whose apocalyptic future we all seem to know" (107). When she speaks of Janine's death, it is as if she were speaking of Beirut's death: "How can one ask her to come back, to rebuild herself, bit by bit, somehow or other, like the city is trying to, ask her to participate in our little occupations, ask her not to wall herself in this starless world, this waterless ocean, in which she went for ever, there where maybe nothingness itself is no more. We can find her nowhere, on no continent, no space, no boat, not even beyond the visible world" (108). When she decides to leave Janine behind "in her dreadful last resting place" (113), she also bids farewell to Beirut. Post war Beirut — a city she can no longer stand, with its noise, heat, pollution and chaos — belongs to its new builders. Even the sea, which represented all the glories of Beirut as she knew them, is flat and of no help: "the sea beyond my windows isn't an ally anymore. She resembles the sun too much and burns my eyes. She has become as terrifying as the militia's heads" (111). The resurrected Beirut, despite its liveliness and moments of nobility (82, 13), is no longer the Beirut in which she felt at home; "everything is gone save the climate. And something of the sea has left, too, because the sea is so messy" (111). In fact, "Our old Beirut is as remote from us as the Stone Age" (82).

As Adnan pays "Homage to Beirut" (1993a, 113), she comes to terms with her loss of it, as with homelessness and exile. Exile, like womanhood, is defined by how it is viewed. "Doesn't the act of looking at an object become also one of its definitions? And isn't a 'woman' all that has been said about her, all that has been seen in her, all that has been done to her?" (22). Exile is paradoxical: it can be powerlessness as well as power, depending on the exile's perception. The condition of homelessness can be remedied as well. Penelope, defined as "pure waiting," may indeed determine the destiny of Ulysses for whom she waits. "Ulysses cannot therefore not return. He is 'programmed' by Penelope's wait. This reverses the whole process: the target does then determine the arrow's path" (59). Insomuch as exile is perceived as equivalent to homelessness, the definition of homelessness — therefore of home — can determine the meaning of exile. An exile's journey home, in other words, does not depend on the conventional notions of home, which is a mental construct built around a physical place, but on how an exile defines it. Beirut the home becomes Beirut the "home" — the word in quotation marks appears for the first time towards the end of her narrative — when Adnan reevaluates the place of Beirut in her heart (111). At the end of her journey, she realizes that the books that she writes are indeed the houses that she builds for herself, and her obsession with houses as locales of home ends (90).

Adnan's ability to transcend convention is a gift of her multiple exile, which serves as a vantage point of many departures and permits her freedom from the restraints of tradition. An exile, as Said points out in *Representations of the Intellectual*, may be forced into restless movement, constantly unsettled and unsettling others (1994, 53). He/she is, however, permitted multiple perspectives from which to examine his/her condition and the world. Writing, freed of the demands of a literary tradition and cultural expectations, can become creative in more ways than one. Given a new function, language becomes the very means by which the self is constructed. Even though the exile's journey of homecoming is long, it is possible. Penelope's strategy to endure her long wait is her weaving, "she weaves and unravels her work" patiently until Ulysses returns (Adnan 1993a, 59). In the case of Adnan, her writing is equivalent to Penelope's weaving; by repeatedly writing her exile Adnan arrives home. Homecoming here is not merely giving new meanings to the idea of home, but also reconstructing the self that was fragmented by exile. In Adnan's narratives there is a relationship between language and the self, or between one's life story and the subject of that story. As she writes elsewhere, "There is a dialectical relation between one's life and one's work. The former obviously influences the latter, but one's work also becomes an influence on one's life. It is a two way affair, a mysterious process where what we call life and what we call creation merge and do not merge, cross feed each other" (1990, 11). As in other exile narratives examined by Kerby, "acts of self-narration" are not to be taken "only as descriptive of the self, but more importantly, as fundamental to the emergence and reality of [her] subject," for her "understanding of [herself] is mediated primarily through language," and her "self-narrating is a matter of becoming conscious of the narratives that [she] already live with and in" (Kerby 1991, 4–5). More importantly, her narratives allow her to construct a home, or what Salman Rushdie (1991) would call an "imaginary homeland," where her imagination is sovereign.

Notes

1. The emergence of the Arab identity as we know it today is tied in with the geographical and political reconfiguration of North Africa and the Middle East, the most parts of which constituted the former Ottoman Empire before the region was colonized by the British, French and Italians. Even though Etel Adnan was born to a Syrian father and Greek mother, she came to define herself as an Arab, deriving her identity from the entity that emerged as the Arab world in the aftermath of colonialism.

2. For discussions of some of these difficulties, see the essays in Part II of this volume, "Reading *Sitt Marie Rose*," especially the essays by Sabah Ghandour and Sami Ofeish, and by Pauline Homsi Vinson.

3. See, for instance, Woodhull (1993, 8).

References

Adnan, Etel. 1977. *Sitt Marie Rose*. Paris: Femmes.
_____. 1982. *Sitt Marie Rose*. Translated by Georgina Kleege. Sausalito: Post-Apollo.
_____. 1986. *Journey to Mount Tamalpais*. Sausalito: Post-Apollo.
_____.1990. "Growing Up to be a Woman Writer in Lebanon." In *Opening the Gates: A Century of Arab Feminist Writing*, edited by Margot Badran and Miriam Cooke, 5–20. Bloomington and Indianapolis: Indiana University Press.
_____. 1993a. *Of Cities & Women (Letters to Fawwaz)*. Sausalito: Post-Apollo.
_____. 1993b. *Paris, When It's Naked*. Sausalito: Post-Apollo.
Alcalay, Ammiel. 1994. "Our Memory Has No Future." *The Nation* (March): 311–313.
Bammer, Angelika. 1994. Introduction to *Displacements: Cultural Identities in Questions*, edited by Angelika Bammer, xi–xx. Bloomington and Indianapolis: Indiana University Press.
Calvino, Italo. 1974. *Invisible Cities*. Translated by William Weaver. San Diego, New York and London: Harcourt Brace.
Curtis, Barry and Claire Pajaczkowska. 1994. "'Getting There': Travel, Time and Narrative." In *Travellers' Tales: Narratives of Home and Displacement*, edited by Geroge Robertso, Melina Mash, Lisa Tickner, Jon Bird, Barru Curtis and Tim Putnam, 199–215. London and New York: Routledge.
Deleuze, Gilles and Felix Guattari. 1986. *Kafka: Toward a Minor Literature*. Translated by Dana Polan. Vol. 30, Theory and History of Literature. Minneapolis and London: University of Minnesota Press.
Dissanayake, Wimal and Carmen Wickramagamage. 1993. *Self and Colonial Desire: Travel Writings of V. S. Naipaul*. Studies of World Literature in English, Vol. 2. New York: Peter Lang.
Gordon, David C. 1980. *Lebanon: The Fragmented Nation*. London: Croom Helm.
Ilie, Paul. 1980. *Literature and Inner Exile: Authoritarian Spain, 1939–75*. Baltimore and London: The Johns Hopkins University Press.
Jameson, Fredric. 1991. *Postmodernism, or, The Cultural Logic of Late Capitalism*. Durham: Duke University Press.
Kennedy, J. Gerald. 1993. *Imagining Paris: Exile, Writing, and American Identity*. New Haven and London: Yale University Press.
Kerby, Anthony Paul. 1991. *Narrative and the Self: Studies in Continental Thought*. Bloomington and Indianapolis: Indiana University Press.
Levy, Judith. 1995. *V. S. Naipaul: Displacement and Autobiography*. New York and London: Garland.
Naipaul, V. S. 1984. *Finding the Center*. New York: Alfred A. Knopf.
Quinlan, Susan Canty. 1995. "The Mysterious Space of Exile: Punishable Songs by Judith Grossmann." In *International Women's Writing: New Landscapes of Identity*, edited by Anne E. Brown and Marjanne E. Gozze, 115–124. Westport and London: Greenwood.
Relph, E. 1976. *Place and Placelessness*. London: Pion.
Rushdie, Salman. 1991. *Imaginary Homelands: Essays and Criticism 1981–1991*. London: Granta.
Said, Edward. 1994. *Representations of the Intellectual*. New York: Pantheon.

Seidel, Michael. 1986. *Exile and the Narrative Imagination*. New Haven and London: Yale University Press.

Trinh T. Miuh-ha. 1994. "Other Than Myself/My Other Self." In *Travellers' Tales: Narratives of Home and Displacement*, edited by George Robertson, Melinda Mass, Lisa Tickner, Jon Bird, Barry Curtis and Tim Putnam, 9–26. London and New York: Routledge.

Tuan, Yi-Fu. 1977. *Space and Place: The Perspective of Experience*. Minneapolis: University of Minnesota Press.

Woodhull, Winifred. 1993. "Exile." In *Post/Colonial Conditions: Exiles, Migrations, and Nomadisms*, special issue of Yale French Studies 82, no. 1: 9–24. New Haven: Yale University Press.

5

On Perception: Etel Adnan's Visual Art

Simone Fattal

The first time I saw Etel Adnan's visual work was in a series of long Japanese folding books in which she had handwritten poetry with accompanying visual equivalents. Through these folding books Adnan had quietly effected a revolution in Arabic calligraphy. She had written out poems by the major contemporary Arab poets, each in a unique book using her own handwriting, not trying to conform to the canons of calligraphy, and had accompanied them with drawings, watercolors, ink and pen work. The books unfolded in front of my eyes as "readings" of poetry taking place in the parallel world of color and sensory perception. The poems were brought to life more rapidly than if one followed the words alone. Also, the tenderness of her line brought an immense emotion and empathy to the text and to its reading, so that the moment of this reading became intensely printed in the imagination. The drawings and watercolors added a dimension of poignancy and urgency to the text, which was seen by Adnan twice, once as a text and once as an image. The reader was thus given three interpretations: that of the poet, the transcriber, and the painter.

Etel Adnan worked in my studio for a few years soon after we met in Beirut, Lebanon. As I was a painter myself, I had a large studio that could offer her space and freedom. The first time she used it was to draw a tree, in watercolor. This flowering tree was a revelation. I looked at it for a long time and all I could say about it was that it was a flowering tree. It had a lot in it of the Arab miniature's world. It stood on the page diagonally, its flowers freshly shivering in the outside air, its colors unobtrusive and discreet, almost shy. A young tree.

I invited her to paint in my studio whenever her work at the newspaper *Al-Safa*, where she was the cultural editor, left her some free time. She would come on the weekends and work. Was it the urgency of time available or her own impatient energy that made her always finish an oil painting in one sitting? I would come later and discover the whole world transcribed on the surface of the canvas. She worked the canvas like a sheet of paper, the canvas laid on the table, using a palette knife instead of a brush. She posed on it squares and masses — vivid bright stretches of color. I was startled by the difference from the original tree that I had seen. All the shyness had disappeared. Etel Adnan in oil had an assuredness rarely seen in other painter's works. The world was summoned and summarized on the canvas.

The first two canvases she painted were entitled *Syria* and *Lebanon*. *Syria* was pink and *Lebanon* was blue. *Syria*: a pink sky, or was it earth? — the pink the desert takes on. The Syrian hills are pink in the sunset and early dawn, and the Lebanon mountains are all shades and hues of blue, what with the proximity of the sea! Strong compact squares, hermetic for the amount of intense color they contained, punctuated their skies and space. One could read the whole *esprit* of a place on one canvas. It was not only that place on that particular day when the sky was gray and some mist was getting in, it was the place the way it will always be, containing as well the very moment that place was portrayed. Adnan said once, "It is not because painting is visual that it is always comprehensible." The visual is a language one has to learn the way one learns French or Spanish or German.

Adnan started as a purely abstract painter, using large squares compactly juxtaposed or floating on a background, or else smaller squares composing a line either dividing the surface or also floating somewhere on the surface of the canvas. Among these hermetic squares, there was almost always a red one. It was as if from the red square that all the rest of the composition emerged. Around it the world — its lines of forces, the large picture — organized itself. During a discussion of a show of Adnan's paintings in California, much later, I heard this comment: "It is as if you are seeing this from very far." Indeed her landscapes are seen from very far — in order to see the whole picture. The landscape rests compressed on a small surface. Only the strong lines, the large undercurrents emerge. There are no people in Adnan's oils; it is the world that she is looking at, the beautiful physical earth with its mountains, hills, rivers and colors. She is a person *in the world*, in the sense Jean Paul Sartre gave to that expression. Much as she talks about the social aspect of the universe in her writing, she talks about the physical beauty of the universe in her painting. As she has said, "Painting expresses my happy side, the one who is at one with the universe" (personal communication).

Adnan is a colorist. "Les coloristes sont des poètes épiques" (colorists are epic poets), said Baudelaire (1967, 965). Who better than Adnan to be in that position, as she is already an epic poet in words? There is an epic vision and rendering in these extraordinary canvases. She is tackling the world, wrestling with it, with love and passion. She told me once, "When I die the universe will have lost its best friend, someone who loved it with passion." She is in love with the beauty of it. She has a need to see color, and not at all to use the crayon as a pen: "I started using oil pastels on their side, i.e. as bands of color, surfaces of color."[1]

In Beirut she was in love with the sea. Most paintings made in Lebanon contained the effect, the reflection the sea had on its bordering earth and mountain. One day in 1973 she went to Iraq to attend a Biennial of Arab painting. When she returned she made a very large canvas. The Biennial had taken place in the early spring when the rains are plentiful, and as always in Iraq, the impression of walking in the mud, of being in the mud, of being the mud was overwhelming. The Tigris carried huge amounts of eroded earth. When she came back to Beirut, she painted a large pink river Tigris in the middle of which stood two rafts—two squares—following the flow to the fresh cadmium green banks of the river. (That is her secret, more often than not she will use color fresh from the tube, as is). The picture was a Persian miniature in its spirit but needed the large scale to express it. That painting was exhibited at Dar El Fan (a Lebanese cultural center that existed between 1967 and 1975) along with another big painting of Mount Sannine. She thought the latter was lost during the civil war when Dar El Fan was sacked and pillaged, but a fellow painter friend, Nicole Harfouche, went in looking for things and rescued it for her, damaged but splendid.

Adnan started painting in California when she was teaching Philosophy of Art and Esthetics at Dominican College in San Rafael. She started teaching there in 1958. One day on her way to class Adnan met the art teacher Ann O'Hanlon. Ann asked her, "How can you teach philosophy of art and not paint yourself?" Adnan heard herself answer, "My mother told me I was clumsy." And Ann said: "And you believed her?" This simple question and answer freed her hands, and soon, at Ann's invitation, she started using a table by a window in the Art department overlooking a little creek and fig trees. She painted on sample pieces of canvas, leftovers, irrespective of their size and shape.

She found her style immediately. Using the palette knife she applied large bands of color juxtaposed to each other. Many thought of Nicolas de Staël when looking at these early canvases; she acknowledges a family spirit. It is as if she and de Staël use the same vocabulary. But unlike in the work of de Staël, there is no hesitation in her choice of colors and the masses. De Staël comes back across an area over and over. At the caesura between colors you will notice the layers and layers of the different colors used, for he almost always leaves traces of them, until he finds and settles on the last one. One can almost read all his different stages. Adnan finds her definitive shape and color at once. Someone said, "your painting is decisive." It is the way her whole being is: no hesitation. In the same way there are practically no corrections in her manuscripts. There is no hiatus between the inception and the laying-down on the page. It is all there from the first moment. When she poses her color on the page, it is the definitive color. She has already mentally mastered her subject and she lands it down. Clear perception, clear execution.

It should also be said that Adnan's paintings are austere, almost severe. No facile effects, no adornments, no concession to the viewer: a simple statement about a proposed moment. Her paintings are succinct in the same way her writing is. She says it all in a few words. She lives in a rarefied atmosphere the way monks live on top of mountains.

Adnan started immediately making mature abstract paintings, and Ann O'Hanlon, seeing them, changed her whole philosophy of teaching Art. She thought, "Well, if Etel can paint so spontaneously then anyone can do it." She started workshops at her house inviting members, teaching that art was just another way of perceiving.

We all perceive.

Adnan continued the journey opened by this first encounter with the canvas. She looked up and painted. The essence of painting is this immediacy between the view and the canvas. We all perceive, but the best rendering is from the one who does not let his or her ego get in the way. She summarized the large picture in strong masses and rendered its lines of strength. O'Hanlon sponsored a show for her at her studio and Professor Pepper, the aesthetics Professor at U.C.-Berkeley, attended and marveled. Indeed, there is an element of marvel in Adnan's work. It is as if a child discovers the way the world works and the way to say it again for the first time. Baudelaire describes it this way: "Le génie est l'enfance retrouvée à volonté" (Genius is childhood found at will) (1967, 1240). And when you say childhood you say first time, therefore you say also innocence, that is, truthfulness.

Ideally she would have liked to create another Bauhaus, to work with a group of artists-artisans and change the world. She was going to build this ideal in Lebanon, in a village, before the war killed a fellow organizer and killed the Lebanon where such a project could have been. She would have organized her artists with the ethics of the medieval guilds. She conceives the artist as artisan too — the artisan of beauty and truth. One enters into art as into religion and pledges truthfulness, for without it one cannot produce a work of art.

In Adnan's case I would add that her truthfulness goes beyond, to a subject almost always situated outside herself. It is never her own "etat d'ame" that is the subject of the art, but rather the outside world, the challenge of a world event or a commission: "l'être-au-monde" of Jean-Paul Sartre using colors and canvas. (This "l'être au monde" was already defined by Baudelaire, for the artist, for him, is necessarily "homme du monde."[3]) When the Apollo program put men on the moon and opened this new dimension to the earth-bound, so that the moon lost its virginity and the universe became somewhere one could go, Adnan produced a large series of brush works entitled "The Apollo Series." For this series she devised her own colors, making yellows and greens with onion skins and pomegranates, adding these dyes to the watercolors and ink.

The juxtaposition of squares of color in Adnan's work means not only that these are the actual colors the earth takes on such and such a day, but that one has to look at what the whole ensemble creates, and the impression these colors are going to produce in the viewer. This is what will inevitably give him or her the feeling of the place, the feeling that is most *sui generis* to a place and the color that is most unforgettable. As the Qur'an says, "He has created for you on earth (things) of different colors, in that fact (the different colors) there is a sign for people who want to remember" (my translation).[4]

Adnan went on with her painting, all the while writing notes on her painting and on perception. After her beginning as an abstract colorist, she turned her attention to Mount Tamalpais. There in front of her window, everywhere she went in Marin County, walking to Dominican from home, or driving to go to the movies, the mountain was there. It became her point of reference, her home far from home. She looked and lived with the mountain even after she came back to Beirut. All the time she was painting the mountain, drawing it in oil, watercolor, ink. She made thousands of these drawings. The natural pyramidal shape of the mountain

"The West Side — Mt. Tamalpais." Watercolor with brush and ink. Etel Adnan.

became embedded in her whole being. It became her identity. She could draw it while in Lebanon, at night and at dawn; the mountain was for her the ever-revealing mystery, the on-going manifestation.

I wonder whether in those days she loved someone as much as she loved Mount Tamalpais.

Her involvement with the mountain lasted until she published *Journey to Mount Tamalpais* (1986). When I published *Journey* at the Post-Apollo Press, Adnan had been working on the mountain for 23 years. Her philosophical training and her specialty in aesthetics came together in this book, a philosophical meditation on her praxis which she wrote over a period of twenty years, piling up her notes. (The element of time is telling, when we know that she wrote *Sitt Marie Rose*, her novel, in a month!) I chose 16 drawings for the book. I did not want to use color plates for I did not want the color to interfere with the reading of a text, and the text had to be with black and white characters.

The book is a meditation on the relationship between Nature and Art, in other words, on the meaning of perception. Through her praxis as a painter Etel Adnan discovered her basic philosophy — we can also call it her credo — that the Universe is One. But she would have never arrived at that conclusion with only an academic education. The relation of her journey into this praxis is that of a student to the meaning of art. She is in dialogue with the painters she likes, whose works she toured the world to see — Kandinsky, Paul Klee, Cezanne and Dürer — painters who are also theoreticians and who wrote extensively on painting. She was also teaching writings by painters in her aesthetics classes, believing that these were more important and more accessible than the writings of dry theoreticians like Hegel or Panovsky. Her paintings are conceived of in regard to those artists. Those are the correspondents she argues with, on whose work she builds. They are familiar and family.

In Lebanon, during the years she spent there from 1972 to 1979, Adnan created a body of work on landscapes focusing on Lebanon. Lebanon's high Mount Sannine was never able to replace Mount Tamalpais in her work — although who knows, if she had stayed in Lebanon. In these landscapes she no longer used compact, tense, actual, recognizable hills and rivers. The landscape was nearer to what we expect to find on a canvas entitled "landscape." It was still made of stretches of color, but the point of view had come nearer to the subject. It was as if these squares had opened up and one could see what each of them contained.

When she was a child Etel Adnan was asked what she wanted to be when she grew up, and she said she wanted to be an architect. It was a scandal for a woman then to even aspire to be an architect, and so she attended the Ecole des Lettres, because it was a night school and she could go there after her daytime job. Her early paintings possessed a solid structure, an inner organization, the vocabulary of an architect: squares and cubes mounted on each other or next to each other, containing the possibilities of matter.

And so the square made room for the Mountain. The square divided itself into a Pyramid, which happened to be the Mountain's form — a Pyramid soon inhabited by spheres. To draw a sphere one needs a line, and the line led to an innumerable number of watercolors and drawings of the Mountain. She drew the Mountain everywhere and all the time. She imagined the essence of it. She saw underneath its surface the number of Indians locked inside. A Mountain of glass. As she writes in *Journey to Mount Tamalpais*, "One October night I dreamed that the whole mountain was made of glass, a thick, greenish glass, with long and rusty streaks of kelp within it. I was lying over it, looking in, and discovering Indians telling me with sign language and impatient gestures that they were imprisoned for centuries" (1986, 23).

Adnan reached the moment where she was (not quite) finished with the general shape of the mountain — seen at dusk, when the blue hues invade the whole universe, seen with rain and clouds and as a Powerful Woman — so she started painting close-ups, details. It was the end of the winter when the mountain is green. This series of green patches of mountain earth are quite astounding; they are a harmony of all greens, signed with only a line of red to uphold the whole composition.

There are very few of these paintings, because she had to stop in order to have a show of the Mountain series at the San Rafael Civic Center. This is where the book, the paintings and watercolors and folding books on the mountain were exhibited, in the gallery of this building designed by Frank Lloyd Wright, another of her great loves. I was especially able to appreciate his design when the show was taken to Paris later that year. The straight white lines of the Paris gallery did not convey the same magic. What a great artist is Frank Lloyd Wright! The curving walls and the red color of his building only enhanced the strong colorful paintings.

Adnan's paintings play the role the old icons used to play for people who believed. They exude energy and give energy. They grow on you like talismans. They help in living everyday life. More often than not I have noticed that people who have Adnan's paintings will keep them in their innermost chambers, and not in their living rooms as *objets d'art*. The quickness of their making, the fact that they are finished in one sitting, their compactness— with nothing diluted or lost, joins to the happiness experienced while painting, the joy of using color. They reflect the praise of the universe, the experience of it, immersion in it, participation in its formation. No lamentation, no elegy. Love.

> Do Colors have the power to break the Time barrier, and carry us into outer space, not only those made of miles and distances, but those of the accumulated experience of life since its beginnings or unbeginning? [Adnan 1986, 52]

> I am sitting as usual in front of Mount Tamalpais. I can't get over its deep greens. It is clear, it is empty. My spirit is anguished by color. Color is the sign of the existence of life. I feel like believing, being in a state of pure belief, of affirmation. I exist because I see colors. Sometimes, at other moments, it is as if I didn't exist, when colors seem foreign, unreachable, impregnable fortresses. But there is no possession of color, only the acceptance of its reality. And if there is no possibility for the possession of color, there is no possession at all. Of whatever it is [Adnan 1986, 51].

This is the lesson of painting. We are here to perceive, and it is exhilarating, for when perception does happen it is a manifestation and perfect fulfillment. But this fulfillment does not last. Some trace of it gets on the

"Mount Tamalpais — From My Window." Watercolor with brush and ink. Etel Adnan.

paper, if we are able to catch it and freeze it. Painting as a lesson of purity of mind. Purity of purpose. Painting as an affirmation of life, of its very constitution.

We think in metaphors, for when the body is asleep, the mind works in images. It tells us in images what few people understand and know how to decipher. Those who understand this language we impart with special powers.

> I always thought that dreaming was the honor of the human species. The logic of dreams is superior to the one we exercise while awake. In dreams the mind finds at last its courage: it dares what we do not dare. It also creates ... and it perceives reality beyond our fuzzy interpretations" [Adnan 1986, 23].

> Sometimes while painting, something wild gets unleashed. Something of the process of dreams recurs... but with a special kind of violence: a painting is like a territory. All kinds of things happen within its boundary, equal to the discoveries of the murders or the creations we have in the world outside [Adnan, 1986, 26].

Painting as pure energy with which to live one's life — with courage.

Let us go back to the descriptions of Adnan's paintings. The palette knife makes a thick paste, like the grain of earth. The taste of the land is on the canvas. Grainy, uneven, with accidents, with ups and downs, with more or less color, more or less substance. She follows the landscape as it moves:

> Now the clouds are grandiose and turbulent. An autumn storm is coming. Whatever makes mountains rise, and us, with them, makes colors restless and ecstatic. At my right , the Tiburon hills are somberly yellow. They have a strange power in their color. Is this pale gold on the surface of these hills so extraneous to its own place, that it makes my mind jump into the notion of some past I never knew and which, still strangely, I relate to them? Otherwise why do these dark and light hues of yellowish metal make me think of Louis the XIVth, of one of his incursions into Europe, of a particular day of his life, that remains lingering between the known and the unknown, that I see clearly and at the same time cannot pinpoint and give as precise reference? Do colors have the power to break the Time barrier ...? [Adnan, 1986, 52].

Painting, as knowledge.

> But can I ever understand what Cezanne says in Mont-Sainte Victoire, and Hokusai in Mount Fuji, if, after thirty years, I don't know what Tamalpais means to me beyond the sketches, paintings and writings that involved me with her. I know that the process of painting and

writing gives me the implicit certitude of what the Mountain is and of what I see: I perceive a nature proper to her while I work. Tamalpais has an autonomy of being. So does a drawing of it. But they are mysteriously related [Adnan, 1986, 55].

Now to the pen. I call pen work everything that does not use the palette knife. That includes the brush, with ink and watercolors, and crayons, and pencils. Adnan has developed, with years, a masterly brush work that some equate to the Japanese and Chinese masters. During her frequent visits to New York she stayed in an apartment on the 33rd floor overlooking the East river from whose windows she could see six or more bridges. There ensued a whole series of thick black ink drawings of the New York bridges, with barges passing under them or anchored on their pylons. These are on Japanese folding papers so thin they are transparent. The contrast between the strong lines of the subject matter and the fragility of the material on which they stand makes one wonder about the materiality of the world.

She then made a corresponding series of the stone bridges of Paris: smaller, more squarish, closer to the water and to the people, always used, always crossed. One of them is an echo of Baudelaire's poem: "Le Soleil moribond s'endormir sous une arche" (an agonizing sun falling under an arch).[5] Yes, we see the sun setting in the middle of the arch. One can still live the experience as one walks by the Seine's banks at sunset. The New York bridges are different: never walked on or by, rising higher in their metallic structures, belonging more to the pure realm of structure, being only lines.

In the Japanese folding books color comes back, also writing. The Japanese folding books were given to her by an artist who used to sit in San Francisco cafes and draw the faces of the people around him for days on end. She met him in one of these cafes, the Buena Vista, and after a few encounters he gave her one book that he had started and told her: "this is yours to continue."

Unlike a drawing which one sees all at once on a page in one glance, these folding books, Adnan chose to think, were closer to being read as a book should be read, continuously. The fact that they unfolded page after page led her to think that they had to be read this way, page after page, and therefore were closer to traditional writing than drawing. In fact, she was discovering what the Chinese tradition knew all along, that *writing is drawing*. In her particular case she was led to use these books both for drawing and writing.

She immediately thought about poetry. She missed Beirut and the Arab World; also the Algerian war of independence was raging. She embarked on the project of putting the great contemporary Arab poets into drawings. It was for her both an artistic discovery and a political statement.

Using her own handwriting, she wrote each poem in a very legible way, giving it a visual equivalent, each time invoking a totally different feeling, using watercolors, crayons, inks, pen and brush. Sometimes the poem was accompanied by the landscape in which it had been read, other times by signs, numbers, and geometrical symbols. These manuscripts are an anthology of all the major poets she knew or loved: Badr Shaker as-Sayyab, Yusuf al-Khal, Adonis, Mahmoud Darwish, Nazir El-Azmeh, Buland El-Haidari, Fadel El-Azzawi, Georges Shehadeh; sometimes they include her own poems. Later she started doing some books on European and American poets. Although she liked the western written alphabet less, and thought it did not have the same visual strength or flexibility as Arabic letters, she could not help but want to write the poetry of some poets she particularly admired: Anne-Marie Albiach, Claude Royet-Journoud, Guillevic, Barbara Guest, Lyn Hejinian, Wendell Berry, Lawrence Ferlinghetti, Duncan McNaughton and others.

She never made a manuscript of an ancient poet's works. She never wanted to make just an *objet d'art*. These manuscripts are political in the sense that they represent poets who are alive. Most of the time she gave the "book" to the poet, so he or she could see himself or herself "read" in that special way. These are responses to a living text. She was a translator of a text in the way a musician is a translator of a score. She saw the manuscript as collaborative work.

These books are also a way of entering the time element in a painting. One unfolds the scroll as one sees the landscape or the poem, bit by bit, and is therefore closer to the real way these things happen to one in real life. You look at a landscape page after page, you look again and the color has changed, the clouds have moved, the boat has left the harbor. The whole remains in your mind in a composite image; the scroll keeps the different moments alive but allows you to read the composite image in its different stages or in a totally different combination. You open the scroll on page one. You follow the sequence on page two. But if you open page one and you put it face to face with page seven, they are also a perfect sequence. Is it a chance happening? It cannot be, for it never fails: in any of these books the pages work in every combination possible.

These books are also monumental works: they unfold to become, at times, several feet long, and yet can be transported in one's pocket. This is the particular genius of Asia: the books are minimalist and grandiose at the same time. They are also intimate and unobtrusive, they do not sit

Folding book. (Etel Adnan)

on your walls forever until they lose the impact of their beauty. They can be placed in a drawer and looked at only when the time is right for this particular contemplation. These books are her greatest contribution to the contemporary visual arts. They are in many collections and museums, notably the British Museum.

A last word about Etel Adnan's visual work should be about her tapestry designs. Etel worked with the renowned tapestry artist Ida Grae. She wove and dyed wool herself, and wrote a series of letters to Claire Paget on that subject, *Notes on Weaving*, a text that was published in a literary magazine in Lebanon, *Les Cahiers de l'Oronte*, but has not yet been published as a book. Her designs are drawings exclusively made for weaving. Her work is close to the spirit of the Turkish *kilims* in its use of vivid colors and large areas of single colors, while being thoroughly contemporary. Some of her tapestries are in public spaces, others in public collections. She has a file at the Museum of Contemporary Crafts in New York, a file opened for her by the founder of America House herself, Mrs. Vanderbildt Webb, who also acquired one of her tapestries. Her work is on file at the Los Angeles County Museum. All of her tapestries bear what we know, by now, to be her trademark: the large bold strokes of color separating other areas of color. These tapestries are abstract, on the whole. They are also exclusively monumental. They are strong, bold, decisive, engaging.

"Colors exist for me," she said in an interview with Professor Fedwa Malti-Douglas, "as entities in themselves, as metaphysical beings, like the attributes of God exist as metaphysical entities" (Adnan, 1987). When you read the first lines of Adnan's book-length poem *The Arab Apocalypse*— "a yellow sun, a red sun, a blue sun" (1989, 7)—you realize how the two realms of her perception, the verbal and the visual, come together. Yellow, blue and red become attributes of the sun, the way the names of God in Sufism are linked to our knowledge of God.

Etel Adnan's art is as innovative as her poetry and fiction, and like these, has had a recognized and wide influence on contemporary Arab art and beyond.

Notes

1. Conversation with Etel Adnan.
2. The Dominican Convent, full of elegant furniture and paintings, was built by a prodigious Belgian nun as a nineteenth-century mansion in a small paradise of eucalyptus trees and redwoods.
3. The phrase "homme du monde" is taken from a subsection of "Le Peintre de Vie Moderne," in *Baudelaire Oeuvres Complètes*, titled "L'artiste, L'homme du monde, homme des foules et l'enfant." See Baudelaire (1967, 1239).
4. Sourat Al Nahl (Bees) 16, ayat 13: "Wama zara' lakom fil ardi moukhtal-ifan alwanuhou, inna fi thalika la'ayaten likaoumen yatathak-karoun."
5. Baudelaire's *fleurs du mal* (1967).

References

Adnan, Etel. 1986. *Journey to Mount Tamalpais*. Sausalito, CA: Post-Apollo.
_____. 1987. "Woman Between Cultures: Interview with Etel Adnan." By Allen Douglas and Fedwa Malti-Douglas. Jan. 8, 1987. Forthcoming in a volume co-authored by Fadwa Malti-Douglas and Allan Douglas.
_____. 1989. *The Arab Apocalypse*. Sausalito, CA: Post-Apollo.
Baudelaire, Charles. 1967. *Baudelaire Oeuvres Completes* with preface, introduction and notes by Marcel Raymond. Centennial Edition. Lausanne, Switzerland: La Guilde du Livre et Clairefontaine.

6

Variations on an Andalusian Theme: Undated Letters to Etel

Fawwaz Traboulsi

I

Dear Etel,

I guess that I had to follow in your steps in order to begin answering your letters. Tomorrow, I'll be off to Spain for a lecture on "Democracy in the Southern Mediterranean" at the University of Malagua, the city in which Picasso was born.

My French companion confessed to me, with much embarrassment, that he had never visited Granada and wanted to profit from his Andalusian visit to spend a day or two in the city of the Al-Hamra and the Generalife. More embarrassed than him, being an Arab, I admitted that I was in the same situation and we quickly agreed to take the trip together.

Have you ever been to Granada?

I'll write to you from there. Meanwhile, find enclosed my review for *Le Monde* of the French translation of Fares Chidyaq's *La jambe sur la jambe*, maybe it will encourage you and Simone to read this great writer, feminist, satirist and social critic, if not in the Arabic original at least in the French translation. That is, if Simone can take her eyes away from Ibn Arabi. Could you imagine: an Arab male who wrote that he had been

metamorphosed into a woman while writing his book in praise of women and the Arabic language? And when? In the middle of the last century!
Love to both of you.

II

Dear Etel,
I should confess to you that I have long been obsessed with Granada. My childhood was haunted by the specter of a maternal uncle, a romantic poet, who died young and left, among other things, a play in verse entitled "The Fall of Granada." My next encounter with Spain came in student days. That time, it was the Spanish revolution which obsessed us. Hardly a day passed in the Ras Beirut cafés without us recalling a famous saying by the *Passionaria*, or one of the innumerable stories about the heroism of the defenders of Madrid, not to speak of George Orwell's anecdotes on Barcelona's anarchists rushing to the front only to discover, once arrived, that they had forgotten to bring their rifles with them. At night, with the help of a few beer bottles, the nostalgia of those glorious revolutionary years in the thirties would overwhelm us as we recite the poems of Lorca and Neruda, raising clenched anti-fascist fists among the bewildered, yet complaisant, waiters of 'Uncle Sam's' and 'Sheikh and Cousin', shouting with full voices *No pasarán*! before sinking into a *'ashura* of wailing over the betrayed and defeated revolution....
I have often wondered why did the Spanish civil war affect me so much. Perhaps, it boiled down to this: I could never be reconciled with the fascist celebration of death in *Viva la muerte*!
Yet, who would have imagined, in the Beirut of the Golden Sixties, that the Spanish revolution cum-civil war would be reenacted in our tranquil Phoenician metropolis? When the fighting broke out, in 1975, it slowly dawned on me that my glorious Spanish revolution was also a bloody civil war. The sniping, abduction, indiscriminate bombardment, sieges, slayings "on the identity card," etc. released from my subconscience their Spanish precedents: the workers in Madrid burning churches and their comrades in Barcelona disinterring the corpses of nuns to play football with their skulls!

III

Dear Etel,
Your letters bathe in the Spanish sun. Life is an unending afternoon, you say. On my first visit, in 1961, I came from foggy, or better, smoggy,

Manchester on a summer vacation, lodged in a hotel overlooking a large square. Afternoons lingered endlessly until they were slowly dispelled by the breezes of the first hours of the evening. Rapidly, the square swelled with swarms of widows clad in black. These widows were the only relics left of that war that inspired our imagination. Martyrs were indeed glorified, but there were victorious martyrs and vanquished martyrs. On a mount, not far from Madrid, was a collective grave for the dead over which stood a huge cross. Its victims had been reduced to those of one side, the only grave that stood out was that of the patron of the victorious martyrs, the founder of the Phalanges' party.

Nobody wanted to talk about the war. The tourist guide, in the bus that took us to Toledo, brushed off my inquiries. All that I could snatch from him was an explanation why the road to the airport had been lined with kilometers of walls on both sides. He admitted it was to hide the miserable shanty towns behind them from tourists. The man in the Madrid bookshop gave me a strange look when I asked about Lorca's poetry books. Of Toledo, I only remember El Greco's Arab-style house and the visit to the Alcazar. The choice of the site was not innocent. The guide submitted us to the official story about the heroism of the commander of the fort's garrison who preferred to let his hostage son be killed by the Republicans blockading the fort rather than surrender.

What was left for me on that visit was to make do with what is prepared for tourists: drinking wine from a sheepskin, wandering in the streets of Madrid and watching a bullfight in which beginner matadors fought beginner bulls in what is closer to a massacre than to a *corrida*, while tourists awkwardly launched their "*olés*" as the *aficionados* kept silent: they knew better…. I finally left Spain with a souvenir laden with symbolism: a matador's sword which the pretty and kind hostess diligently camouflaged from the French customs. Thus, I made my first entry into Paris with a bouquet of artificial flowers on my arm hiding the deadly blade of the matador….

IV

Spain: a quarter of a century later. In Valencia to attend the Third Congress for the Mediterranean Writers, convened on the theme "The Intellectual and the Struggle for Democracy." With Mahmoud Darwish, Elias Sanbar and Farouk Mardam, we decided to spend a couple of days on the way to visit Barcelona. Immediately fell in love with the city which I fantasized about as an idealized Beirut. Phoned Nawal and told her to prepare herself: we will settle in Barcelona.

The scene you related about the naked woman pushing her way through the throngs on the Rablas evokes in me the epic scenes from Yankso's films. Only the naked body means freedom. No wonder Spanish anarchists vowed such a cult to nudism.

I did not see a naked woman on the *ramblas* of Barcelona; I witnessed Spain finally breaking the self-imposed silence on its civil war. Side by side with the photos of the *Caudillo* were issues of the daily *Diario 16* serializing Hugh Thomas's classic on the Spanish civil war. Finally, the Spaniards can now know about their war what others in the West and the rest of the world had known for decades.

The city of Valencia, last republican bastion to fall in the hands of the Frankists, is the only city which is officially commemorating the fiftieth anniversary of the civil war. Not an easy task anyway. It was imposed by the left faction of the ruling Socialist party, which controls the local government. During the reception at Valencia municipality, we are greeted by the frail figure of the poet Juan Gil Albert, a companion of Lorca and Machado, one of the last witnesses of the war generation.

The Congress itself reveals the plurality and richness of the cultural scene in democratic Spain where there are three semi-official languages in addition to the Castillan: Galecian, Catalonian and Basquian. A writer explains to us that after the extensive decentralization, Spain's unity as a nation still holds thanks to two institutions: the Crown and the Army. Most of the Catalonian delegates insist on delivering their speeches in their native tongue, which sounds like hispanicized French. The prevailing mood among writers is resumed in the saying: language is the only remaining homeland for writers.

On this April 14th, the great tenor, Amancio Prado, sings Lorca's "Ballad of Secret Love." The force of the unavowed overwhelms us during fifty captivating minutes. Juan Goytisolo, leading us in a stroll in the city whose center strangely resembles that of pre-war Beirut, shows us the Victoria Hotel where Lorca lodged during his visits to the city and where he wrote the Ballads we just heard. Juan relates how, after Franco's death, he and a group of friends tried to dislodge Franco's statue in the city center. It took them days. Not only was the statue guarded by Phalangist loyalists, with whom they had to engage in fights, but it was well anchored by metal shafts buried deep down in cement. So much for the deep anchored Frankism in Spanish earth.

Antonio Gades and his flamenco troop mount a version of *Carmen* (already put on the screen by Antonio Saura) in which Bizet's opera is completely recuperated and hispanized. Gades retained only a few couplets of the original opera. You know, the famous "Tarattatiii tarrattataaa"...

about love, a bohemian child. The rest is expressed by the language of the body. Spanish friends reflected that Arabs are perhaps the only people, in addition to Spaniards, who can appreciate the flamenco. I am not so sure. In fact, no Arab dance comes close to reproducing the craze of the gypsy soul. The language of the hands and fingers in the Flamenco may be likened to the *Samah*, the Andalusian collective women's dance based on the *muwashahat*, a tradition which is still preserved in Damascus and Aleppo. But our Arab dance is more melodious and gentle compared to the violence, and fury of the flamenco which is a dance of passion, defiance, violence, even death. Our guide, Carmen by name and a committed socialist, insisted that the violence of the flamenco reflects the violence of the class struggles in Spanish history.

The orientalist Pedro Martinez likes to reduce everything Spanish to the Arabs:

— Regionalism in our country is inherited from the Arabs. Do you know how many Kings of the Ta'ifas were there in Arab Spain?

— ...?

— well, 17 kings. And do you know what is the number of the Spanish regions today?

— ...?

— 17 also...

My turn now.

— and you, do you know how many official Ta'ifas (confessions) are there in present-day Lebanon?

— how many?

— 17 !!

— Can I ask you what were you doing during the war?

My question is addressed to the little man with whom I much sympathized and who has come to bid us farewell:

— everything, came the answer.

Presently, he is advisor to the minister of Culture in the government of the autonomous region of Valencia. Sitting around the table in our hotel café, he reluctantly reveals himself: he ran the underground organization of the Spanish Communist Party in Valencia under Franco. A friend of his tells me that he lived in hiding for ten years with a family in a one-room flat and that he had to hide in the cupboard every time somebody came to visit them. He left the SCP after the famous Khrustchev speech in which the Soviet leader denounced Stalin's crimes. Presently, he is an independent, close to the socialists.

— They say my family name is of Arab origin, and goes on enumerating localities in the Valencia named after Arab tribes.

The most important thing for him is that the situation in his country does not degenerate into armed conflict. "After all the pains of Frankism, our most valuable achievement is democracy," he insists, "even if that happens at the expense of other achievements." Does he regret anything from his experience? Most of all, having to kill an anarchist leader in Valencia, on orders from the Party. He does not want this to recur ever again.

His turn to submit me to a number of precise questions on Lebanon. I do not find it difficult to explain, by reference to their own experience fifty years ago. He admits that he doesn't understand much of what is happening. Jokingly, I said that I feel the same. More seriously, I tell him to imagine that the Spanish civil war lasted well into the forties, the splinters and divisions inside each of the original two camps would have resembled much those of today's Lebanon. On taking leave, he says: we've grown old, maybe we've become too pessimistic, my advice to you of the younger generation is hope.

— Not to worry about that, hope is our incurable malady.

A stop in Madrid on the way back to Paris to meet *Guernica* in person. I found it much bigger than I had imagined, but the colors are impressive: I hadn't guessed that the painting contained so many shades of blue and grey. The initial shock of the encounter is much attenuated by the innumerable reproductions I had been working on, studying and analyzing every detail. The magic touch of the first encounter isn't there. It's too late, my Guernica manuscript is already under print. Further, the bulletproof glass cage that protects the mural and the Guardia Civil soldier standing on guard beside it, kept on distracting me from being completely absorbed in the masterpiece, constantly under the impression that the painting is a well-guarded political personality.

I had always imagined *Guernica* exhibited in a public place. In this annex to the Prado, it figures as the last witness of the civil war: you wonder whether the painting is being sheltered from oblivion or whether it is condemned to seclusion because it evokes so many sad memories that the Spaniards of today want to simply forget....

Dear Etel,

How does one forget a civil war?

IV

Again in Valencia to attend another commemoration, that of the International Congress of Anti-fascist Writers which was held in the city in 1939. We suffer a severe jet-lag. Still thinking of civil wars, while most of the intellectuals of Europe and the Americas, including the few survivors who had attended the initial congress like Stephen Spender and Octavio Paz, are delivering their *mea culpas*: if the enemy in the thirties was Fascism, now the enemy to combat is Communism, is the gist of what they are saying. A recycled Cohn Bendit joins the older generation in delivering a similar message. The panel on Arab-Spanish relations under the Republic and the Civil War must have made us look from another age. Vargas Llosa could not bear even to listen to our interventions: he opened a newspaper and started reading into it.

How strange of you to say: "I like what is happening now in Spain. Neither poor, nor rich, it's a 'worker's world' as communism dreamed of, but could not accomplish." While in Spain, it suddenly struck me that this country could be the best model of development for the Arab World, neither the U.S.A. and certainly not the U.S.S.R. Industrialized, yet with a large agricultural sector; urbanized yet so anchored in tradition, united yet so decentralized and respectful of national, linguistic, regional and cultural diversities. Hard-working people yet so lively, especially the young. Democratic but with a keen sense of social equality.

VI

Dear Etel,

If cities are women, then Granada is a city.

Much that I hate this worn out comparison between cities and women, you cannot escape it in Granada. "If you consent, Granada / I shall be your man," proposes Don Juan in the *Spanish Romancero*. Granada replies: "I am with husband, Don Juan, / married and not widowed / and the Arab who possesses me / loves me with a great love." After a lengthy visit to the Al-Hamra and the Genaralife, spontaneously sat silent on the stone steps in the garden next to a small pond, just meditating. Tourists passed by. Tourists amaze me with their habit of comparing what they see with what is drawn on maps or written in guide books. Ever anxious until they discover that the information in the guide or the detail on the map matches with what is in front of their very eyes. As if a site, a monument, a painting or a statue would not exist unless it appears in the book or on the map!

Still musing in the garden, I jot down a few disconnected words in my notebook:

Granada, architecture of shade
gypsy pomegranate
water narcissus,
traces of the Soul on stone

Slowly, it dawned on me what made my visit to Granada so special. No other sight would have been more appropriate after the Gulf war. One had to feel that he belongs to a people who has done something after that catastrophic electronic beating. Yet, a crazy thought kept on nagging: What use is it to belong to a nation loaded with such a glorious past? It could well console you after national defeats. But, what else? To begin with, you acquire such a sense of satisfaction, conceit and self-fulfillment so that you do very little about your present or your future. You spend your time telling people, the West in particular: you misunderstand me, I wasn't like that, I am the inheritor of a great civilization. A glorious past fixes you premanently to that Past, the dead control the living. Not only that, it infests you with the dream of a millennium which will magically reenact that past intact and project it in your present and future. Satisfaction turns into cosmic frustration....

Wherever you are on this fortified hill, you look down on the Albaicin quarter (al-Bâ'icîn, in Arabic). I translate the word to my companion: "the wretched." What a strange relationship between the Al-Hamra on top and the Albaicin below. Al-Hamra and the Generalife are the paradise as imagined by the Arabs. As if the inhabitants of the castle had just to look down on the poor underneath in order to be confirmed that they were living in paradise. Conversely, you should take a seat in one of the cafes that lounge the river in the Albaicin, in order to experience what it meant to be on that other side of Paradise. Especially at night, when all the beauty and awe of Alhambra castle is revealed under the floodlights. From their quarter, the Andalusian al-bâ'icîn could very well imagine this as the paradise they have been promised, yet dissimulated and forbidden behind its formidable walls, towers and huge trees. Offered, promised and unattainable at the same time. Ever present, yet invisible like Iram Dhat al-'Imad. Now I understand what Lorca meant when he said: "Mysterious Granada, enigma of what could never exist / and yet, does exist."

At times, the poor of the Albaicin quarter would revolt. Their last revolt was against Abi 'Abd Allah, last king of Granada, last monarch of Arab Spain. He remained entrenched in his castle until the revolt was bloodily crushed by the soldiers. At that time, Granada was already besieged by the army of Isabel and Ferdinand. The fall of Granada signaled paradise lost for the Arabs, to quote Lorca once more. The Arab who lost it sneaked out from the castle's back-door so that nobody sees him. He was crying. He "cried like a woman / a realm he could not defend like a man."

Cannot evade the comparison between Abi 'Abd Allah and Saddam Hussein: both weak vis-à-vis their enemies, strong only against their own people; both surrendered to their enemies but massacred their own people in revolt. Yet Saddam is devoid of the feminine that Abi 'Abd Allah had in him. I doubt if Saddam ever shed a tear in his life....

Talking of victors and vanquished, you cannot evade the comparison between the palace of Charles the Fifth and the palace of the Nasserides. The Arab palace, open to all directions, represents the most intricate and sophisticated attempts at breaking down the barriers between outside and inside, between nature and culture, between the arch and water, between stone and spirit. By contrast, Charles's palace, built to commemorate the victory against the Arabs, is the Reconquista's architectural massacre. Huge blocks of stone seem to weigh personally over your very heart: the voluminous square building, with a round piazza inside it, representing a circle inside a square, is the absolute symbolism of repression and containment: a dead end, with no outlet except upwards, through the circular opening, towards the sky.

Two kinds of spirituality contrasted: one ethereal, intricate, in which the arabesque of the Spirit thins out stone; the other, the crushing geometric weight of spiritual mass over men.

VII

Dear Etel,

I had wanted to write to you about Yemeni women in Aden and their long struggle for their rights. But, I'll have to stop for now. I was putting my letters into English when the new Blood Wedding was celebrated in Qana.[1] The Lebanese now want to believe that Qana of Southern Lebanon is the same as the Qana of Galilee in which Jesus attended the famous wedding. Whatever, water in Qana was not transformed into wine. Blood simply turned into blood.

The Israelis are the only people in the world who commit mistakes. Other peoples commit assassinations, crimes, terrorism, genocide, ethnic purification, crimes against humanity, what have you. Only the Israelis commit mistakes when they kill civilians. But one should admit that they are capable of such neat surgical mistakes. They kill on the map. The mistakes they commit are misreadings of maps. Or do they misread? Mistakes or no mistakes, this cruel unjust world still treats this spoiled brat nicknamed Israel as one who is only capable of committing ... mistakes.

Just back from Qana. A procession of some 300 intellectuals observed five minutes' silence sang the first couplet of the national anthem and then, each in turn, laid a red rose on the mass grave. A TV cameraman asked me to repeat the movement of laying my rose on the grave so that he can film it. I obeyed mechanically. Bending down I noticed a picture of the Virgin Mary put there for the Christian woman from Qana who was killed with the rest of the 108 victims. In fact, I would have repeated the movement indefinitely. I still imagine myself laying a red rose on the mass grave of the women, children, elders and men of Qana. Yes, men. Why shouldn't we cry over men too? They say we should not, because men are capable of defending themselves. Who can defend himself against a cluster bomb that falls upon his head in a tin-covered barracks at the UN camp in Qana?

Thought of you.

On the way out, I was telling someone what a neat surgical mistake it was, when, beside me, Joseph Samaha, hesitantly muttered, "why?" and immediately retracted, "what a silly question!"

Love,

Fawwaz

Notes

1. This is a reference to the Israeli artillery bombardment of the United Nations compound in the Lebanese village of Qana on April 18, 1996. As a result of this bombardment, 107 Lebanese civilian refugees were killed.

SECTION II

Reading *Sitt Marie Rose*

7

Mary Rose

Haas Mroue

Mary Rose planted flowers in a forgotten square
painted the walls yellow and made a swing and a slide
from leftover shrapnel. The children sang to the snipers
from behind the wall.

Mary Rose on rooftops, sipping warm tea with snipers,
giving them crayons, "draw yourselves dead," she told them.

Mary Rose, her earrings tinkling in the heat
driving to the other side of town over the Ring Bridge,
pleading to men in black turtlenecks to spare the children.

Mary Rose, Paul and Rima waiting for her after their bath.
Will she come say good night?

Mary Rose, her laughter shattered the Green Line
a thousand times and her warmth cradled the children
in their graves.

Mary Rose disappeared on the Ring Bridge
somewhere between West and East Beirut.

If only I could go back
no more a child
and hold Paul and Rima tight
their pyjamas still damp from their bath
and wait with them. A cup of sweet, warm milk
and they sleep and never dream of Mary Rose
their mother
four pieces under a bridge.

8

The International Reception of *Sitt Marie Rose*

Annes McCann-Baker

Etel Adnan's novel, *Sitt Marie Rose* was first published in France by Editions des Femmes in 1977. This novel, only 105 pages long, poetic in its conciseness and its emphasis upon formal structure, has since come to be known as an "underground classic." It subsequently won the Amitié Franco-Arab Prize, an award created in 1969 by the Association de Solidarité Franco-Arabe. In 1982 it was translated into English by Georgina Kleege and published by the Post-Apollo Press in Sausalito, California. It is currently in its sixth printing in English. Other translations have been published in Arabic, Italian, Dutch, German and Urdu.

When Adnan wrote *Sitt Marie Rose*, in 1977, she was well known in Lebanon as a poet and journalist. During 1972-73, when the civil war was brewing, she had written about the political situation in her front-page editorials in *al-Safa*, a daily Lebanese newspaper in French. She had also written the texts for two documentary films on the war. *Sitt Marie Rose* was written, in French, while Adnan was staying for a period in France. The novel was translated into Arabic by Jerome Chahine that same year, and was published in Lebanon by al-Mu'assasa al-'arabiyya lil-dirasat wal-nashr in 1979.

The Arabic translation was controversial from the beginning. While the West Beirut leftist newspapers applauded the book, the Christian Phalangists did not, and the book was not marketed in East Beirut. When

Adnan returned to Lebanon after the publication of *Sitt Marie Rose,* she found that the newspaper from which she had been on leave, *l'Orient-Le Jour,* had been advised never again to publish her work. Adnan describes the sequence of events: "So when in 1978, during one of the cease-fires, I returned to Beirut to take up my work again, the editor-in-chief said literally, 'who asked you to write what you think?' I replied, 'But your paper was paying me to write what I thought.' There was a long pause. I was paid to write on painting, not on politics" (Adnan 1985, 120). Adnan had dared to question the psychological, historical, sociological and political causes of the war. However, her provocative themes were allowed little discussion in the official forums of Beirut of that time, and the book is not available in Lebanese bookstores today. According to Le Levant, the largest book distributor in Beirut, the novel is not in stock and has not been distributed for commercial use for a very long time, although it has occasionally been ordered for use in university literature classes.

The Arabic version of *Sitt Marie Rose* was also read in Syria, where the real Marie-Rose Boulos, upon whom Adnan's protagonist was modeled, originated. Nour Press, a women's publishing house in Egypt, planned to publish another translation for the Arab world, but was unable to do so for lack of funds. However, an Arabic translation, now out of print, was published in Beirut and Amman by the Arab Institute for Research and Publishing. In 2000 the original Arabic translation was reprinted in Cairo (see Adnan 1979a).

Des Femmes, the original French publisher, printed 6,000 copies, which are still available through the company's catalogue. The fact that the book did not sell as well in France as in the United States, and has not been reprinted in France, may be a result of Adnan's fairly explicit condemnation in the book of French religious schools in Lebanon. However, the book did receive excellent French reviews in such periodicals as *Jeune Afrique, Nouvelles Littéraires, Libération, Politique Hebdo, Dimanche Diplomatique* and *Tribune Socialiste;* the latter called the novel "a symbolic and lucid testimony." Perhaps because the French version of the novel was published by a feminist press, the critiques in that country often seemed to focus on what the book had to say about women and their attitudes about the war. The writer for *Politique Hebdo,* speaking particularly about the Palestinian cause, stated, "More than a testimonial, this book launches an appeal: that other women continue to fight, as long as the words 'exile,' 'torture,' and 'massacres' continue to be the daily language, as it has been for a whole people for the last thirty years" (G.R. 1978). The reviewer in *Jeune Afrique,* like many other reviewers, praised the literary quality of the language: "This very beautiful book of Etel Adnan brings back to life what two years of war regularly destroyed: the power of speech and inner freedom" (Eddi 1978).

The Dutch publisher, Novip, published *Sitt Marie Rose* in 1979, only a year after the novel's original French publication. It has printed two editions of the novel. Novip received a prize from the Ministry of Foreign Affairs for its publication of important foreign books, among which was *Sitt Marie Rose*. Adnan was invited to Holland to attend the ceremony and was interviewed on Dutch television. In addition, an interview with Adnan was featured in the Arab World section of the Dutch anthology of international women's literature, *Ongehoorde Woorden* (see Adnan 1985). According to the book's American publisher, the Dutch version also sold well in Indonesia.

Although the Italian feminist press that printed the Italian translation in 1979, Le Donne, has gone out of business, the publication of *Sitt Marie Rose* in Italy brought attention to Adnan's other works. In 1993 Multimedia Editzione in Salerno published *Viaggio al Monte Tamalpais* (Journey to Mount Tamalpais) and *Crescere per Essere Scritrice in Libano* (The Woman Artist in Lebanon). A collection of Adnan's short stories, translated from Arabic, English and French, was published in Italian by Ed. Jouvence in 1995 under the title *Confini della Luna*.

A Spanish translation is needed, as shown by an anecdote told by writer Sarah Miles. While doing a series of articles on the war in El Salvador, Miles was one of the last to enter a building where the headquarters of the trade unions had been entrenched for years. She saw a well-thumbed copy of the English version of *Sitt Marie Rose* on a bench. She was told that a journalist from Canada had brought it and that the single copy had been read aloud by whomever could orally translate it into Spanish over the years. (Later, the building was stormed by government forces and most of the people there were killed.) In addition, there has been discussion of a translation into Turkish (personal communication).

Sarah Miles' anecdote shows why the novel has been called an "underground classic." However, the book has not had an underground status in Germany. Published in 1988 by one of the most prestigious presses in the country, Suhrkamp Verlag, the first run of 7,300 copies is now out of print. The book was extensively reviewed, and Adnan is well-known in Germany, where she was invited twice in the fall of 1995. *Sitt Marie Rose* is on the reading list of high-school classrooms in Bavaria (Das gute Buch 1990). German critics tend to focus more on Adnan's analysis of the different strands of Lebanese culture than on the feminist or pacifist themes in the book. However, one critic did write about the feminist theme, and another explored the religious significance of the book (see Review of *Sitt Marie Rose* 1989 and Radio Station 100, 1989). In 1999 Suhrkamp Verlag also published *Paris, Paris*, a translation of *Paris, When It's Naked*.

The English version of the novel, published in the United States by Post-Apollo Press, has had an amazing trajectory and subsequent influence. The director of the Post-Apollo Press, Simone Fattal, says the book was never marketed in an aggressive way; rather, it became known through word of mouth. As the novel began to show up on syllabi across the country, Adnan's fame spread through the creative and philosophical world. Feminist professors, including well-known poets Adrienne Rich and June Jordan, have used the book as a classic example of a strong female character, in this case one based on an actual female martyr. Indeed, June Jordan has described Adnan as "the visionary, great Lebanese poet," and *Sitt Marie Rose* as a "transcendent, miraculous novel" (1985, 84). The novel is now taught in undergraduate and graduate classrooms within many different contexts. Many California campuses, in particular, use it, since Post-Apollo is a local publisher. Literature classes approach the book as a masterful work of symbolism and as a powerful narrative, while history and political science classes examine the story as a portrayal of opposing political and sectarian factions in Lebanon during the civil war.

In 1988 the Center for Middle Eastern Studies at the University of Texas, where I edit the Modern Middle East Literatures in Translation series, carried out a survey in conjunction with the Middle East Studies Association annual meeting to determine whether Middle Eastern fiction translations would appeal to classrooms. We discovered that social scientists and humanists had begun to use imaginative forms of writing as representative cultural products, in addition to reading them as individual texts. When social science as well as literature faculty responded to the question of which, of any, fiction works they used, *Sitt Marie Rose* was listed over and over. Our sales records since then indicate that translations of Middle Eastern fiction and memoirs are being used in anthopology, sociology, political science and history classes, as well as in literature classes. Indeed, it may be fair to say that we can thank, in great part, Etel Adnan and her profound rendering of a cataclysmic period for the current proliferation of translations from Middle Eastern literature. As *Sitt Marie Rose* continues to reach new readers, its success makes clear the growing importance of Adnan's work in an international context.

References

Adnan, Etel. 1977. *Sitt Marie Rose*. Paris: Editions Des Femmes.

_____. 1979a. *Sitt Marie Rose*. (Arabic). Translated by Jerome Chahine. Beirut: al-Mu'assasa al-'arabiyya lil-dirasat wal-nashr. Reprinted with an introduction by Ferial Ghazoul, 2000. Cairo: al Hay'a al-'Amma Li-Qusur al-Thaqafa.

_____. 1979b. *Sitt Marie Rose*. (Dutch). The Hague: Novip.

_____. 1979c. *Sitt Marie Rose*. (Italian). Milano: Le Donne.

_____. 1982. *Sitt Marie Rose*. Translated by Georgina Kleege. Sausalito, CA: Post-Apollo.

_____. 1985. "Interview with Etel Adnan." By Hilary Kilpatrick. In *Unheard Words: Women and Literature in Africa, the Arab World, Asia, the Caribbean and Latin America*, edited by Mineke Schipper, translated from the Dutch by Barbara Potter Fasting, 114–120. London and New York: Allison and Busby.

_____. 1993a. *Crescere Per Essere Scritrice In Libano* (The Woman Artist In Lebanon). Salerno, Italy: Multimedia.

_____. 1993b. *Viaggio al Monte Tamalpais* (Journey to Mount Tamalpais). Translated from the English. Salerno, Italy: Multimedia.

_____. 1995. *Al Confini della Luna*. (The Border of the Moon) Rome: Ed. Jouvenance.

_____. 1997. *Sitt Marie Rose*. (Urdu). Pakistan.

_____. 1988. *Sitt Marie Rose*. (German). Frankfurt: Suhrkamp.

_____. 1990. "Das gute Buch in der Schule, Empfehlenswete Bucher fur die Bibliotheken der Gymnasien und Realschulen Bayerns." 1990. Folge (1): n.p.

_____. 1999. *Paris Paris*. (German translation of *Paris, When It's Naked*.) Frankfurt: Suhrkamp.

Edde, Dominique. 1978. Review of *Sitt Marie Rose*, by Etel Adnan. *Jeune Afrique* (March) 1: n.p.

G.R. 1978. Review of *Sitt Marie Rose*, by Etel Adnan. *Politique Hebdo*, March 25.

Jordan, June. 1985. *On Call: Political Essays*. Boston: South End.

Schipper, Mineke ed. 1984. *Ongehoorde Woorden*. Weesp, Netherlands: Het Wereldvenster.

_____. 1985 ed. *Unheard Words: Women and Literature in Africa, the Arab World, Asia, the Caribbean and Latin America*, translated from the Dutch by Barbara Potter Fasting. London and New York: Allison and Busby.

Review of *Sitt Marie Rose*, by Etel Adnan. *Der Tagesspiegel* no. 13, Issue 197 (February): n.p.

Review of *Sitt Marie Rose*. Radio Station 100. Berlin: June 1989.

9

Transgressive Subjects: Gender, War, and Colonialism in Etel Adnan's *Sitt Marie Rose*

Sami Ofeish and Sabah Ghandour

Etel Adnan's *Sitt Marie Rose* (1982) tells the story of a Lebanese Christian woman who, during the Lebanese civil war, was abducted by Christian militiamen for working with the "enemy," and then murdered in front of her students. This is a novel about transgression in both a literal and figurative sense, a text that problematizes questions of gendered, sectarian,[1] and national control, and that highlights the implications of these questions for Lebanese state and society. In particular, the novel investigates the possibility of constituting a subject identified with a religious community who can, at the same time, adhere to the notion of secular citizenship. The identity problem of the Lebanese subject explored in this novel reflects to a great extent the larger conflict of national identity at the root of the Lebanese state. The novel's protagonist, Marie Rose, an assertive woman who transgresses the "normal" code set for women to follow, defies not only her abductors' assumptions of sectarian-affiliated, nationalist and communal solidarity, but also their entire hegemonic patriarchal structure. In addition, she shakes up their parochial understanding of modernity and westernization, concepts they have imbibed through a legacy of colonialization and French education. By narrating the story of Marie Rose, the novel explores the role that patriarchy, sectarianism and colonialism play in identity formation among the Lebanese, and examines the possibilities of resistance to these categories.

The first sections of this chapter discuss the historical and theoretical context of colonialism and neopatriarchy within which Adnan's narrative is set. Subsequently, the chapter provides a reading of *Sitt Marie Rose* that grounds the novel within this historical and theoretical context.

Patriarchy, Nationalism, and Postcolonialism

Colonialism as a historical phase in the formative history of Lebanon theoretically ended with the termination of the French Mandate in 1946. Nevertheless, the effects of colonialism are still present in various facets of Lebanon's socio-political and cultural life. We are using the term "post-colonialism" without a hyphen, following the suggestion of some critics, to represent an ideological orientation rather than the historical linear stage indicated by a hyphenated "post(-) colonialism" (Mishra and Hodge 1994, 284). Such a distinction allows for a reading of *Sitt Marie Rose* as a novel that makes plain the socio-cultural construction of subjectivities while at the same time interrogating the consequences of a political system instituted and propagated by colonialism.

Our understanding of nationalism and patriarchy in the novel benefits greatly from the works of Frantz Fanon and Hisham Sharabi. In his seminal work *The Wretched of the Earth*, Fanon highlights the problematics of nationalism in colonial and postcolonial settings. He examines several factors that impede the development of nationalism in the Third World: the lack of inclusive incorporation of various groups under the national project, the vulnerability of the dominant elite and their pro-western ties, and the ensuing competition among "primordial" groups for access to resources. Addressing "The Pitfalls of National Consciousness," Fanon notes that the national bourgeoisie of emerging Third World states frequently failed to cultivate national consciousness. As a result, this bourgeoisie could not unite the citizens and develop their sense of national and civic responsibilities. Fanon's conception of national consciousness goes beyond the love and admiration of one's country. It implies that every single citizen must be educated to believe that that s/he belongs to the nation and should actively participate in its growth and development. It also suggests that nationalism should not be entwined with the extension of exclusive benefits to one group in power (Fanon 1963, 200-1).

Fanon's national bourgeoisie is in many ways a comprador bourgeoisie (agent of foreign interests) which is mainly engaged in intermediary economic activities rather than national production. This bourgeoisie's failure to transmit its vision effectively to the masses facilitates a fallback to old tribal attitudes and loyalties among the general population. It also allows for the spread of religious rivalries, through which people split up into different religious-affiliated communities "kept up and stiffened by colonialism and its instruments." Fanon provides examples to that effect from different regions in Africa. For instance, western missionaries in some areas constantly reminded people how the "great African empires were disrupted by the Arab invasion" as a prelude to instilling hatred towards Arabs and discriminating against Muslims (Fanon 1963, 160). Discrimination was reversed in other areas, where indigenous Christians were resented as "conscious, objective enemies of national independence." In areas where Catholicism and Protestantism predominate, the masses were pitted against each other along these religious-affiliated lines (160-61).

According to Fanon, religious-affiliated tensions in Africa led in turn to the rise of racial feelings. Such sentiments divided the continent into a northern White "Mediterranean" and "cultured" Africa viewed as a "continuation of Europe," and a southern Black "inert, brutal, uncivilized" and "savage" Africa. The bourgeoisie of each of these regions, which had "totally assimilated colonial thought," imitated the colonial powers by reinforcing this racial discourse and acquiring an arrogant and paternalistic attitude (161-62).

Moreover, colonialism has reinforced patriarchal structures in many parts of the Third World. Hisham Sharabi suggests that western-dependent Arab states have not achieved "modernity." Instead, their social structures fall under the category of neopatriarchy, which is a case of "modernized" traditional patriarchy (Sharabi 1988, 3-4). Neopatriarchal society, according to Sharabi, reflects "a conservative, relentless male-oriented ideology, which tends to assign privilege and power to the male at the expense of the female" (33). The extension of modernized social structures into the postcolonial period does not necessarily translate into social liberation or justice for women. In the absence of a fundamental challenge to patriarchy, a postcolonial state will inevitably reproduce patriarchal structures.

Lebanon from Inception to the Civil War

The case of Lebanon is illuminated by the theoretical insights of Fanon and Sharabi. Modern Lebanon within its current borders is the offspring of the common interests of the French colonials and the influential

Maronite comprador. Lebanon was created in 1920 by joining two regions together. The first region incorporated the Ottoman-supervised governorate of Mount Lebanon; the second included coastal and interior areas to the north, south, and east of Mount Lebanon that were under direct Ottoman control. These two regions differed in terms of the socioeconomic and religious-affiliated composition of their residents. They also had varied perceptions of national identity, and differentiated access to power and resources.

The region of Mount Lebanon had a heavy concentration of Christian, particularly Maronite, residents. It subsequently developed into Lebanon's service-based center, where residents had relatively better access to services, employment, and professional training. The idea of a pro-western "eternal" Lebanese nation flourished among many Maronite residents of the center. This nationalist belief, coupled with privileged access to power and resources for some residents, was facilitated by their co-religionist leaders, the influential Maronite comprador.

The coastal/interior region was more multisectarian in composition, with a heavier concentration of Muslim residents. This region developed as the disadvantaged periphery, where the general population had less access to services and more limited control over power and resources in comparison with the advantaged center. Although feudal lords and members of the national bourgeoisie constituted the political and economic elite of this region, they were kept at a relative political disadvantage vis-à-vis the comprador between 1920 and 1975. Support for Lebanon's inclusion into a larger Syrian or Arab state was predominant among the periphery's residents even after independence, fueled by their resentment of an imposed "Lebanese nation" promoted by the Christian comprador.[2]

The inception of the postcolonial state in 1943 was based on a verbal elite agreement called the National Pact. This agreement strengthened the sectarian system on various levels. Considering sects as primary communities, the sectarian system promoted sectarian representation as the more legitimate form of political representation. This system also allowed for distribution of state resources and political control among the elite along religious-affiliated lines, with a particular advantage given to the Maronites. The sectarian elite used this system to maintain their class control and to divide the underprivileged lower and middle classes.[3]

The National Pact also included an agreement over Lebanon's identity. The Maronite comprador sacrificed its notion of Lebanon's primary attachment to the West, while the Muslim elite of the peripheries withdrew their insistence on unity with a larger Syrian or Arab nation (Petran 1987, 33). But with the development of a service-based economy, led after

independence by the Maronite elite in association with western invest-
ments, the state and its ideology had a clear western tilt.

Colonialism also fortified the patriarchal social structure. By allying
with the indigenous male elite and recruiting men, exclusively, as civil ser-
vants, the French primarily asserted men's authority. Continuous waves
of emigration, the result of frequent economic crises from the late nineteenth century, significantly added to the burden of women left behind in
Lebanon. The dual development of the sectarian and clientalist systems
by the independent state's elite also strengthened patriarchy. As a result,
subordination of women became increasingly prevalent by the early period
of independence (see Bashshur 1978).

Western influence over Lebanon was maintained after independence
through the system of education. The sizable western missionary schools and
universities continue to be the wealthiest and most prestigious units in this
system. The predominantly western pedagogical orientation in missionary
schools remained largely unchanged. In addition, the majority of courses
offered in all schools and at most universities used French and/or English as
the primary language of instruction. As a result, the post colonial generations
have been heavily socialized towards the West (Sharara 1983; Sabban 1988).

Thus, the causes for conflict in modern Lebanon since the state's
inception are rooted in colonial tutelage. Socioeconomic and regional disparities, along with lack of unity over national identity, were associated
with the French-initiated Greater Lebanon in 1920. The discriminatory
sectarian system gradually expanded under the French Mandate and was
fully developed by the state's 'Founding Fathers' in 1943. The process of
dissociating from the Arab East and adhering to the West, a process reinforced under colonialism, continued between 1943 and 1975.

The advancement of the service-based economy after 1943
significantly destabilized the livelihood of agricultural producers and led
to a massive rural-to-urban migration. With the emergence of other crises
associated with restrictions on political participation, a growing socioeconomic gap, and lack of equal access to quality education plus limited
job opportunities, demands for reforms pounded the state from the late
1960s onwards. The multisectarian movement for change, which had a
strong secular orientation, included a broad range of unions, students,
intellectuals, and women's groups (Ofeish 1996, 378-92). This movement
was allied with the Palestinian resistance forces in Lebanon, and shared
with these forces a common Arab vision of change and a resentment of
the anti-reformist pro-Western Lebanese state.

The state and its supporters rapidly organized to defend the status
quo. The ensuing tensions soon led to the outbreak of the civil war in

1975. At the forefront of the state's protectors were the Maronite-based sectarian militias who incited sectarianism to mobilize their co-religionists to their side. The Phalange party had the largest and most well-trained militia in this group at that time.

One of these militias' early aims was that of maintaining full control over "their" territories. They initiated a zealous campaign of sectarian and political cleansing in the Christian-concentrated areas they were able to occupy during the war's first two years. This campaign targeted Muslims, Christians who disagreed with their political views, and Palestinians (Petran 1987, 182-87). "Their" territories were clearly marked and separated from the more diverse territories of the "others" by the force of roadblocks, check points, shelling, and snipers.

Palestinians were particularly targeted by the Maronite-based sectarian militias for more than one reason. Most importantly, the Palestinians' alliance with the reformist Lebanese coalition had greatly strengthened the latter's internal position. Secondly, a Palestinian–Lebanese alliance as such would tilt Lebanon towards the Arab East, thus threatening the Maronite elite's project of westernizing Lebanon. Thirdly, the Palestinians were considered anti-western due to their conflict with Israel and its western allies. Finally, the militias' projection of Palestinians as the "enemy" helped them in rallying the troops and deflected the more accurate assessment of the war as a class-based conflict among the Lebanese.

Thus, another hierarchy of control reinforced by violence was established by the Maronite-based sectarian militias at the war's outset. Their "enemy" list included the movement for change that challenged the dominance of sectarian privileges, westernization, and patriarchy. Integration of the Palestinians into this list was partially aimed at camouflaging the internal strife and representing it instead as an internal/external one. The value-laden nationalist hierarchy of friends and foes did not even change with friendly moves by neighboring Arab states. Although Syria's intervention in spring 1976 rescued the Maronite-based sectarian militias from an inevitable defeat, the Syrian Arabs remained to them the "less civilized" suspicious elements.

Fanon's theoretical arguments discussed earlier are very useful in facilitating a better understanding of Lebanon's situation. Fanon was concerned about the destructive effects of a non-inclusive ruling elite on the nation. Lebanon's ruling elite had failed to create a unifying and comprehensive national project during either the 1920–43 colonial era or the 1943–75 postcolonial era. The project of a "Lebanese nation" that developed out of these two eras was exclusively synonymous with the privileged Maronite elite. Thus, feelings of frustration and resentment were growing among many groups, leading to the creation of a determined opposition that force-fully stressed Lebanon's Arabness and called for change. The sectarian sys-tem initiated by the French colonials and developed by the 1943 state promoted unequal access to resources among the population along with stereotypical imagery to facilitate its goals. Fanon had noted colonial efforts to divide African groups along stereotypical faults. In Lebanon, stereo-typical presentations of enemy groups promoted by the most dominant (Maronite) elite in the 1970s were set along the dichotomies of civilized/less civilized, Christian/Muslim, Lebanese/Arab, and western/Arab, respec-tively. The systematic violence following the outbreak of the civil war in 1975 was strongly associated with a forceful campaign of stereotyping the "other," a process amply evidenced in *Sitt Marie Rose*.

Violent Hierarchies: Sectarianism, Patriarchy and Power

Sitt Marie Rose is Etel Adnan's fictional and political response to the civil war crisis. The novel is divided into two parts: Time I, in which an unnamed female character tells the story in the first person, and Time II, in which the action is narrated through the voices of various characters. Time I, which is divided into many unnumbered texts, sets the scene for the male characters, their hobbies and interests, and specifically their fas-cination with hunting and killing birds. This part also introduces us to the general war atmosphere in Lebanon, particularly in Beirut. The second part is divided into three main sections, each of which is divided in turn into seven short chapters. Each of the seven chapters is narrated by one of the characters: the deaf-mute children, who speak with a collective voice; Marie Rose; Mounir; Tony; Fouad; Bouna Lias; or the unnamed narrator. These characters appear in the same order throughout the three main sec-tions. Although the unnamed narrator is a participating character in the first part of the novel, she disappears as a character in the second part, retaining only the privilege of narrating, summarizing, and commenting on events.

The male characters in *Sitt Marie Rose*, Mounir and the other militi-amen (the *Chabab*)[4] are associated with the Phalange. The *Chabab* believe themselves to be representing "legality" and "defending the power of the state" (Adnan 1982, 57–58). As Mounir makes clear, they believe the end of the war will be "clean and definitive. There will be a victor and a van-quished, and we'll be able to talk, to reconstruct the country from a new base" (33). It is precisely this "clean and definitive new base," which

Mounir dreams of reconstructing, that the novel problematizes for us. The binary opposition of "victor" and "vanquished" through which he understands and rationalizes matters can no longer work in a country devastated by war. As the war later shows, the positions of the "victorious" and the "defeated" constantly changed places, and the rigid dichotomy which Mounir aspires to achieve proves to be unattainable.

Violence plays a central role in the *Chabab*'s determination to maintain control. Their infatuation with violence is presented very early on in the novel as we learn about their fascination with hunting. They create self-righteous categories that divide people and issues, creating oppositions between themselves and others (the "enemy"), right and wrong, good and bad, civilized and less civilized, who should live and who should die. Violence, associated with absolute order, power, and efficiency (Adnan 1982, 37), and loaded with a multitude of "good" values, is used as a forceful tool to achieve their goal. As Fouad, one of the *Chabab* believes, "It's violence that accelerates the progress of a people" (55).

The value system of the *Chabab* is greatly affected by Lebanon's educational system and by its western missionary schools in particular. The *Chabab* had received an education valorizing anything not Arab; they were taught to make fun of "Arab cinema and everything that belonged to the region" (Adnan 1982, 47). Marie Rose, herself an educator, blames the Jesuits for the *Chabab*'s western orientation; she believes that the missionary schools "oriented them toward Paris and the quarrels of the French" (47). In one scene, the narrative takes us back to a time when Marie Rose and Mounir were teenage sweethearts. Marie Rose tells Mounir, who is dressed up like a Crusader in a white tunic while at the same time wearing an Arab "kefyeh-and-agal," "'You come from here. You're not a foreigner. You don't come France or England. You could never be a Crusader.'" Mounir's response is indicative of his confusion over identity: "'Are you sure?' he asked with a sadness that misted his eyes, 'Then what am I going to become?'" (48).

It is precisely this question — "What am I going to become?" — that reflects the dilemma of many Lebanese over their national identity. Mounir can only understand what it means to be an Arab or European on the superficial level of attire. Although he aspires to be modern — in this instance identifying himself with the Crusaders, i.e. the Westerners/Europeans — Mounir expresses his confusion about his identity by wearing an Arab headdress. As Thomas Foster pointedly remarks, "He [Mounir] cannot acknowledge that modernization can lead to irrecoverable loss or that the narrative of Europe and that of its others may significantly impinge on each other. The war foregrounds both the necessity and the difficulty of displacing the dualistic categories of modernity and tradition, self and other, that Mounir takes for granted" (Foster 1995, 61).

It is this dichotomy between "self and other" that Mounir rigidly applies to issues and people. According to him and the *Chabab*, to be Europeanized is to categorize people and place them on a hierarchical scale. Mounir, who places the French on a higher pedestal than himself, and by implication, the Lebanese people, considers himself to be of a higher status than the Syrians. Talking of his hunting trip to a Syrian village, Mounir remarks, "When we arrived, we were the first Europeans they had ever seen. Excuse me, I mean Lebanese" (Adnan 1982, 5). Even his adolescent infatuation with Marie Rose is based on her resemblance to the Europeans; she doesn't "look like an Arab ... because [she has] blue eyes ... like girls in the movies ... so modern" (34). This hierarchization of people and issues only allows Mounir to see matters in a comparative fashion: "You see, a young Syrian in Beirut, it's like us in Paris" (6).

Adnan's novel probes whether it is possible to construct a subject indoctrinated from childhood into identifying individuals on a sectarian basis who can yet be tolerant of other people's beliefs and convictions. Sectarian identification encourages individuals and groups to see power as something acquired only by adhering to one's sectarian community. Such behavior becomes more intense when sectarian individuals perceive themselves as fighting against members of other sectarian communities over power and resources. While the challenges of the war pushed the Christian militiamen, with whom the *Chabab* are associated, to the extremes of ethnic cleansing, it also provoked their deepest fears regarding their own status and affiliation. These anxieties over identity are evidenced throughout the novel in the behavior and self-representation of the *Chabab*.

The *Chabab* see themselves as Christians. Already "oriented toward Paris and the quarrels of the French," Mounir and the other young boys at school were proud to walk in processions led by the French priests, singing "I am a Christian. This is my glory, my hope, my support..." (Adnan 1982, 47). Moreover, the *Chabab* see themselves as competitors with Muslims. Notwithstanding the existence of Palestinian Christians, they identify the Palestinians as Muslims. Thus, Tony proclaims: "My name is Tony and it will never be Mohammed.... We are the Christian youth and we are at war with the Palestinians. They are Moslems. So we are at war with Islam, especially when it crosses our path" (36).

To the *Chabab*, being a Christian is equated with being "western," which in this context implies non-affiliation with Arab causes, and with being privileged within the status quo. Thus, they perceive any challenge to their "Lebanese Nationalist" identity as a threat to their state dominance and power. As the narrator puts it, "The civil war is a laser which has hit the center of their identities. It's a nuclear explosion, not from a bomb, not from the exterior, but from the very heart of their race's memory" (Adnan 1982, 40). According to the *Chabab*, any Christian Lebanese should adhere to their worldview (and, they imply, should be subject to their control), otherwise become a suspicious element, especially if this person challenges the status quo they are defending. Following this logic, they set about fighting "the dissident Christians to save the real Christians" (75). One of those dissidents is Marie Rose.

Gender Challenge

As an autonomous free-thinking woman, Marie Rose poses a challenge to the *Chabab*'s conceptualization of women and of their role in society. For the *Chabab*, women should be dependent on men because they are non-thinking subjects incapable of being autonomous. The opening scene in the novel exemplifies the *Chabab*'s attitude towards women. The "modernized" women gather in Mounir's luxurious apartment in Beirut, surrounded by his male friends. Mounir wants to make a feature film about the cultural shock of "backward" Syrian workers when they first move to "sophisticated" and "westernized" Beirut. For this movie, he would like to "bring" some Syrian workers to Lebanon during one of his hunting trips to Syria. He wants the narrator to write the scenario for his film.

Mounir's offer to the female narrator to write the film's scenario could be perceived as an attempt to include women in men's projects. However, his attempt only serves to belittle women's contributions. Despite her efforts, the narrator's intervention is minimalized, and is confounded by Mounir's conceptualization of the film's theme and scenes. He has also made it clear from the outset that he wants the movie to reflect not the Syrian laborer's perspective, as the narrator wishes, but "the point of view of the hunters," that is, of the *Chabab* (Adnan 1982, 6). As Denise Kandiyoti aptly points out in her discussion of women and the nation, "Women are no longer excluded from the public arena, but subordinated within it" (Kandiyoti 1994, 377). It is not simply that women are given secondary roles but that they have little control over their input.

Women mix with men in Mounir's house, but they are passive listeners. Their mingling in the men's world is characterized by the absence of a dialogue between the sexes. There is only indirect speech reported in this setting. When one of the women expresses her interest in joining the men on one of their hunting expeditions, the reader learns that the "men" refused because "they didn't want to be bothered" (Adnan 1982, 2). While explaining the beauty of the Syrian desert, Mounir retorts: "I can't tell you what the desert is. You have to see it. Only, you women, you'll never see it. You have to strike out on your own, find your trail with nothing but a map and a compass.... You, you'll never be able to do that" (3-4). The *Chabab* not only find women's presence to be a nuisance to their hunting expeditions, but feel that women will "never" be able to see or experience what men explore. Mounir's discourse marks an important issue; he sees women as subservient to men, and as unable to think and act "on [their] own." He also sees them as accessories or ornaments that both beautify the men's world and make that world look "modern." In such a context, women as "icons of modernity" are "less a comment on changing gender relations than a symbolic evocation of the dynamism of a 'new' nation" (Graham-Brown 1988, 220). Although the "new" nation which Mounir dreams of constructing will have to include women, these women are manipulated by men like chess pawns.

Mounir feels baffled by Marie Rose, who is very unlike the women with whom he associates. She is a Lebanese Christian who has been working for the social services of the Palestinian resistance for a long time. She has been involved in the movement for change, including educational reform and "women's liberation." She has chosen to move to multisectarian West Beirut, and lives with a young Palestinian doctor. However, Mounir admits to himself that the war changes people's perspectives on issues: "Things have evolved in this country. Yes, it's taken nearly a year of civil war, hundreds dead every day in Beirut, and an upsetting of the old alliance between heaven and earth, for me to conceive of a woman as a worthy partner, ally or enemy"(Adnan 1982, 35). Autonomous and an activist, Marie Rose fully challenges the *Chabab*'s prototype of what a good Christian and a respectable woman should be. The possibility of a woman as "a worthy partner, ally or enemy" (35) frightens Mounir and the *Chabab*. They consider Marie Rose a "traitor" because she works for the 'enemy's' camp and defies their love of hierarchy. The fact that she "strike[s] out on [her] own" and finds her own "trail" infuriates the men. As a result, they not only suppress her actions, but physically "eliminate" her (4).

Marie Rose does not confine herself to women's issues, but also invades what the *Chabab* consider to be their sacred territories. Her transgression of public space constitutes a major 'intrusion' into their realm. As with the national and sectarian hierarchies that Mounir abides by, the patriarchal hierarchy he endorses prevents him from seeing and accepting

Marie Rose as a woman with her own rights and freedoms. Mounir's parochial understanding of his nation-state is synonymous with "political actors whose definitions of who and what constitutes the nation have a crucial bearing on notions of national unity and alternative claims to sovereignty as well as on the sorts of gender relations that should inform the nationalist project" (Kandiyoti 1994, 378). Differently put, Mounir and the *Chabab* believe that the "nationalist project" can only be visualized, defined, and implemented by men. Consequently, women cannot and should not have equal rights to men in the public realm. As mentioned earlier, although the men in this novel adopt a "modernizing" outlook on women, their actions exhibit a "traditional" understanding of solidarity that is based on sectarian affiliation. Their stance is thus similar to that which Sharabi describes as "neopatriarchy," that is, a modernized patriarchy. The novel presents the ways in which sectarian control and patriarchy reinforced each other in Lebanon, resulting in a neopatriarchy as Sharabi suggests, where power and privilege continued to be assigned exclusively to males.

Mounir does not allow his reluctant realization of "woman as a worthy partner" to overcome his sectarianism, for such a realization would alter the "old alliance" of the patriarchal system, with its dominance of men over women, of the privileged over the deprived, of the powerful over the weak, of the sectarian over the secular. If these alliances based on power hierarchies are shaken, then new alliances based on equality, freedom of speech and action, and social justice would replace them, and that would disrupt the dominance of Mounir's group.

Marie Rose not only challenges the men's patriarchal attitudes and actions, but also tries to rectify their misconception of the civil war as a religious-based one. She gives voice to a sensitive issue in Lebanese politics. Instead of accepting the *Chabab*'s sectarian explanation of the war, she highlights the Lebanese civil war's class and ideological dimensions, emphasizing the growing socio-economic disparities and political conflict between the haves and have-nots in Lebanon as a primary cause. Marie Rose reiterates that the status quo forces made the fight "into a religious war to cloud the issues"(Adnan 1982, 63). She realizes that the conflict is "not really religious. It's part of a larger Crusade directed against the poor. They bomb the underprivileged quarters because they consider the poor to be vermin they think will eat them.... They have turned those among them that were poor against the poor 'of others'" (52). The issues, then, although appearing to be religious in texture, are political and economic in substance (Ofeish 1996, 432–34). As discussed earlier, the dominant Maronite elite have instigated sectarian solidarity among their middle and lower class co-religionists to counter the secular and popular movement for change that emerged in the late 1960s.

Sitt Marie Rose implicates the religious establishments, Christian and Muslim alike, in the propagation of violence in Lebanon. Instead of being concerned with "human pain" and "human mercy," "their shared existence is a dry flood whose passage leaves more cadavers than flowers" (Adnan 1982, 65). The Maronite friar Bouna Lias supports the *Chabab*'s violence and legitimizes their actions on a religious basis. He further emphasizes the religious nature of the war, explaining to Marie Rose that the war should be placed "under the sign not of politics but of the divine. In this century no one has fought with holy medals on as many chests, the Virgin on as many rifles, the crucifix on as many tanks, the name of God on so many lips, the vision of Heaven before so many eyes, as our young men" (96). Presenting himself as "the guardian of justice" (64), Bouna Lias calls on Marie Rose to confess her sins for aiding the "enemy" and to regret her actions so that he can save her from torture and death. Religion here is used as a substantial determinant of "right" and "wrong" regarding political, socioeconomic, and national issues.

While the discourse of Bouna Lias and the *Chabab* reflects a sectarian approach, the discourse of Marie Rose offers a completely different vision. Contrary to their clan solidarity and exclusiveness, she embraces diversity and inclusiveness. Her worldview emphasizes "a common culture and a common history" among the Arabs, including Lebanese and Palestinians, both Christians and Muslims. She realizes that, in order for the Arabs to be liberated, "there are knots to untie, abscesses to drain" (Adnan 1982, 57). These "knots" and "abscesses," which have to be extracted from the Arab "race's memory," refer to the "concentric circles of oppression" that the novel depicts. The first and foremost of these circles surrounding the individual is that of the family. These circles continue to expand in scope and dimension, engulfing the Lebanese civil war within a larger regional and global context. For after the circle of the family "comes the circle of the state, then the circle of the Brother Arab countries, the circle of the enemy, the Super Powers, and so forth.... These circles of oppression are inevitably circles of betrayal.... [They] have also become circles of repression" (103-4).

In her attempt to break some of these circles, Marie Rose, who takes on a "mutative" role, suffers and dies. "[E]veryone warned me not to cross the line," she acknowledges (Adnan 1982, 31). But perceiving herself to "represent love, new roads, the unknown, the untried" (58), she defies the established norms. She is executed for crossing, in a literal sense, the imaginary line between sectarian communities and opposing ideological fronts.

She is also persecuted for crossing, in a figurative sense, the line that contains women within an already-molded framework of permissible actions and behavior. Her intrusion into the domain of politics, customarily taken to be men's exclusive territory, merely confirms Tony's belief that "when whores like this get mixed up in war, now that's something to get disgusted about" (60).

Conclusion

Marie Rose contests the militiamen's claims to power, challenges their patriarchal system, and questions the sectarian foundations of their very existence. The *Chabab* try to bring her back to the "right path" by "readmitting" her to her sectarian community. But by trying to force her to adopt a sectarian identity, they are depriving her of her right to be a free citizen practicing her own beliefs and convictions. In this sense sectarian oppression as opposed to secular freedom is inextricably intertwined with the *Chabab*'s rigid boundaries between male/female, public/private, and colonizer/colonized.

Sitt Marie Rose portrays the complex intersection of gender, colonialism and war's violence as these constitute subjectivities through well defined hierarchies. For the *Chabab*, "freedom" is defined by conforming to these hierarchies and avoiding contradiction. Knowing that "they wouldn't be able to conquer either her heart or her mind," they have to eliminate Marie Rose physically, to "deduct" her from the community. As the narrative voice tells us, "Power is always obscene. It's only in thickening the sensibility that the human brain attains power and maintains it, and all power finally expresses itself through the death penalty" (Adnan 1982,104). It is this "thickening" of sensibility that allows one of the *Chabab*, who has "reduced all truths to a formula of life and death" (37), to boast thus about his violent act: "I quartered her with my own hands" (92).

Notes

1. For a theoretical discussion of sectarianism and the sectarian system, see Ofeish (1999, 97–100).
2. For an elaborate discussion of the crisis of national identity associated with the creation of "Greater Lebanon," and the differences between the two regions, see Ofeish (1996, 169–175).
3. For an extended discussion of the principles and aims of the sectarian system in association with the National Pact see Ofeish (1996, 203–208).

4. The term Chabab is the plural of chab; it usually means "youths" in the Lebanese dialect. This term also signifies strong, muscular men who boast about their power and accomplishments.

References

Adnan, Etel. 1982. *Sitt Marie Rose*. Translated by Georgina Kleege. Sausalito, CA: Post-Apollo.

Bashshur, Munir. 1978. *Bunyat al-nizam al-tarbawi fi Lubnan*. (The Structure of the Educational System in Lebanon). Beirut: al-Markaz al-Tarbawi Iil-Buhuth wal-Inma'.

Fanon, Frantz. 1963. *The Wretched of the Earth*. New York: Grove Weidenfeld.

Foster, Thomas. 1995. "Circles of Oppression, Circles of Repression: Etel Adnan's *Sitt Marie Rose*." *PMLA* 110, no. 1 (January): 59–74.

Graham-Brown, Sarah. 1988. *Images of Women: The Portrayal of Women in Photography of the Middle East 1860-1950*. New York: Columbia University Press.

Kandiyoti, Deniz. 1994. "Identity and its Discontents: Women and the Nation." In *Colonial Discourse and Post-Colonial Theory: A Reader*, edited by Patrick Williams and Laura Chrisman, 376–391. New York: Columbia University Press.

Mishra, Vijay and Bob Hodge. 1994. "What is Post (-)colonialism?" In *Colonial Discourse and Post-Colonial Theory: A Reader*, edited by Patrick Williams and Laura Chrisman, 276–90. New York: Columbia University Press.

Ofeish, Sami A. 1999. "Lebanon's Second Republic: Secular Talk, Sectarian Application." *Arab Studies Quarterly* 21, no. 1 (Winter): 97–116.

_____. 1996. "Sectarianism and Change in Lebanon: 1843-1975." Ph.D. diss., University of Southern California.

Petran, Tabitha. 1987. *The Struggle over Lebanon*. New York: Monthly Review.

Sabban, Rima. 1988. "Lebanese Women and Capitalist Cataclysm." In *Women of the Arab World*, edited by Nahid Toubia, 124–138. London: Zed.

Sharabi, Hisham. 1988. *Neopatriarchy: A Theory of Distorted Change in Arab Society*. New York: Oxford University Press.

Sharara, Yolla Polity. 1983. "Women and Politics in Lebanon." In *Third World, Second Sex*, compiled by Miranda Davies, 19–29. London: Zed.

10

Ever Since Gilgamesh: Etel Adnan's Discourse of National Unity in *Sitt Marie Rose*

Mohomodou Houssouba

Sur la surface lisse de l'Euphrate descend la trahison...

...

O soleil pacifique père éternel des enfants de Canaan
O déluge babylonien aïeul des Arabes

[Adnan 1980, 8, 4]

Treason floats down the smooth surface of the Euphrates...

...

O peaceful sun eternal father of Canaan's children
O Babylonian Deluge ancestor of the Arabs

[Adnan 1989, 21, 33]

Etel Adnan's novel, *Sitt Marie Rose*, chronicles the eruption of the Lebanese civil war as the culmination of the continual fraying of the post-colonial Arab world. This tragic turn deepens the psychic agony of the central character, Marie Rose, a Christian Lebanese teacher who participated in the relief effort on behalf of Palestinian refugees after the Arab-Israeli war of 1967. In the larger history, thirty years before, Lebanon had helped to create the Arab League, which was set up to reunify the peoples of Arab descent. In all its activities—from maintaining a joint front in the first Arab-Israeli war to creating various development institutions—the organization projected the ideal of Arab solidarity, of different postcolonial states coming together to forge one strong, forward-looking nation. Geographically, this entity stretched from Syria to Morocco, thus including most of the old Islamic empire. But what should constitute the basis for unity among such disparate peoples, besides the language they share?

The opening scenes of Adnan's novel dramatize, instead of unity, subtle conflicts. Despite their long, common history, the Lebanese and Syrians relate to one another as accidental neighbors with their relationships — between Lebanese tourists and Syrian villagers, Syrian migrant workers and Lebanese overseers in Beirut — shaped by economics. In fact, these opening scenes play on the dark irony of a presumed Arab brotherhood replaced by a master-slave dialectic. As the war drags on, causing more acts of cruelty and sadism, the irony darkens too, becoming more didactic as the two female narrators — foils for the sadistic male order of economic exploitation and political oppression — ponder the minds of their fellow male Arabs. The result is a sequence of reflections on Arab identity. The motif of common ancestry and temperament recurs throughout the novel. Arabs are portrayed as the descendents of Sumerians, Babylonians, and Canaanites, with the hunting ethos feeding the warmongering impulse in the Arab world, the perversion of both Christianity and Islam in the hands of tribal patriarchs, and the propensity for fragmentation and resignation in the face of immense suffering all portrayed as parts of a common heritage. This unsettling psycho social picture confronts the reader with the problem of Arab unity, which the prevailing order of things negates. There is neither solidarity nor unity among Arabs.

But should this failure be attributed to atavism, or rather, to commonplace materialism? The question is important in that it forces us to consider the terms of the debate more closely. Simply put, there are at least two choices of analysis: class-struggle economics or group psychology. The latter is particularly challenging because it involves fuzzy concepts like common (racial) attributes. Do Arabs share traits that predispose them to self-destruct? If so, how then can such an essential character be altered? Is there any room left for chastising greedy merchants, cruel despots, or even fatalistic slum dwellers? Does the story restore individual agency, which the narrators find particularly lacking in their world? Or does it simply reproduce more particularist myths in the attempt to make sense of collective suffering?

At the outset, we are confronted with the economic gulf between the rich and the poor, as well as with individual lifestyles and mindsets that contradict the discourse of Arab solidarity held in official circles. The narrative unfolds against the backdrop of several panoramic views which project a subtle yet disturbing picture of the social economy of prewar Lebanon. The juxtaposition of the affluent Lebanese Christian districts, the poor Muslim quarters, the "pristine" villages of southern Syria, and the Syrian migrant workers' squats in Beirut foregrounds the geopolitical implications of such a layered economic system. The narrative fragments of the different communities reflect the fractious political culture of the region, of which Lebanon is both a microcosm and a crossroads. In this regard, the failure of economic justice as well as democratic principles to take hold in this small, prosperous country offers a study in the predicament of the larger Arab nation, whose ruling and other privileged classes have consistently put their personal and group interests above the urgent needs of the collective.

Adnan's novel explores the roots of this fateful disconnect through implied questions: Why, despite all formal declarations of united Arab states, does all-Arab national unity remain so elusive? Will there ever be any genuine united Arab nation, as a community based on the ethic of mutual care? What precedents might support one's answer one way or the other?

In effect, the answers Adnan offers pass through mythology and social psychology. The story of the Arab peoples is mixed with the history of the world — especially the successive rise of organized religions, which would reshape the identities of so many distant societies. Again, Lebanon exemplifies the stronghold monotheistic religions have had on the Arab destiny. Historically, it has been a port of entry for invaders and traders venturing into the region of "Greater Syria." The occupiers included the Roman and Byzantine administrations under which Christianity became established in Lebanon. The Maronite confession endured and evolved even during the rise of Islam in the seventh century. In fact, beside religious pluralism, Lebanon has proved to be fertile ground for distinct, hybrid confessions. For example, the Druze and Maronite traditions derived respectively from Islam and Christianity; still they have developed their own particular practices. Consequently, each community shapes its identity around religious rituals, like the annual Crusade processions in which Adnan's character Mounir and other Christian students once marched, chanting in the streets of Beirut, "I am a Christian. This is my glory, my hope, my support..." (Adnan 1982, 47).

This scene becomes particularly important when viewed against the background of the destructive inter-confessional war which Adnan's novel portrays. Religious allegiance becomes the most obvious element in the tragedy of the war. Has religion been sent to the Arabs as a recipe for unrelenting, mutual annihilation? In the end, the narrator cannot see any peace or justice in the lives of Arab peoples managed by religious institutions. Instead, the worst terror, born of internecine quarrels, has been visited on this community out of religious zealotry, which the narrator considers yet another manifestation of the persistent tribalism among her people.

Indeed, this is a troubling commentary in the options it entails. The present offers little hope while the grim signs of war dominate the cityscape of a bombed-out Beirut. So the narrator steps back to the distant past when an epic hero, Gilgamesh, sets out on a journey to find a truth on his own, without making his personal quest a state affair or the prescribed path for his subjects (Adnan 1982, 58). Then, what does this allusion imply for the future of the Arab world? Where does the individual's solitary departure lead a community traumatized by war and the breakdown of solidarity so lamented in the novel?

Interestingly, the opening scenes of the novel depict the departure, not of an inconsolable, aging king (Gilgamesh), but of groups of cheerful, young Lebanese males leaving their comfortable houses to seek adventure in the wilderness of Syria and Turkey. The economic and discursive gap surfaces here, when the Lebanese men speak of their hunting forays into the Syrian countryside. Syria emerges as a larger but backward neighbor: "One leaves Lebanon, and comes to know the neighboring (and enemy) country of Syria. The Syrians are not as rich and well-equipped, and lack the proper style ... to hunt as well. Before, it was the Europeans with the faces like the ones we saw on the screen, who went hunting in Syria and Iraq, and elsewhere. Now it's the Christian, modernized Lebanese who go wherever they like with their touristo-military gear (Adnan 1982, 3). This observation exposes the critical issue of identity in the Lebanese context, an issue that is central to Adnan's argument — especially for the ethos of an inclusive Arab identity that would drive the quest for a unified homeland. However, through their lifestyle, the Christian Lebanese play the role of the affluent class once constituted by European expatriates. The reference to the European leisure class of the past evokes the colonial order under which a small elite has access to vast privileges while the masses toil for bare subsistence. The reproduction of an economic model predicated on such inequity not only illustrates the lack of vision on the part of the privileged group, it betrays the cause of Arab solidarity.

The novel dramatizes the danger that the inherent contradictions of the Lebanese system pose to the rich as well as to the less fortunate. The result is a time bomb. Like the calm surface of the Euphrates, the established order gives the affluent class a false sense of serenity. For a while, everyone seems to play out their assigned roles— the rich allowed to live content and undisturbed, the poor resigned to their fate — until a spark ignites the tinder. In this regard, Adnan posits the allegory of the postcolonial socio economic contract, especially the abandoned promise of mutual sacrifice, the practice of delayed gratification needed to bolster solidarity. Without a stake in the system, the masses will not pull ranks to protect it.

The elite's ability to enjoy such opportunities without compunction signals an ethical lapse that the narrator of *Sitt Marie Rose* considers highly perilous. Sheltered by their immense wealth, the rich have invariably lost sight of the poor, taking refuge in consumption and escapism. But the teeming slums and refugee camps, with their invisible masses, are not about to go away. Instead, they are allowed time to fester with despair and subdued rage — the signs of defeat inscribed on the faces and in the voices of the Syrian laborers literally brought into the picture at the opening of the story. While Mounir plans to produce a film about an authentic Syrian village of mud huts, the story line he envisages will use the experiences of Syrian seasonal laborers in Lebanon.

The film project occasions the first close-up of the relationship between Mounir and the unnamed female narrator who is supposed to interview the workers on a construction site. Her attempts are frustrated by the Syrian men's reluctance to divulge anything consequential about their experiences and feelings. But the silence enables the narrator to report directly on the laborers' harsh working and living conditions. Her central observation about the site exposes the obvious divide that Mounir's escapist plot elides or tries to resolve in a melodramatic dénouement: "The contractor is fierce. He talks to the workers like to subhumans, like to beasts of burden who go on two legs only because the narrowness of the stairways makes it impossible to go on four. He is neck tied and suited. He arrives in superb and enormous cars, cars made obscene by the size of their trunks, Buicks and Chevrolets. The workers are small, supple, muscular, shy, furtive, and above all, silent" (Adnan 1982, 10). To be sure, there is nothing neutral about this juxtaposition of the contractor and his day laborers. The former wields the power of a feudal lord, who never fails to ask the most physically demanding tasks from the men, even at the cost of efficiency. The narrator's observation implies an allegorical extension of the scene. The contractor embodies the archetypal character of cruelty, which will become central to the narrator's direct commentaries on the social and political culture of the Arab world. At this stage, Adnan makes the narrator's point of view the dominant filter through which the reader learns about the beginning of the Lebanese civil war and the roles of the various actors in its unfolding. The metonymic use of the Syrian village and Beirut to represent the dynamics at work across the Arab community of nations remains one of the elements that make this simple story so compelling.

On the other hand, through the surrealistic reenactment of the Crusades conducted by French priests, we see the ongoing connection between Christian identity and a pro-European political outlook that contrasts with the sentiment of pan-Arabism seemingly prevalent among Muslim communities. The narrator retraces this basic faultline to the capital, Beirut, where modern Christian neighborhoods and Muslim quarters sprawl from the center outward, looking to the west or east — a fragmented cityscape that conjures up an image of collective martyrdom. In the wake of the "events," the sophisticated façade of the Christian quarters and the outward decrepitude of the Muslim enclaves fall into a spatial gap: "Everyone feels a prison closing in, and keeps making a lot of phone calls. Space shrinks" (Adnan 1982, 14). A parallel time warp ensues, as the pace of the tragedy quickens: "Minutes seem to have fewer than sixty seconds. They go faster. The mechanism of time is out of order" (15). This play on time and space is important to the larger scheme of historical representation in the novel. The two elements frame historical consciousness — as territory and collective unconscious. In the case of Lebanon, the carnage of the moment follows an established pattern. The narrative focuses on the consistency of reciprocity in the infliction of pain — the source of despair on the part of the narrator who sees a sure repetition of the horror, once the current victim gathers enough strength to reverse power relations.

The preoccupation of Sitt Marie Rose, who is abducted by Mounir and his Christian militia forces in the second part of the novel, stems from an understanding of local and regional history. The Palestinian refugee camp is the "open sore" of the Arab world — a testimony to the betrayal of one member of the "family" of the Arab nation. To Sitt Marie Rose, its existence exposes the hypocrisy of leaders and individuals who publicly posture about the Palestinian predicament to give it a semblance of urgency while doing their best to undermine the Palestinian cause. In this regard, the Israeli defeat of Arab armies in June 1967 remains the pivotal moment in the region's contemporary history, a moment when different Arab parties made fateful choices.

On the whole, suggests Adnan, the Palestinians were sacrificed for the larger community. Sitt Marie Rose impresses the portent of this deal on Mounir during her interrogation: "For the first time in Arab history one group has died for another. You do not represent the half of the country, made up of as many Christians as Moslems, who are fighting for and with the Palestinians. I'm not the only one to do it" (Adnan 1982, 57). By joining the Palestinian resistance, she has hoped to help forestall the systematic suppression of their militant presence in the midst of different host countries. She warns the dominant Christians against the temptation to get rid of the new wanderers: "You who love victory, beware that the defeat of the Palestinians will act as leaven in the Arab psyche. You're tearing their throats out. I repeat tearing their throats out. I can hear their death-rattle. Their blood fills your mouths. But things are on the move. They are moving in Rabat, moving in Algiers, in Kairouan and in Tripoli of Libya, in the Fayoum and in Damascus, in Bagdad and much further ... people are arriving barefooted to claim their dues" (58). This picture dismays Mounir and other Christian militiamen who blame the civil war on the same Palestinians. Tony is quite sanguine about using the war to bring about a final solution to the perceived problem: "She's a Christian and she went over to the Moslem camp. She's Lebanese and she went over to the Palestinian camp. Where's the problem? We must do away with her like with every other enemy." His tirade ends on a vow of brutal efficiency: "And in this war, there are no prisoners. There's nothing to be taken. That's how it is. We must suppress them" (36).

However, this articulation does not surprise Sitt Marie Rose, who detects in the militiaman's bravado a symptom of the neurosis among her people. Sectarian loyalty constantly eclipses the larger bond between members of the Arab family. Ironically, the idea of nation itself — Lebanon for the Lebanese — falls into the category of tribal allegiance, not nationalism as such. To Marie-Rose, the Christian men's conception of the Lebanese nation-state flows from a deeper exclusivist consciousness, the driving energy in their hunting frenzy. The Palestinians are the lightning rod of the moment but the scope of the campaign is much broader. Tony explicitly invokes a religious war: "We are the Christian Youth and our militia is at war with the Palestinians. They are Moslems. So we are at war with Islam, especially when it crosses our path" (Adnan 1982, 36). This statement makes religion the most divisive element of the Arab community. More than any other factor, it inspires machinations that preempt any effort to form a united front against the outside enemy.

In this regard, Sitt Marie Rose attributes even the loss of Jerusalem to the Arab Christians' lack of spiritual attachment to the Holy City. She discovers this emotional void to her surprise after founding an association to support Jerusalem: "I thought that in this country where Christians hold the power, many people would feel cut off with the loss of the Holy City. But Jerusalem has no friends in this city [Beirut]" (Adnan 1982, 50). Taking stock of this detachment, she muses over a possible deeper meaning — that charity, the cornerstone of authentic Christianity, has long ceased to drive the Christians of the region: "They have perverted Charity at the heart of its root. Jerusalem is the great absent. That city, founded a few thousand years ago by the Canaanites, their ancestors, where Christ died and rose — they've never been there. They don't plan to go. The spiritual Jerusalem is dead, in their consanguineous marriage, and under the weight of their hatred. It is no longer in the Middle East" (52). The evocation of Jerusalem as the homeland of the Canaanites brings to the fore the issue of common ancestry, for Canaan represents the double heritage of race and religion that Arabs have failed to reconcile.

On the surface, the primacy of religious identity can be deemed the root of the "hatred" which has triggered the present "apocalypse" (Adnan 1982, 86). In a sense, then, Canaan is a reminder of a common, pre-confessional origin. It is a potential rallying point where the Arab community realizes its destiny without sectarian delusions — the thought that any single group can strike up external alliances and survive as a self-contained island of prosperity, be it the Saudi kingdom or the Lebanese republic. However, Sitt Marie Rose's understanding of history does not allow her to expect such a critical awakening. She cannot escape the disturbing historical realism that colors her reading of past and current events. She constantly retraces tragic turns in regional history to some over-determining atavism. Tribal loyalty — manifestly a confessional badge — always takes precedence over Arab identity:

> For ten thousand years in this part of the world we've always been tribal, tribal, tribal. But Gilgamesh left alone, all ties forever broken, searching for life and death. Since that distant day we haven't invented a single man who didn't found a religion. We haven't had a single man who was effectively alone, who sought on his own account, to understand good and evil, who could stand up crucified without anyone knowing it, and carry his adventure and his secret to a grave that didn't open on either Heaven or Hell. Shepherd or sheep you always have defined yourselves in terms of herds. [58]

Undeniably, Sitt Marie Rose's charisma puts her in control here, even as she faces a potential executioner. The statement is poetic in its economy, as it weaves together historical, sociological, psychological, biblical, and literary allusions to Arab history. In a way, it also echoes the earlier references to an ancestral heartland in Canaan (and Jerusalem). But the valuation of historical memory is quite different. While the narrator deplores the absence of a collective commitment to the defense of Jerusalem — even for parochial reasons — her allusion to Gilgamesh implies that group solidarity constitutes the greatest impediment to self-actualization in the Arab world.

Gilgamesh's heroism comes from his solitary quest for the meaning of life and death. In the Sumerian epic, Gilgamesh, fifth king of Uruk

(Erech in the Bible), carried on a tyrannical rule and hedonistic life; for example, his entitling himself to the virginity of every young bride. This monotonous self-indulgence changes as a result of his interaction with a new persona: Enkidu. According to one version of the legend, Enkidu is a feral man living on the edge of the steppe in the company of wild animals, who undoes the hunters' traps to free the prey. A young hunter observes him one day in the act of getting a gazelle out of a trap. On hearing of the incident, the hunter's father dispatches him to Gilgamesh with a curious proposal: to send a woman who would seduce Enkidu and make the animals ashamed of him. In the meantime, Gilgamesh has a dream in which his own people gather around to admire a star that has just fallen from the sky. It is a scene so disturbing to the king that he immediately seeks an interpretation from his mother, Ninsun. Then he has the vision of an ax that he fails to lift despite his best efforts. Ninsun explains how a friend of unfailing loyalty will enter his life and "lift" him in times of duress.

The hunter's scheme works. Soon the animals desert Enkidu, who allows the woman to shave and dress him, and take him to Uruk. Enkidu's arrival triggers a spectacular duel which proves only the parity between the two men. The seal of their newly found friendship bolsters Gilgamesh's decision to fight Humbaba, the guardian of the cedar forest. Despite his informed reluctance to challenge this deity of nature, Enkidu follows his friend and ends up bearing the brunt of an aggrieved Humbaba's fury. He is nearly killed before Gilgamesh recovers from a petrifying shock and helps kill Humbaba.

The death of Humbaba offends Ishtar, the goddess of love and war, "patronness" of Uruk, who entreats her father Anu (father of Sumerian gods) to punish Gilgamesh for the crime against the cedar forest. In the end, Anu agrees to send down the Bull of Heaven whose rampage will kill three hundred men and nearly reach Gilgamesh before Enkidu can gather his last strengths to slaughter the beast. That night, Enkidu reports his vision of the god's decision that one of them must die as penance for killing Humbaba and the Bull of Heaven. Since Gilgamesh is "two-thirds god," Enlil, the god of earth and war, has decreed that he — Enkidu — must die. In retrospect, Enkidu has foreseen his own death in the battle schemes of Gilgamesh, who now realizes as much. The sudden death of Enkidu during the ensuing rampage plunges Gilgamesh into the deep anguish that will force him to walk away from Uruk and the abundance of possessions and pleasures at his disposal.

To this extent, Gilgamesh's departure from Uruk could be understood as an emotional crisis precipitated by the death of his devoted companion — his alter ego in reality. Considering his previous libertine, noncommittal lifestyle, the loss of Enkidu cuts short his emotional and moral reformation. For the first time, he has learned to value a person out of care, not for a use. Enkidu's willingness to sacrifice himself for Gilgamesh has taught the latter the essential moral lesson that the female personae of Adnan's novel find missing in the ethos of male-bonding (from falconry to militia service) that makes the masculine space so exclusionary in Arab culture.

The narrator of *Sitt Marie Rose* imputes the warmongering mentality of the militia men to "a sick sexuality, mad love, where images of crushing and cries dominate" (Adnan 1982, 66). Curiously, the pathology is linked to the "exclusive love of the mother":

> The exclusive love of the mother sets the cycle of violence in motion again. When a stranger appears on the horizon, or the poorly-loved, he is the dispossessed whose hatred sprouts and grows before the eyes like jungle plants that don't even wait for the rain to stop, to proliferate, then he, the one loved by his mother and blessed with wealth, takes his rifle and goes to the attack. He feels he's the strongest, and doesn't know that those bullets will carve bloody words on his naked chest. Deadly, like the stranger, he too will disappear. [67]

The woman on the pedestal equally risks violent death once she decides to step down and confront the imposed consecration that deprives her of all agency to the point that "a woman who stands up to them and looks them in the eye is a tree to be cut down, and they cut it down" (67). There is a poignant related image in *L'apocalypse arabe*: "une femme crucifiée de fleurs" (a woman crucified with flowers) (Adnan 1980, n.p.).

The narrator's reflections on atavism generate a coherent commentary on social history. From Sumer to Canaan, the narratives of the past are distilled into a storyline of racial history. More importantly, the recent "events" fall into a seemingly predictable pattern of fratricidal violence. It becomes logical to construe some collective psychology from the persistent musings. Perhaps unwittingly, a coherent narrative of the past unfolds. Gilgamesh takes center stage as a racial ancestor, and Canaan becomes the homeland of Arab Christians. But this picture is problematic in that it collapses space (territory) and race. Can we accept the implication that such direct lineage exists between the contemporary Arab subject and the ancient world?

A critique of the novel also has to contend with the peculiar problem of representation in the genre. The notion of reality in the text is shaped by elements of fictional narration. For example, the combination of plot and point of view in this story creates a specific perspective. In effect, the plot reenacts an episode of actual history. The narration of the Lebanese civil war is straightforward: "On the thirteenth of April 1975 Hatred erupts. Several hundred years of frustration re-emerge to be expressed anew" (Adnan 1982, 11). But even in these first lines, the superposition of history and the narrator's attitude toward the history takes hold. The present situation becomes overdetermined. It is mediated by the collective memory of violence, and expressed through individual voices like the female narrator, Marie Rose, or the priest Bouna Lias.

The novelistic rendition of history is potentially even more dialogic because the genre accommodates a conversation between conflicting worldviews in a way that textbook history usually does not. Etel Adnan's novel at least juxtaposes the monologues of the antagonists, and in this regard, conveys a realistic picture of the uncompromising polarization fueling the war. Still, the manipulation of point of view favors Marie Rose's intellectual and ethical positions. The narration is suffused with a moral discourse that appeals directly to the reader. Consequently, a responsible critique of the novel must account for the ethical portent of the recurrent plea—the narrator's case against the order of things, and her outrage—intended to prod the collective conscience. The agony is expressed with stark explicitness. Change is indispensable, yet hard to predict from the facts on the ground: "How long must we wait for the impossible mutation? It's fear, not love, that generates all actions here. The dog in the streets looks at you with terror in his eyes. The combatant has the mentality of a cave man, and despite his courage, goes forward with a mask, or huddles for hours behind sandbags" (67-68). In this sense, every strike ricochets, feeding the fertile enemy-memory of the victimized group. The consciousness of collective grievance undermines the sense of subjectivity necessary to separate the individual from the collective in the discourse of victimhood.

The evocation of Gilgamesh's solitary departure represents an allegory of grief management. The hero retires from the world of sensory overload to conduct an ascetic meditation on the meaning of death, loss, and the possibility of resurrection. The tumultous journey becomes a pilgrimage to the house of Utnapishtim, the guardian of the secret for immortality. During this voyage across the "sea of death," he refuses to heed all the warnings that his quest is vain. In the end, his persistence pays off—Utnapishtim indicates to him the river plant that brings back "new life." Once Gilgamesh finds it, he is instantly restored—jubilant and eager to cross back and return to Uruk. Then, his decision to bathe before resuming his journey creates the tragic climax: a serpent takes advantage of a brief moment of distraction to steal the magical plant. It is a rather anti-climactic turn (a familiar motif in the genre—compare, for instance, Orpheus's losing forever Eurydice because of an inadvertent glance back at the underworld). The double loss awakens the tragic hero to the irreversibility of death:

> In time he recognized this loss
> As the end of his journey
> And returned to Uruk.
>
> Perhaps, he feared,
> His people would not share
> The sorrow that he knew.
>
> *[Mason 1972, 91]*

Even Gilgamesh, then, longed for a certain communion in the experience of grief. His own epiphany will not be sufficient unless it is shared by his people. It is the balance between individual and collective grieving, or penitence, that needs to be introduced to the culture on which Marie Rose reports. Arguably, she is pleading for more individualism to counter the oppressive power of group loyalty, which imposes onerous duties on the subject.

But how do we reconcile this argument with the discourse of solidarity, which assumes loyalty to a certain collectivity or imagined community with definable interests? The depiction of the Arab community at the mercy of a fractious political culture poses such a dilemma. Since national unity is predicated on a shared goal, can its discourse avoid prescribing the tyrannical form of group loyalty faulted for the persistence of violence and sadism in the culture? More concretely, what system of government will implement the unification project without imposing a totalizing political discourse?

Such questions point to the complexity of the implications of pan-Arabism. One troubling aspect relates to the construction of an Arab race through epic or biblical stories. The result is the sort of fuzzy genealogy that animates passionate claims on any one strip of land. Each group arms itself with a version of the biblical narrative that favors its claims. The dispute over Jerusalem is a case in point.

The Holy City for Judaism, Christianity, and Islam, continues to be disputed on the basis of exclusive ownership. Marie Rose's genealogy (Arabs as the direct descendants of the Canaanites) may only compound the problem. It creates a concrete lineage where the historical and demographic data are most blurry. In other words, the admonishment intended to awaken Christian Arabs to the common destiny that Palestine represents, though compelling on the surface, cannot account for the density of history. In the same vein, the use of the wandering Palestinian to exemplify the onset (or enabling) of the "impossible mutation" from atavism seems to build on the theme introduced in relation to Gilgamesh — but this too leaves a troubling gap. It is claimed that the uprooted refugees will not revert to nomadic life and the hunting ethic that shapes Arab clan loyalty. But the novel states that: "The scouts of the clan hunt and bring the prey back to the fold. This is a common good, be it in Islamic tribes in southern Tunisia, or in Christian tribes from the Lebanese mountains: the trapped gazelle is always shared by all" (Adnan 1982, 101). Indeed, the notion of sharing here implies expectations regarding the individual's duty to join the hunt — a significant detail considering the hunting-war nexus in the novelistic commentary on collective psychology.

This connotation of communal sharing enables the narrator to project the wandering Palestinian as a new phenomenon on the scene in the Arab world. Compared to the urbanized nomads of all religions, the refugees occupy a totally different social and psychological sphere: "They were no longer nomads comforted by their tribe and their herd, but a people perpetually pursued, as if by some cosmic agreement, by both an outer and inner enemy, by their proclaimed brothers as well as the adversary, without a single square meter of certainty or security under their feet. They would have to forge a nation in the midst of total hostility. They breathed an air laced with betrayal" (Adnan 1982, 71). In effect, the novel suggests, the Palestinian predicament will engender more than another enemy-memory — an aggrieved group clamoring for revenge. Instead, the wanderers "represent a new beginning" beyond the narrow scope of an Arab world "made up of sects, sub-sects, ghettos, communities, worked up by envy, rotten, closed back on themselves like worms" (57). But should the Palestinians be expected to carry the burden of this historic role as "leaven in the Arab psyche" — at the expense of their collective memory of betrayal and suffering?

Sitt Marie Rose's activism within the Palestinian resistance implies the realization of a broader vision that will reconcile suffering and mutual forgiveness. Against the general trend, Lebanese activists have joined the Palestinian cause, in which they recognize their own destiny. These individual choices carry the energy that would start the social revolution, of which the Lebanese "events" are but a catalyst: "Besides things have started to explode. It's already too late for you to crawl back to the cocoons of the past. Mixed in the blood of the dead Palestinians is as much Lebanese blood, Lebanese who died for them, and with them" (Adnan 1982, 57). Marie Rose stresses this development as a watershed that will shake up the cultural and political foundations of the Arab world. It is a relational revolution: "For the first time in Arab history one group has died for another" (57).

Symbolically, Gilgamesh's solitary quest appeals to Marie Rose because it signals a departure from the trappings of inherited privilege and a search for self-knowledge. He owes his life to Enkidu who stopped the rampage of the Bull of Heaven. In this sense, his mournful journey is a show of gratitude; it softens Gilgamesh's rough edges and projects the possibility of personal redemption.

Yet even this opening confronts us with a nagging discomfort. As in the social context depicted, the use of symbols invariably falls back on the past — to what Edouard Glissant calls "identité-racine" (root-identity) and which he considers the source of pain in places torn by modern civil wars: "Mais, cette identité-racine unique, qui nous a fait tant de mal, continue encore à sévir et à dévaster la terre, comme en Yougoslavie" (But this exclusive root-identity, which has done us so much harm, still persists and continues to devastate the world, as it is doing in Yugoslavia) (Glissant 1995, 97).

In the case of the female narrators of *Sitt Marie Rose*, the treatment of the past sometimes results in curious dichotomies. For it is ironic that while the narrator of Time I implicitly abhors Mounir's exotic depiction of the Syrian countryside, her description of the Christian and Muslim quarters of Beirut falls into a discourse of exotic authenticity: "The Muslim enclaves still retain the disorder of the Orient which is still the last good in these essentially bastard countries which have no precise culture except the one that developed from a pell-mell of values in a state of disintegration. You would have to seek out someone squatting in a corner, someone not yet fanaticized by the tornado in order to touch some semblance of humanity, which, like a compass, still marks the magnetic North of the human species (Adnan 1982, 21). This passage exhibits the dichotomies through which Marie Rose filters her relationship with each community. To be sure, there is more than the Christian-Muslim divide in the Lebanese civil war. But the narrative insistently construes such a strict polarity. A striking example is the absence of significant references to Christian Palestinians, their stake in the loss of Jerusalem, or their overall perspective on the crisis.

The description above replicates the clear-cut delineation that demagogues use to appeal to their constituencies, but it does not account for the density of the cultural amalgam — a blending which, on some level, appears unnatural to Marie Rose herself. Yet she recognizes the dynamic of the disorder, the porosity that enables simple human feelings to flow between people and subdue the dehumanizing sectarian dogmas surrounding them. There is probably a hint of dramatic irony in the way Marie-Rose sees this powerful picture — but still sees it only partially.

In the end, the critique of political Christianity, which has transformed Christ into a "tribal prince" (Adnan 1982, 104) remains a persistent commentary running throughout the novel. It illustrates effectively the allegory of the corrupt social pact predicated on the defense of sectarian interests at the expense of the national community's well-being. The resulting breakdown of civil society in Lebanon becomes a cautionary tale to the Arab world. No group should delude itself into believing wealth and power can insulate it from the violent consequences of social injustice. In time, the tinderbox catches fire and burns down houses in rich as well as poor quarters of the city.

However, it is worth noting the danger of essentialism in a reading that limits itself to the social contradictions within Lebanese society as represented in the novel. Although the narrative captures the polyphonic diversity of the historical conflict, readers who are unfamiliar with the history of this civil war might construe a clear-cut distinction between the victim and victimizer categories. In this case, Christians become the embodiment of the cruelty that dehumanizes everyone as the battle intensifies. Such reductionism needs to be warned against, primarily because it constitutes a serious misreading of the allegory at the core of the narrative. Adnan's return to a prehistoric, collective unconscious of the Arab world actually seems to suggest that the problem lies not with religious faith, but rather in the self-serving use of sectarian labels as rallying cries. A holy war involves manipulative practices that rob the individual of independent judgment. Its conduct continually feeds a superficial fanaticism, which blinds the combatant to the absurdity and sadism inherent in the act of war. In other words, the role of political Christianity should be understood in a specific social and historical context, which remains subject to debate. The confessional-class dichotomy represents the dangerous social divide that the privileged class failed to appraise until it engulfed everybody. The absence of an inclusive vision among the Lebanese elite also symbolizes the ineffectual leaders of the Arab nations, who, at decisive moments, have continually opted for self-preservation and sold short their brethren. Regrettably, they only compounded their losses this way. But this reading of history transcends the Arab context; indeed, it captures the worldview of expectant, frustrated peoples across the postcolonial world.

References

Adnan, Etel. 1977. *Sitt Marie Rose.* Paris: Des Femmes.

———. 1980. *L'Apocalypse arabe.* Paris: Papyrus.

———. 1982. *Sitt Marie Rose.* Translated by Georgina Kleege. Sausalito: Post-Apollo.

———. 1989. *The Arab Apocalypse.* Sausalito: Post-Apollo.

Glissant, Edouard. 1995. *Introduction à une poétique du divers* (Poetics of the Diverse). Montreal: Presses de l'Université de Montréal.

Mason, Herbert. 1972. *Gilgamesh: A Verse Narrative.* New York: Mentor.

11

Among Good Christian Peoples: Teaching Etel Adnan's *Sitt Marie Rose*

John Champagne

In an essay entitled "Teaching Deconstructively," Barbara Johnson provides the following definition of the teaching of literature:

> Teaching literature is teaching how to read. How to notice things in a text that a speed-reading culture is trained to disregard, overcome, edit out, or explain away; how to read what the language is doing, not guess what the author was thinking; how to take in evidence from a page, not seek a reality to substitute for it. This is the only teaching that can properly be called literary; anything else is history of ideas, biography, psychology, ethics, or bad philosophy. Anything else does not measure up to the rigorous perversity and seductiveness of literary language. [1985, 140]

Johnson adds in a footnote that "this is not meant to imply that nothing should be read outside the text at hand, or that a text is unconnected to any discourse outside itself," as the "inside" and "outside" of a text are themselves not a "'given'" (148). As Johnson herself concedes, it does, however, submit that "history, philology, biography, the 'spirit of the age,' and the 'material conditions of production' are not less problematic — or less textual and interpretively constructed — than the literary text they would come to explain."[1]

How is the teacher of postcolonial literature in particular to read Johnson's advice?[2] Given, for example, the history of western imperialist expansion into, withdrawal from, and lingering influence over peripheral regions, and the way this history necessarily structures the writing and reading of the texts of postcoloniality, what are we to make of Johnson's emphatic interest in the literary? In raising this question, I am reluctant to suggest that postcolonial novels, poetry, and drama represent some kind of "special case" of literature that needs to be read differently from other literary texts. Obviously, history is inscribed in all texts and all readers, not just the texts and readers of postcolonial literary works. It is not something we are necessarily required to import to a text; in a cultural climate that diligently attempts to erase the traces of history, however, perhaps postcolonial texts appear to confront the problem of history more directly than other literary works.

It would seem, then, that any attempt to think through the possibilities of Johnson's account as it may apply to the teaching of postcolonial literature in particular must confront a number of problems: In the case of a postcolonial novel, what counts as textual evidence? What is it evidence of? To what end is something noticed? What particular kinds of things does a metropolitan "speed-reading culture" tend to "disregard" in a postcolonial text, and how does the reader's inscription in history inflect what can and cannot be read?[3]

At least once every year for the past several, I've taught in translation Etel Adnan's experimental novel *Sitt Marie Rose*. The novel is one of several that I currently use in an undergraduate survey course called "The Theme of Identity in World Literature." This essay will examine the teaching of Adnan's novel. Interweaving an account of my experiences teaching the novel with a close reading of appropriate passages, the essay will implicitly argue for a pedagogy that requires students to be attentive to their own historical positionings as reading subjects. Such a pedagogy ideally implicates the western reader in, among other things, the torture and death of Sitt Marie Rose.

Clearly, my assumption here is that "history" is not necessarily something "outside" the novel that one must bring to a reading. While students do seem to benefit from having done some research on the history of Lebanon in general and the 1975 civil war in particular, such research is not sufficient; students must also learn to address the way the transaction between subject and text we call reading is necessarily structured by a history always already inscribed in their own subjectivities, as well as in the text. This history inflects not only their interpretation of any given novel, but also any attempts to understand something of the historical context out of which that novel was written and in which it circulates today. As Antonio Gramsci might say, history has deposited within the reading subject an infinity of traces; it is up to the reader to compile an inventory of such traces. Teaching literature can provide an occasion for the compiling of such an inventory.

I would thus propose rewriting Johnson's formulation as follows: teaching postcolonial literature in the metropolitan center is teaching students how to read their own positionings as subjects: how to theorize their own practices of reading as necessarily structured by, among other things, the history of imperialism, a history in which they are woven as subjects; how to interrupt and complicate their desires to over- or dis-identify with the Other (as character, as implied author); how to recognize themselves as implicated in the text of the Other. This is the only teaching that can avoid treating postcolonial texts as either 1) simply another commodity for western consumption (this time, under the guise of a benevolent "appreciation" of "foreign" literature), or 2) a representation verifying the savageries of "underdevelopment" and the need to reinvigorate the exportation of western humanism to the Third World.

Teaching Sitt Marie Rose

Sitt Marie Rose tells of the kidnapping, torture, and execution of its title character. Set in Lebanon, it recounts a time period immediately preceding the 1975 civil war, as well as the initial year or so of the war itself. Marie Rose, a teacher of deaf-mute children, is a Christian who, owing to her work with the social services of the Palestinian Resistance, is perceived by a paramilitary faction of fellow Christians as having gone over to the side of the enemy.

The novel is divided into two sections. The first, entitled "Time I: A Million Birds," is narrated by an unnamed woman screenwriter. She is asked by a character named Mounir to work with him on a film about Syrian workers in Lebanon. Also described are two friends of Mounir's, Tony and Fouad. The novel begins with a scene in which these characters are watching Mounir's film of themselves hunting. The scene provides character insights into these men, noting the joy they receive from hunting, and their tendency to identify themselves as European. The section also describes some of the events leading up to and including the beginning of the civil war. Detailing some of the atrocities of the war, it concludes with the narrator's realization that she can't possibly make the kind of film Mounir desires—a film that ignores the way many Syrian workers have become casualties of this war. As Mounir complains, the kind of film the narrator wants to make is "too violent. It's too political" (Adnan 1982, 24). Written in the present tense, the narrative is fragmented and elliptical, the language at times extremely rich with images. Students often characterize this language as poetic. Sometimes, the narration provides few overt clues to such things as setting, time, and place, and simply "inserts" the reader in the middle of the situation. At other times, it offers specific dates and refers to concrete and actual historical events.

The second half of the novel is entitled "Time II: Marie Rose." It is divided into three unnamed sections that are further divided into seven unnamed subsections. Each of the three sections designates a different period of time; the sections are arranged chronologically. Within the three sections, the seven numbered subsections are each narrated by a different character or provide an account in reported discourse of Sitt Marie Rose's interactions with that character. The first subsection is told by one of Marie Rose's students; the second is the voice of Marie Rose herself; the third, a character named Mounir; the fourth, a character named Tony; the fifth, a character named Fouad; the sixth, a peasant friar named Bouna Lias; and the seventh, an unnamed narrator whose diction, sensibility, and point of view seem to be that of the unnamed narrator in the novel's first half. This pattern is replicated in all three sections.

Narrative "events" are thus sometimes repeated within each of the three sections, the same event presented from the viewpoint of each of the seven different "characters." At times, it appears as if a character is speaking directly to the reader, or else we are privy to his or her thoughts, which take the form of monologues. Mounir, Tony, and Fouad have captured and imprisoned Marie Rose. Mounir is the leader, Tony and Fouad, the executioners. Bouna Lias has apparently been called in as some kind of witness. While the novel never states that Mounir, Tony, Fouad, and unnamed narrator of the first half are the same as those who speak and act in the second half, the description of these characters is so similar that the reader might be led to this conclusion. The final section of the novel describes the death of Sitt Marie Rose at the hands of her captors.

Whenever I teach Adnan's novel, a series of questions arise once we have unraveled some of the formal difficulties of the novel and are well into class discussion: how is it possible for Marie Rose's torturers to commit these brutal acts? Why are these men — Mounir, Tony, Fouad, and Bouna Lias — the way they are? What is it about their identity that allows them to interrogate, torture, and murder Sitt Marie Rose? What relationship is the novel drawing between masculinity, religion, and the way in which Marie Rose's torturers attempt to rewrite themselves as "European"?

Finally, why does the novel present this problematic through what appears to be the idiom of high European modernism rather than through, say, realism? I would now like to move to a discussion of how these questions might be used to problematize students' tendencies to dis-identify with the characters in Adnan's novel, and how this initial dis-identification can be understood as, among other things, a repression of the history of imperialism. Such a problematization ideally brings to the foreground elements of the students' own historical positioning as subjects— particularly those of the student who shares (albeit unevenly) with Adnan's characters a similar set of identifications (i.e., Christian, western, male).

Pedagogy and the Postcolonial Novel

In an effort to contextualize something of my students' responses to Adnan's novel, however, I need to back up and take a bit of a detour through something of my own history of teaching *Sitt Marie Rose*, as well as offer a somewhat sketchy and incomplete account of my pedagogy as a teacher of postcolonial literature. I first taught *Sitt Marie Rose* as a graduate student at the University of Pittsburgh in a course called "Contemporary Literature in Context," an introductory undergraduate course in "global" or "multicultural" literature. This course required students to examine how the problem of historical context— the context in which a given novel was written, the context (if any) in which its plot is set, the context in which the book is currently read— shaped their understanding of the texts under discussion. In an initial effort to get at something of these contexts, students were required to keep a reading journal. Drawing whatever information they could from the book's cover, they were to begin their reading by noting whatever they might discern about these contexts. What did they know, for example, about the history of the Middle East? What other experience might they have with "war literature"? (These issues are raised by the back jacket of Adnan's novel.) During their reading, students were to indicate passages in the novels with which they were having some difficulty. The class attempted to define difficulty broadly as any time students had some trouble "becoming" the implied reader of the novel. These difficulties could thus range from a lack of knowledge of specific intertextual and cultural references within the novel, to boredom, to an even more willful "resistance" to reading "with" the text — with the understanding that both implied author and reader are fictions we must necessarily construct as we read, and, as such, are subject to interpretation.

Students were then asked to provide an account of how they managed to cope with these difficulties—how they managed to continue reading despite their desire to put the book away, for example. Finally, students were asked to use these difficulties to explore what the implied author was attempting to accomplish. In other words, rather than attributing these difficulties to some failure on the part of either the implied author or the novel itself, we were to assume that these difficulties were precisely what the two solicit. Why would this particular novel deploy these particular difficulties? To what end? For what purpose? Students were then required to formulate these notes into a paper. These papers were used in a variety of ways as a basis for class discussion. Sometimes, they were read aloud. Sometimes, they were distributed to the class.

We began the course with one work of nonfiction, Immanuel Wallerstein's *Historical Capitalism*. A critique of capitalism as a historical system, this text provided a starting point for the class in that it offered an analysis of the larger global context in which these novels were written and continue to circulate. While not specifically "about" literature, Wallerstein's book made it possible for us to think about such issues as how it was historically possible for a group of students in the United States to read, in English, a handful of novels written out of a rather divergent yet related set of historical circumstances. It also allowed us to develop and share an initial vocabulary for the course, a vocabulary we could bring to each of the novels we read. For example, Wallerstein's study offered us a theory of racism, sexism, the international division of labor, core-periphery relations, anti-systemic movements to resist capitalism, the relationship between state structures and the accumulation of capital, and so forth. This vocabulary facilitated our reading not only of the novels themselves—many of which dealt with such subjects as colonialism, postcoloniality, nationalism, and what Gayle Rubin has called the sex-gender system (Rubin 1975)—but also made possible an exploration of the material relations out of which these novels were written and in which they continue to meet their readers. Following our initial discussion of Wallerstein, we read a number of novels, including Graham Greene's *The Quiet American*, Bruce Weigl's *Song of Napalm*, Chinua Achebe's *Things Fall Apart*, Maryse Condés's *A Season in Rihata*, Adnan's *Sitt Marie Rose*, Dennis Denisoff's *Dog Years*, Jeanette Winterson's *Oranges are not the Only Fruit*, and Arturo Islas's *Migrant Souls*. Approximately two weeks of discussion were devoted to each book.

Additionally, students were required to choose one of the novels we were reading that semester and present a small group research report on that novel. These research reports were an opportunity to gather some information on the context in which the novel was written, set, or read, and then to share that information with the class. In an effort to prevent these research reports from degenerating into a simple recounting of "facts," students were also required to say something about some of the problems they faced in attempting to theorize these contexts. Problems might range from an account of the difficulties of even finding information on, say, Etel Adnan, to a critical reading of a particular historical account of, say, the French presence in Lebanon. In this way, we were trying to heed Johnson's warning that history is "not less problematic — or less textual and interpretively constructed — than the literary text [it] would come to explain" (1985, 148). My job was to act as facilitator, to add whatever knowledge I might about these varying contexts, and to complicate any attempts to simplify the problem of context — whether that simplification occurred in the students' reports or in the texts they cited in their reports.

"The Theme of Identity" and Sitt Marie Rose

The next time I had the occasion to teach a course similar to "Contemporary Literature in Context," it was at a different school, Penn State Erie, the Behrend College, where I continue to teach today. Behrend is a small college within the Penn State system. It attracts a somewhat homogeneous population — the majority of our students are white, middle to working class, and from the Pennsylvania area; men outnumber women approximately three to one. Penn State has a course on its books called "The Theme of Identity in World Literature: Race, Gender, and Other Issues of Diversity." In this new version of the course, I wanted to retain the interest in context, but shift some of our focus to the question of identity in particular — what is it, from where does it arise, how can literature both help and hinder our efforts to understand what is meant by identity? In the first incarnation of this new course, I dropped *The Quiet American, Song of Napalm,* and *Dog Years,* and substituted Mariama Ba's *So Long a Letter* and Manuel Puig's *Kiss of the Spider Woman.*

The first half of the course focused on colonialism and postcolonialism, allowing us to talk about such matters as national identity, gender identity, religious identity, and familial relations and their effect on identity. The second half of the course added the question of sexual orientation to the mix, and ended by focusing on the United States as a kind of postcolonial culture — not in terms of its former relationship to Great Britain (a very specious analogy indeed, given, for example, the historical policy in the United States of exterminating indigenous people) — but in terms of the way it attempts to "manage" a variety of diasporic and "marginalized" identities. The course also offered a sustained attempt to critique the very notion of identity by complicating attempts to assign characters' "stable" identities, and problematizing a sense of identity as "chosen."[4]

This shift to the problem of identity provoked a slight change in the tenor of the class. Specifically, this new course required me to deal at some length with what is apparently the predominant reading strategy of under-graduates at my institution. This strategy requires the reader to understand and evaluate a given novel with reference to its characters: were they lik-able or irritating, "round" or "flat," "believable" or lacking in verisimili-tude, and so forth. While I tried when appropriate to interrupt and complicate this reading method, it nonetheless emerged again and again. This was not necessarily a hindrance to our work, as it led us to a semes-ter-long discussion of the appropriateness or inappropriateness of this reading strategy, its limitations, blind spots, and possibilities.

As one might expect, a frequent theme of my students' papers was the difficulties (or lack thereof) of identifying with either the characters or the implied author. Over the course of the semester, I came to the fol-lowing provisional conclusion: undergraduate students in this particular context often respond to postcolonial literature in one of two ways, argu-ing that the characters or the implied authors are either "just like us" or "nothing like us." Both of these maneuvers homogenize both Self and Other, and cover over the complexities of the students' and implied authors' own subject positions. I have a number of problems with the for-mer response: what this allegedly benevolent reading strategy of "just like us" sometimes occludes is the ways that some of these similarities are pre-cisely the product of the project of colonialism and its lingering influence in and on the present. It is obviously no coincidence that "they" are "just like us." This has often been the explicit goal of the colonialist enterprise. What is sometimes lacking in this reading strategy is an awareness of the violence that has accompanied this attempt to produce "them" as "us," and any effort to think through the limitations of historically dominant sub-jectivities and epistemologies, dependent as they are upon such (histori-cal) factors as racism, sexism, universalism, and ethnocentrism.

Concerning the second response: "they're nothing like us" seems gen-erally to emerge from two apparently contradictory ideologies: an ethno-centrism that more readily and enthusiastically acknowledges the "barbarism" of other cultures than that of its own, and a pluralism that argues that since all cultures hold different values, it is impossible to make value judgments about the practices and beliefs of the Other. Both of these are unsatisfactory. The first provides the rational for western expansion and conquest; the second often thwarts any attempt to propose a position on, say, such complicated issues as the continuation in the diaspora of the practice of the removal of the clitoris, and efforts by western nation states to intercede in this continuation.

All of these responses are predicated upon a tendency to treat postcolonial literature as a simple reflection of the "real" conditions of colonialism and postcolonialism. This tendency assumes that the link between postcolonial literature and the historical real is somehow more "transparent" than is the case with the (high modernist) literature of the West. Such a strategy necessarily elides the historical complexities of a project like Adnan's, which is attempting to deploy French high modernist literary techniques to critique the very influence of France on the Middle East.[5] It also necessarily minimizes the formal complexity of such novels as *Sitt Marie Rose*.

In any case, my emerging sense of the teacher's role is one of bringing to crisis one ("just like us") or the other ("nothing like us") of these responses, depending on a variety of factors including considerations such as which response predominates, at what point in the semester a given text is being read, and so forth. In an essay in *College English*, I provide an account of teaching Ba's novella in the context of this same course, arguing in particular the dangers of the "just like us" approach (Champagne 1996). This present essay is a kind of companion piece to that one, in that I will be attempting to explore the other side of the coin: in the context of a course like "The Theme of Identity," *Sitt Marie Rose* is a novel which often produces a response of "they're nothing like us," and this response is arguably a kind of reaction-formation to the novel's explicit attempts to invoke the West and its role in producing a version of subjectivity congruent with that of the torturer. The reader response of distanciation is perhaps proportional to the novel's attempt to implicate the western subject.

Christianity and Sitt Marie Rose

My students, most of whom, through class discussion and their written work, self-identify as Christians, are almost uniformly horrified by the behavior of Sitt Marie Rose's torturers. When asked to comment on the difficulties they faced in reading the novel, they frequently assert that they are puzzled by the fact that Marie Rose's torturers claim to be Christian. Good Christian peoples don't behave in this way, they insist; Christians are not violent. This insistence becomes the grounds of their dis-identification with Marie Rose's torturers.

The first time I taught this new version of the course, the infamous events of the Oklahoma City bombing helped complicate this discussion. Barring such "real life" events in the future, through my comments on students' papers and in the course of class discussion, I would continue to use Adnan's text to complicate these claims about Christianity. Specifically, when I teach *Sitt Marie Rose* in a course like "The Theme of Identity," I focus on the ways in which the text suggests that the tortur-ers' religious beliefs are connected to their masculinity and sense of their own national identity. I often begin such a discussion by asking students to write in class about a particular series of questions—questions that they themselves raised in their papers: How does the novel answer the ques-tion of why these men are the way they are? What makes possible their participation in the torture and execution of Sitt Marie Rose? Students are always required to cite specific passages from the text in their answers. These answers then become the basis of class discussion. I myself write an answer to these questions along with my students, and so I feel free when it is warranted to take them to any passages they may have overlooked— though I try to delay this strategy for as long as possible.

Adnan's novel draws an extremely rich and suggestive connection between Europe, Christianity, masculinity and masculine sexuality, and violence. It suggests that it is precisely the convergence of a variety of identifications with the (former) colonizer that produces a subjectivity capable of murder. Torturers are apparently made in Lebanon through a confluence of identifications made possible by a lingering history of colo-nial domination. This connection between European Christianity, mas-culinity, and violence is not spelled out in any one section of the novel; rather, over the course of reading the text, meanings accumulate and asso-ciations consolidate, layered one on top of the other: "Europeanness" is linked to Christianity; Christianity is linked to Lebanese masculinity; Christianity is linked to violence; violence is linked to Lebanese Christ-ian masculinity—and so forth.

This "layering" of meanings draws attention to some of the formal qualities of the novel. As many modernist novels do, *Sitt Marie Rose* pro-vides a clue as to how it demands to be read: the narrator in Time I tells us that "[a]ction is fragmented into sections so that no one has an exact image of the whole process" (Adnan 1982, 17). Attempting to account for its own aesthetic, the novel insists that this particular story can only be told in this particular way; simultaneously, it reactivates the familiar mod-ernist dictum that "form" and "content" are irreducibly linked.

While it would be presumptuous and disingenuous to suggest that the novel actually reproduces the fragmented subjectivity of the war-torn, it is perhaps not too far-fetched to suggest that, considered in its entirety, the overall form of the novel attempts to mimic a version of this subjectivity. This explanation of the novel's form is persuasive in that it strengthens a sense of the congruity between *Sitt Marie Rose*'s "avant-garde" form and overtly political "content," and does not depend on reading the novel through the eyes and sensibility of one or more character. It requires us, rather, to contemplate the novel as the performance of a certain rendering of a subjectivity — that subjectivity we designate by the term implied author.[6]

When read carefully, the opening passages of the novel testify to the influence of the West in general and Europe in particular on the characters who will later become Sitt Marie Rose's torturers. In the initial film of the hunting expedition undertaken by Mounir, Tony, and Fouad,[7] the men travel in a Volkswagen jeep (Adnan 1982, 1); the images of their hunting are punctuated with the strains of a song by Pink Floyd (2). Watching the film, the narrator tells us, "Before, it was the Europeans with faces like the ones we saw on the screen, who went hunting in Syria .... Now it's the Christian, modernized Lebanese who go wherever they like with their touristo-military gear" (3). In describing the reactions of Syrians to Lebanese tourists, Mounir makes the error of suggesting that "we were the first Europeans they had ever seen. Excuse me, I mean Lebanese" (5).

Given the work we have done in the course prior to reading *Sitt Marie Rose*, even without a specific knowledge of Lebanese history, students are capable of discerning from these passages the ties of the Lebanese Christian right to economic interests in Europe in particular. Significant in this regard is the narrator's claim that "Mounir's family is extremely rich" (2). Once the war breaks out, a friend of Mounir's suggests that the Phalangists "defend ... the Lebanese Right and business" (16).

Clearly, the identities of Mounir, Tony, and Fouad are predicated upon an identification with the European, Christianized West over and against any kind of identification with the identity "Arab." As one of Marie Rose's captors declares, "My name is Tony and it will never be Mohammed" (36). As children, most of these boys believed that "unless one resembled Europeans one was nothing" (47); when Sitt Marie Rose pleads that the Palestinians "belong to the same ancestral heritage the Christian party does. They're really our brothers," (54) her words are largely ignored.

Students have sometimes suggested that the "problem" is one of a mistaken identity: these Lebanese men aren't "really" Europeans. They've simply confused their true identity with that of the former colonizers, muddled their own sense of self by allowing themselves to dream of "Paris and the quarrels of the French kings" (Adnan 1982, 47). Of course, given the history of Lebanon, the long standing presence in the region of both Christians who looked toward Europe and Muslims who faced Mecca, as well as the more recent burden of a government proportioned out by religion, it is impossible to determine what and who is "truly" Lebanese. In class discussion, we try to use Wallerstein, then, to think about how all ethnic and national identities are necessarily fabrications, attempts to cover over discontinuities and differences in the name of solidifying state structures in particular.

This (mis)identification with Europe on the part of those who will become Marie Rose's killers is further complicated both by the role of the Christian church in Lebanon and the attempts by these men to forge a political identity that simultaneously mobilizes ethnic and religious affiliations and alliances, "imaginary" and "real." As Tony puts it, Sitt Marie Rose is "[a] Christian and she went over to the Moslem camp. She's Lebanese and she went over to the Palestinian camp" (36). The link between national identity and religion here is readily apparent. Such a link also elides the presence of the non-refugee Muslim population in Lebanon. Mounir and his cohorts, presumably members of the Phalangist party, see the struggle against the Palestinians as both a religious war and a war to determine the rightful rulers of Lebanon. They turn to Europe for guidance, drawing in particular on the image of the Crusades.

In the second section of Time II, Sitt Marie Rose speaks of the role the Crusades have played in the formation of these men's identities. She draws our attention to the ways the Christian school Mounir and his friends attended performed certain rituals of interpellation, including a yearly procession commemorating the Crusades. Led by the French priests, such a procession hailed the students as Christian warriors. "The next day at school," Sitt Marie Rose tells us, "they were proud of having defeated the Infidels. They dreamed of a Christianity with helmets and boots, riding its horses into the clash of arms, spearing Moslem foot-soldiers ...." (47-48). When Marie Rose tries to convince her own (Christian) children of the "obscenity" (her word) of the civil war, they respond that the Bible tells them that "God hates the enemy" (50).

In its depiction of the Lebanese conflict, the novel's sympathies are clearly with the Palestinians. Without portraying the Palestinians as blameless, *Sitt Marie Rose* nonetheless emphasizes the brutal acts of violence committed by the Christian Right. The novel's account of the events that initiate the civil war leads the reader to conclude that the Christians are chiefly responsible. The connection between violence and Christianity is transparent: outside the church where the head of the Phalangist party is celebrating mass, a bus full of Palestinians is shot by Christian militiamen, one victim after another (11).[8] Later in Time I, the narrator adds that the Christian enclaves of Lebanon are "[m]ore Westernized and efficient in war as in everything" (21).

Perhaps the novel's most sustained attempt to link a certain version of Christianity with violence occurs in the passages in which Bouna Lias the friar speaks to Marie Rose (subsection 6 of Time II). While he himself is not sure why he has been called to witness the indictment of Sitt Marie Rose, he soon takes on the role of inquisitor. Bouna Lias reminds Marie Rose that the civil war is also a religious war: "we are at war with Islam whether you like it or not. They can't separate their religion from their culture, from their heritage, and neither can we. We're fighting for the road that leads to the Divine" (63). When she tells him that he doesn't know what love means, he reminds her that she is a Christian who has gone over to the enemy (64).

In their final discussion before her death, he tries to warn her that "Christianity is in danger" (93). He chastises the Palestinians with whom he allegedly once felt sympathy, arguing that they turned to "international crooks" to further their cause; he says nothing, however, about European support of the Phalangists. In what is perhaps her most telling critique of Christianity, Sitt Marie Rose responds that religious iconography has hailed Christian subjects as torturers:

> Yes, you've made them insensible to pain by glorifying thorns and nails, glorifying blood as a beverage and human flesh as nourishment. They exalt themselves with flagellation, and passed their childhoods hearing terrifying stories of Hell. In your schools that smell of incense and sweat they identified with Christ and the executioner, taking themselves first for one and then for the other. They kill and mutilate with a rosary in their hands, believing that they serve the Virgin. And you want me to bow before such a fantasy? [96]

Bouna Lias's response: while Sitt Marie Rose is being killed, he excuses his participation in her execution, claiming that he and the others are defending God's interests on earth, and that is God's will that Marie Rose be reduced to "a pile of dislocated members that was a sinner" (97).

In addition to drawing attention to the relationship between violence and Christianity, the novel also links violence to a certain version of heterosexual masculinity and sexuality. In the opening passages, the narrator makes clear that Fouad the hunter "prefers jeep-speed-desert-bird-bullet to girl-in-a-bed-and-fuck" (2). She suggests that none of these men receive as much pleasure having sex with a woman as they do either hunting or car racing with one another (3). Hunting in particular is treated as a sexualized activity between men. At the initial screening of the hunting film, a number of women, including the narrator and several relatives of Mounir and Tony, are present. The novel suggests that these women receive scopophilic pleasure from watching their men in action (4). The narrator later tells us that the atrocities of war are treated "like an evening of scores between men" (13).

A passage in Time II develops this sense that masculine identity is linked to violence. Referring to Marie Rose's captors as "that gang of boys" (39), the narrator suggests that "the nearer they are to the paroxysm of violence, the more they become themselves" (40). In this particular historical context, masculine violence thus makes possible the "fabrication" of a male identity. The name of Time I, "A Million Birds," is linked directly to this image of men as hunters. As the narrator insists, "I tell myself that it would be better to let loose a million birds in the sky over Lebanon, so that these hunters could practice on them, and this carnage could be avoided" (17). This imagery is repeated in Time II: Marie Rose: "These four men set upon that passing bird," (100) the narrator tells us; "Like a bird flying alone in a seemingly untroubled sky, Marie Rose was cut down by hunters on the look-out" (103).

Interestingly, while the novel foregrounds the bonds of homosociality between these men, it also refrains from sexualizing their interactions.[9] At two different moments, *Sitt Marie Rose* goes to some trouble to detail the repugnance these men feel toward all sexuality, homo and hetero. About Fouad, the narrator insists, "Even orgies bore him. ... He is always disgusted by promiscuity" (2). "And these four are particularly pure," she tells us. "They never sleep together" (3). In Time II, the narrator offers a similar account of these men:

> They are moved by a sick sexuality, a mad love, where images of crushing and cries dominate. It's not that they are deprived of women or men if they like, but rather are inhibited by a profound distaste for the sexual thing. A sense of the uncleanliness of pleasure torments them and keeps them from ever being satisfied. [66]

Significantly, both of these passages make reference to homosexual activity as something these men might abhor. For some readers, this is politically important: for example, too often, male fantasies of violence against women have been facilely labeled as "homoerotic" — as if gay men have cornered the market on gynophobia, and as if homoeroticism is necessarily marked by violence. The passage also suggests that the sexual act itself might put into peril the precious male identity fabricated by and for these men. Their phobias around sexuality are symptomatic of both the precariousness of this identity, and their fear of "losing it."

Adnan's novel proposes that masculine heterosexual violence is linked specifically to a fear of women. As the narrator in Time II suggests, "But a woman who stands up to them and looks them in the eye is a tree to be cut down, and they cut it down" (67). In a passage analyzing Sitt Marie Rose's torturers, the narrator insists, "Feminine symbols tear at them with their claws" (69). Beginning with Isis and ending with the Virgin in Beirut, she then details seven thousand years of female mythological figures that "loved Power, their Brother or their Son." This anticipates Marie Rose's critique of Christianity: "You [Bouna Lias] taught them that the ideal family consists of a Christ without a father, and a mother who like the Arab woman loves no one but her son" (97).

The novel seems to suggest that one of Marie Rose's crimes is simply being a woman. As Tony insists, "This woman is nothing but a bitch. Mounir should not regard her as an ordinary person" (36). Fouad refers to her as "[t]his female monster" (92). The narrator suggests that these men are terrified of a woman who can stand up to them (68). Such misogyny requires the drawing and quartering of Sitt Marie Rose with their own hands; the threat that she represents to their masculine identity must be annihilated. "They love destruction because it's a process of peeling away" (40), the narrator of Time II tells us. Drawing and quartering is an act in which the men "find" their identity by "destroying" the identity of a woman. "I quartered her with my own hands," Fouad brags.[10]

Students tend to find the character of Mounir, who turns out to be a former lover of Marie Rose's, particularly vexing in this regard. They note, correctly, I think, the way the novel invites them to "empathize" with him, and are confused by his apparently "sympathetic" portrayal. Marie Rose has some fond memories of their courtship, sympathetically noting that while he had "an obsessive fear of failure," he was nonetheless "extremely sensitive" (46). Mounir seems more reasonable, less prone to violence, than the other captors. "He's never killed anyone with his own hands," Tony tells us (90). Speaking of her as a "worthy partner," (35) he is willing to discuss Marie Rose's political commitments at some length, and does what he can to secure Marie Rose's release by offering to exchange her for her current lover, a member of the Palestinian resistance (88). The narrator tells us that up until Marie Rose's capture, Mounir had managed to avoid being party to, and feeling responsible for, murder and torture (74).

However, Mounir is nonetheless the leader of this group, and he is ultimately responsible for the order to kill his former love. Mounir thus sometimes strikes the more mimetic-minded as an "unbelievable" character; according to the assumptions of some such readers, "good guys" don't become torturers. Of course, this is precisely one of the ways in which the novel wants to intervene in our understanding of the relationship between violence and sexuality. The novel goes to some lengths to show us that the same guy who left kisses in your hair at sixteen (53), who loved Chopin études (46) and received an education at the hands of the Jesuits (48), can later be the same guy who oversees your execution.

By the novel's conclusion, the pattern is complete: Europe, Christianity, violence, masculinity and male heterosexuality — all are interwoven to form the identity of Sitt Marie Rose's killers.[11] The novel thus suggests that identity is "ideological": it works through a process of interpellation that draws upon a variety of different discourses in an effort to produce subjects "useful" for global, postcolonial capitalism. Wallerstein's argument helps make this connection to capitalism clear. As nation-states have been one of the most useful tools for maneuvering within capitalism, it is no surprise that identities might coalesce around nations, and that such a process would necessarily rely for support on congruent forms of identification. This is not to suggest that there is not also *resistance* to this particular figuration of that which appears to operate as a subject; the fact that so many different discourses are called upon to formulate the subjectivities of Sitt Marie Rose's torturers reminds us that the process of nation subject-formation is anything but seamless, as does Sitt Marie Rose's own resistance in the face of her torturers.

I recently had the occasion to teach *Sitt Marie Rose* in a slightly different context: an honors section of "The Theme of Identity." Teaching this novel for the fourth time, I received an unanticipated response from my students: rather than arguing that the Christians represented in the novel were somehow foreign, nothing like themselves, a handful of students wanted to take the novel's point of view on Christianity in another direction. Specifically, they wondered if the novel either "recuperated" Christianity in any way, or problematized all efforts to do so. Given the novel's portrayal of this version of Lebanese Christianity, *can* Christianity be recuperated, they asked, or is it necessarily structured by misogyny, violence, ethnocentrism, and sexism?

These questions emerged from our discussion of a particular student paper. In his essay, Brian Emick offered a response to the novel that asserted that Marie Rose was "a Christ-figure" (1996, 1). "She died for her beliefs and that is exactly what Jesus did. She truly was a martyr" (2). In support of this reading, he cites Sitt Marie Rose's deathbed prayer: "God, whoever you are, protect the future generations from the genocide that awaits them.

I want to make peace with everyone. Even with my captors, I want to make my peace" (Adnan 1985, 85-86; cited in Emick 1996, 2). He ends his essay with the insistence that Sitt Marie Rose "succeeded in spreading the true Christian beliefs even though it took death to do it. When no one else had the courage to fight for what he/she believed, Marie Rose did have the courage to engage in actual Christian service. I truly believe that Marie Rose was what the Christian way is all about, and that is love and generosity" (1996, 4).

The writer seems to be attempting here to wrestle a "true" Christian identity from a "false" one. He is not quite assuming that the Lebanese Christians portrayed in the novel are not "like us": rather, he recognizes their behavior as a familiar distortion of Christianity. His reading is in some sense "symptomatic" of the text itself, which, despite its critique of Christianity in Lebanon, also insists, through the narrator of subsection seven of Time II, that "the true Christ only exists when one stands up to one's own brothers to defend the Stranger. Only then does Christ embody innocence" (104). Another way to phrase this: perhaps the writer is attempting to wrestle Christ away from Christianity — a familiar gesture in certain liberal Christian churches today, given their displeasure with the "official" stances on such topics as birth control, homosexuality, and war, for example.[12]

Other students, however, were less sanguine about this image of Sitt Marie Rose as Christ. They had a number of objections to the paper's argument, objections that were formed into questions for discussion: given the charges leveled by Sitt Marie Rose against Christianity, can there exist a Christianity that does not "[glorify] thorns and nails, [glorify] blood as a beverage and human flesh as nourishment" (Adnan 1982, 96)? A Christianity that does not imagine that "the ideal family consists of a Christ without a father, and a mother who like the Arab woman loves no one but her son" (97). Also important to consider is Marie Rose's critique of certain aspects of the Christ image. As Marie Rose laments of the "tribal" Arab world, "We haven't invented a single man who didn't found a religion. We haven't had a single man who was effectively alone, who sought on his own account, to understand good and evil, who could stand up crucified without anyone knowing it, and carry his adventure and his secret to a grave that didn't open on either Heaven or Hell" (58). Furthermore, given its history, can the Christian Church end its complicity with violence? Finally, given the novel's critique of Lebanese Christian masculinity, what does it mean that Marie Rose is rewritten by the student writer as a (male) Christ figure?

Following the emergence of these questions, I asked my students to take us to particular passages in the novel that we might read in an effort to answer these questions. I also asked how useful it might be to approach identities as "true" or "false." Perhaps we need some other vocabulary. The emergence of such unanticipated questions helps me to remember that one of the pleasures of teaching literature is surely the exfoliation of unforeseen readings— particularly readings prompted by students' careful attentiveness to the text.

Conclusion

In the course of class discussion, then, numerous passages in *Sitt Marie Rose* might be used to complicate students' attempts to insist that the Christian men portrayed in the novel are nothing like "us." Additionally, in a class like "The Theme of Identity" in particular, we might occasionally move "beyond" the novel to discuss how it might speak to us about the ongoing processes of our own identity formation. This move is in fact encouraged by a novel like *Sitt Marie Rose*, which goes to such lengths to establish that many of "us" are in fact quite like "them." We might, for example, think about the role of the Christian church in America. What is the Church's stand on violence? How does it feel about capital punishment? War? Torture? This is sometimes an interestingly difficult process: many of my students who identify themselves as Christian know very little of church history and doctrine; a majority of them don't even know the Bible; often, those who appear most familiar with the Bible seemed not to have read very far beyond the Old Testament.

Given the subject matter of Adnan's novel, we might also be tempted in class discussion to think about a variety of recent right-wing attempts to link "American" and "Christian" identities through such points of contention as school prayer and the teaching of "national," "Christian" values. Reacting to Bouna Lias, we might ask, can we separate our religion from our heritage and culture?

We might also examine some contemporary discourses activated in the production of the U. S. male, and see what relationship, if any, these discourses have to some of the ones unraveled in Adnan's novel. (Significantly, hunting is one of Pennsylvania's most popular sports.)

Finally, we might think about the problem of ethnic identity in the United States After all, the Lebanese are not necessarily any more "hybrid" than any other citizens of a nation-state. While in the United States the ideology of the melting pot provides for a homogenization of conflicting identities and an erasure of certain more visible "signs" of ethnicity, this does not change the fact that the majority of families first arrived in the United States as "foreigners."

Students' resistance to exploring the way the novel implicates western readers in the death of Marie Rose, however, is strong. In reply to the assignment asking him to write an essay on the difficulties he faced in reading *Sitt Marie Rose*, one of my very brightest students titled the first draft of his paper "Jihad"— typical of a certain kind of student response to Adnan's novel. In commenting on this initial draft, I asked him to analyze his title as itself symptomatic of some of the problems western readers face when they confront Adnan's text. I had hoped this comment would encourage him both to think about how such things as the media's distorted portrayal of Arab Islamic culture as fanatically predisposed toward violence had led him to use the term "jihad" to describe what is at least a conflict in *Sitt Marie Rose* that finds historical precedent in the Crusades, and to use this "error" as an opportunity to consider the ways in which his own positioning as a reader is inflected by such things as the history of Arab–U.S. relations. Instead, the second draft of the paper featured a long paragraph explaining that the term "jihad" referred to a "holy war"— as if I hadn't understood the meaning of the term. He also argued that his rationale for using the term was that the novel also portrayed a war that some of its participants perceived as holy. The fact that the "holy war" described in Adnan's novel is portrayed as an act of aggression undertaken by Christians against Muslims seemed unimportant to my student.

I am willing to believe that my use of the term "symptomatic" in responding to his paper was perhaps overly subtle; perhaps my student was not deliberately avoiding the problematization of his own thinking I'd hoped my question would provoke, and merely misunderstood my comment. He did, after all, attempt to respond to my query in the manner in which many of our students have been trained: he assumed that the teacher was asking him to "clarify" or "explain," rather than substantially revise his position. This suggests some of the limitations of our efforts to deploy new literary pedagogies. Schooling has necessarily produced a particular kind of student, one who is perhaps unprepared to examine such things as his or her historical position as reading subject.

In presenting this account of the teaching of *Sitt Marie Rose*, have I problematized Johnson's account of an appropriate literary pedagogy? Similar to Johnson's approach, the pedagogy outlined here asks students to notice what is important in a text. Approaching the work with a particular set of questions that suggest what must not be disregarded, overcome, edited out, or explained away, it remains attentive to the letter of the text. It neither considers questions of the author's motives, nor ignores the seductiveness of the work's language. What it does do, however, is insist upon a notion of textuality that prevents us from disqualifying a consideration of such things as history. As deconstruction has taught us, the "insides" and "outsides" of a text are extremely permeable. There is no necessary reason to insist either that the literary text "ends" at its final printed word, or that literature has no pertinent relationship to the historical real. That transaction of meaning we call *reading* particularly problematizes any efforts to bracket off the literary text from its alleged outsides.

This pedagogy also presupposes that texts are always read with a particular set of concerns in mind, regardless of whether or not such concerns have been fully articulated by a reader. It is a pedagogy that extends to students a series of questions that they might not yet have been offered. While students are not required to enjoy reading with this set of concerns in mind, nor to "like" the answers they find when they read through these series of questions, they are expected to have learned some of what kinds of readings such questions both make possible and impede. Here, again, I would agree with Johnson: teaching literature is teaching to read.

Notes

1. I don't necessarily disagree with Johnson here, and yet, as someone whose own work is significantly influenced by deconstruction, I am obliged to note a certain incompatibility between what Johnson's text intends and what it does (142). If we were to apply Johnson's argument here to her own text, engaging in "a careful teasing out of the conflicting forces of signification that are at work within the text itself" (140–141), we might notice that "what the language is doing" in Johnson's text is attempting to shore up the boundaries of the literary even as it confesses the impossibility of doing so. In attempting to define the "proper" method of teaching literature, Johnson's language works to discredit a variety of "inappropriate" methods by defining them in opposition to the literary. While Johnson's footnote attempts to hold in abeyance certain anticipated objections (from within deconstruction, it should be noted) to her analysis by problematizing the boundaries of the (phantom) "text itself," a corollary problematization of the literary is necessarily and symptomatically absent. Rather than, say, reverse and displace the binaries literary/nonliterary, the footnote instead adds to the list of "inappropriate" approaches to the study of literature detailed in the body of the text.

Read alongside one another, then, the body of the text and the footnote provide us with a kind of summa of those "other" methods — history of ideas, biography, psychology, ethics, bad philosophy, history, philology, the "spirit of the age," and the "material conditions of production" — Johnson's text designates in opposition to the literary. Part of what seems to be operating here is the securing of an object of study for a discipline through both a self-policing of the boundaries of that discipline (Johnson's argument reminding practitioners in literary studies that the teaching of literature must not be confused, for example, with the teaching of the history of ideas) as well as through a warning to those in other disciplines who might be tempted to make an "inappropriate" use of the literary text in their own teaching and scholarship. The proper method of teaching literature is apparently the property of a certain version of the deconstructionist literary critic. "Anything else" just doesn't "measure up." (Recall here that the terms proper, appropriate, and property all come from the same Latin root — proprius, meaning "one's own.")

2. In speaking of "postcolonial" literatures, I am obviously not suggesting that the postcolonial represents some kind of definitive rupture with the colonial period. As Gayatri Spivak has argued (1989), postcoloniality necessarily activates a rupture that is also a repetition. See "Who Claims Alterity?" in particular. Another way to frame this argument would be through Fredric Jameson's account of postmodernism (1991), in which he suggests that postmodernism doesn't simply "exceed" the modern: there will always necessarily be something of the modern within the postmodern.

3. We might also note that Johnson's advice seems inadvertently to privilege postcolonial literatures that are stylistically competitive with the West — that is, experimental or avant-garde works. This particular version of deconstruction seems to value high modernist experimental or avant-garde works over traditional realist texts. While Roland Barthes, for example, has demonstrated that even a realist text such as "Sarrasine" can be read in such a way as to reveal the "rigorous perversity and seductiveness of" its language (1974), such a reading is made possible by the deployment of (French) post-structuralist theory. An attempt to use such theory to read postcolonial texts in particular necessarily reactivates the well-rehearsed debates concerning the use of western theories to analyze non-western texts — a debate that is obviously complicated by the question of how "non-western" a postcolonial novel, for example, might be, given the fact that many of its conditions of possibility are directly linked to colonialism's project of "educating" the conquered.

4. Puig's book works particularly well here, complicating as it does the line between "hetero" and "homo" sexualities.

5. Adnan here is shorthand for the implied author of the novel. I have had no access to her own thoughts on this topic. While there are necessarily historical limits to this project of using the language of the colonizer, it is nonetheless an interesting and complex approach to postcolonialism. The other novels I use in the course similarly problematize the notion that postcolonial texts simply reflect the conditions of postcoloniality. Given the historical circumstances out of which *Things Fall Apart* was written, for example, its main character, Okonkwo, must be portrayed as both "subjected" — not only to and by colonialism, but his indigenous culture as well — *and* capable of resisting historically and culturally dominant modes of subjectivity. These pressures are not only dictated by "reality," but by the discursive situation in which the novel meets its readers. Achebe (1959) attempts to speak back to a history of representing the African as savage — using the very language that has contributed to this representation.

6. In their admirable efforts to understand and account for the fragmented quality of this book, students sometimes suggest that the use of multiple points of view allows the reader to understand the depicted situations from all sides, as it were. This is no doubt an effect of the desire to read the book primarily through the lenses of characters and their motivations. Such a reading strategy (mistakenly) suggests that the implied reader does not leave the book with a sense of

subjectivity as fragmented, but rather with the opposite, the reader achieving the kind of omniscient perspective offered by the traditional realist novel. Additionally, less careful readers using this strategy have difficulty determining which characters the implied author is inviting us to side "with," and which we are to perceive critically. This sometimes leads to the kind of pluralism mentioned earlier, in which it is suggested that we cannot judge either Sitt Marie Rose or her torturers, and, by implication, we cannot discern any possible relationship or connection between Eurocentrism, Christianity, masculinity, and violence — as if the novel were a realist text that merely "represented" individualized and isolated perceptions of postcoloniality through the eyes of some of its randomly selected subjects, and did not attempt to intervene in its history in any way. Such a "pluralistic" reading necessarily blunts the force of whatever kind of "political" intervention the novel might have made possible. It reads the novel as an apparently "neutral" portrait of the postcolonial condition in Lebanon without being attentive to the way in which such a portrait might also be activated as a proxy in the continuing efforts to "cope" with the history of western intervention in Lebanon. Clearly, I am drawing here on Gayatri Spivak's well-known distinction between representation as portrait and representation as proxy (1998). I am also not unaware of the fact that "western intervention" in Lebanon is a vexing phrase, given the hundreds of years of, say, Christianity's influence in the region. I think, however, that we can be aware of this rich history and still turn a critical eye toward the particular forms of "Eurocentric" interventions in Lebanon that have occurred in the nineteenth and twentieth centuries in particular.

7. A fourth character, Pierre, joins them, and is also mentioned in this initial section. He does not, however, appear in Time II.

8. While the novel notes that a Christian was shot outside this same church earlier that morning, it qualifies this by suggesting that it may have been either "[a] laid trap or simple chance, no one knows" (11).

9. Obviously, this discussion relies on Eve Kosofsky Sedgwick's work (1985) on homosociality, a dynamic which deploys elements both homoerotic and homophobic.

10. This depiction of the relationship between masculinity, male heterosexuality, and violence resonates with a number of nonfiction studies of masculinity, including Klaus Theweleit's *Male Fantasies* (1987).

11. One passage in particular encapsulates this connection. When Sitt Marie Rose tells Mounir that as a young man he must have looked silly dressed up as a Crusader, he responds, "'You're just a girl. You don't remember what it's like to be a twelve-year-old boy'" (48).

12. Many Christian theologians themselves seem to be moving in this direction, although such movement is largely "covert." It is sometimes hard to remember that, for example, prior to the present pope, it was not unusual for Catholics to question such doctrine as the Virgin birth and the bodily resurrection of Christ. Such talk has most recently been driven underground, given the way the threat of excommunication is bandied about (although I did hear a Catholic nun recently describe "mother Church" as "the mother who eats her young").

References

Achebe, Chinua. 1959. *Things Fall Apart.* Greenwich, CT: Fawcett.

Adnan, Etel. 1982. *Sitt Marie Rose.* Translated by Georgina Kleege. Sausalito: Post-Apollo.

Ba, Mariama. 1989. *So Long a Letter.* Translated by Modupe Bode-Thomas. Oxford: Heinemann.

Barthes, Roland. 1974. *S/Z.* Translated by Richard Miller. New York: Farrar, Strauss and Giroux.

Champagne, John. 1996. "'A Feminist Just Like Us?': Teaching Mariama Ba's *So Long a Letter.*" *College English* 58, no. 1 (January): 22–42.

Condé, Maryse. 1988. *A Season in Rihata.* Translated by Richard Philcox. Oxford: Heinemann.

Denisoff, Dennis.1991. *Dog Years.* Vancouver: Pulp.

Emick, Brian. 1996. Unpublished class paper on *Sitt Marie Rose.*

Greene, Graham. 1992. *The Quiet American.* New York: Modern Library.

Islas, Arturo. 1990. *Migrant Souls.* New York: Morow.

Jameson, Fredric. 1991. *Postmodernism, or, The Cultural Logic of Late Capitalism.* Durham: Duke University Press.

Johnson, Barbara. 1985. "Teaching Deconstructively." In *Writing and Reading Differently,* edited by Douglas Atkins and Michael L. Johnson. Lawrence: University Press of Kansas.

Puig, Manuel. 1991. *Kiss of the Spider Woman.* Translated by Thomas Colchie. New York: Vintage.

Rubin, Gayle. 1975. "The Traffic in Women." In *Towards an Anthropology of Women,* edited by Rayna R. Reiter, 157–210. New York: Monthly Review.

Sedgwick, Eve Kosofsky. 1985. *Between Men: English Literature and Male Homosocial Desire.* New York: Columbia University Press.

Spivak, Gayatri Chakravorty. 1988. "Can the Subaltern Speak?" In *Marxism and the Interpretation of Culture,* edited by Cary Nelson and Lawrence Grossberg, 271-313. Urbana: University of Illinois.

_____. 1989. "Who Claims Alterity?" In *Remaking History,* edited by Barbara Kruger and Phil Mariani, 269–92. Seattle: Bay.

Theweleit, Klaus. 1987. *Male Fantasies, Volume 1: Women, Floods, Bodies, History.* Translated by Stephen Conway. Minneapolis: University of Minnesota Press.

Wallerstein, Immanuel. 1983. *Historical Capitalism.* London and New York: Verso.

Weigl, Bruce. 1988. *Song of Napalm.* New York: Atlantic Monthly.

Winterson, Jeanette. 1985. *Oranges Are Not the Only Fruit.* London: Pandora.

12

Voice, Narrative, and Political Critique: Etel Adnan's *Sitt Marie Rose* and Nawal El Saadawi's *Woman at Point Zero*

Pauline Homsi Vinson

In "Can the Subaltern Speak?" Gayatri Chakravorty Spivak declares: "If, in the context of colonial production, the subaltern has no history and cannot speak, the subaltern as female is even more deeply in shadow" (1988, 287). Noting the lack of attention to resistant voices in Spivak's comment, Benita Perry questions the silencing impulse implicit in such an omission and maintains that "a conception of the native as historical subject and agent of an oppositional discourse is needed" (1995, 44). Appearing two years apart, Etel Adnan's *Sitt Marie Rose* (first published in French in 1977) and Nawal El Saadawi's *Woman at Point Zero* (first published in Arabic in 1975 under the title *Imr'ah 'inda nuktal al-sifr*) share a striking similarity in the attempts of both their writers to record in literary form the silenced voices of actual women whose defiance of hegemonic structures cost them their lives. As postcolonial women writers whose own voices are subject to being silenced by dominant social groups, both Adnan and El Saadawi manage to gain literary voices of their own through their attempts at giving voice to the would-be silenced "subaltern."[1]

In spite of important differences between Etel Adnan's *Sitt Marie Rose* and Nawal El Saadawi's *Woman at Point Zero*, significant similarities link the two works. Both texts explore the nexus of historical fact, literary narrative, and gendered political critique. In so doing, they contribute to a common strand of feminism among various Arab women writers whose distinctive voices nonetheless join together in a common project, namely, to situate the root causes for the silencing of specific women's voices within social, political, and institutional structures.

Explicating her own project in *Sitt Marie Rose*, Adnan declares, "I was trying to show how some cultural values which have their good side in time of peace can, in time of war, lead to genocide." The main such value for Adnan is "tribal behaviour" (1983a, 51). Significantly, her critique of tribal behaviour is articulated in specifically feminist terms. As Adnan puts it, "In traditional societies women were not allowed in wars.... Today we cannot tell women to stay at home and not to fight.... I took sides by writing a book. I didn't take a gun, because I did not want to add violence to violence" (1983b, 32). In writing her novel, Adnan takes political action of sorts, signaling the conjunction of issues related to gender, writing, and politics.

In a similar way, Nawal El Saadawi maintains that, for her, writing is an empowering act of political intervention: "Writing to me is exactly like breathing. ... It is a feeling that I have to give back what I have been given. I feel oppression, the injustices in life ... so I become furious and want to fight back against this by writing. Writing is power: it gives you power, by being known, by communicating with people" (1986, 1735-36). Like Adnan and many other Arab feminists, El Saadawi insists that the position of individual women in society is inextricably linked to social, economic, and political factors that are not necessarily gender-specific. She declares, "The emancipation of Arab women cannot be achieved unless the root causes of, and conditions leading to, oppression are swept away. Real emancipation can only mean freedom from all forms of exploitation whether economic, political, sexual or cultural" (1980, 6).

Adnan's and El Saadawi's words find their echoes in the expressions of such writers as Ghada Al-Samman and Shirley Saad. Al-Samman maintains that "No revolution can take place without a total human revolution on all levels: economic, ideological, political, and social.... That is to say, the sexual revolution, in the last analysis, is only part of the total revolution against a deprivation in human freedoms" (1977, 392). Saad too identifies the impulse to write as a personal response to socio political conditions: "I started writing while I was living in Abu Dhabi and feeling very frustrated with the restrictions imposed on me by the weather and the local customs. Although most of the restrictions didn't really apply to foreigners, only to the local women, I met some of them and sympathized with their plight. Some of them were obviously content with their lot, but some were eager for more freedom, more education, more opportunities to achieve something other than children. This is basically what pushed me to write 'Amina' and other stories as well" (quoted in Badran and Cooke 1990, 48). The list of Arab women who conceive of their literary writings as responses to feminist, political, and social needs goes on.[2] Suffice it to say that for many Arab women writers, giving voice to "the subaltern" becomes a literary project of great personal as well as social significance.

In *Sitt Marie Rose* and *Woman at Point Zero* the attempt to give voice to the "subaltern" is explicitly linked to the question of narrative voice. Significantly, both novels open not with narrative accounts of the actual women whose life stories they depict, but rather with accounts of the narrators' relationships to their texts. *Sitt Marie Rose* is divided into two major parts. Time I takes place before the outbreak of the civil war, and concentrates on the struggles of a woman writer to assert her own voice. Time II, which utilizes a variety of narrative voices, focuses on the abduction and murder during the war of Marie Rose, a character based on an actual woman by the same name (Cooke 1988, 10). *Woman at Point Zero* is also divided into several narrative sections. The first and last deal with the writer-narrator's account of her own encounter with the real-life Firdaus, a prostitute who was condemned to death for having murdered a man. The middle section is a first person narrative record of Firdaus's life story. Both Adnan's and El Saadawi's works are depicted as necessary expressions of would-be suppressed female voices. The death of each female protagonist is shown, ironically, as at once the consequence of and the only means left for her to preserve her personal integrity. Each can remain true to herself only through a defiance that she knows will cost her her life.

Because they offer such striking points of conjunction as well as contrast to one another, Adnan's and El Saadawi's texts function as foils for each other, illuminating each writer's contribution to a politicized Arab women's literary tradition. Each novel begins not with an account of the protagonist's life story, but rather with a description of the narrator's own involvement with her subject. While Adnan's text, though based on the life of a real woman, nowhere signals this indebtedness, El Saadawi's text pointedly highlights the fact that the protagonist Firdaus is in fact a real-life woman. The first line of the text asserts: "This is the story of a real woman" (El Saadawi 1983, 1). In spite of this important difference between the two works, however, both texts nonetheless insist on the universality of their individual protagonists' predicaments. By situating Marie Rose's abduction and murder within the context of the war in Lebanon specifically, and tribal mentality in the Arab world generally, Adnan manages at once to address the particularity of individual experiences and to universalize them. As the narrator puts it: "Death is never in the plural. There are not millions of deaths. It happens millions of times that someone dies" (Adnan 1982, 84). El Saadawi manages to achieve a similar effect through her depiction of a woman who insists that her particular experiences extend beyond class lines: "Only my make-up, my hair and my expensive shoes were 'upper class.' With my secondary school certificate and suppressed desires I belonged to the 'middle class'. By birth I was lower class" (1983, 12). For El Saadawi, whether upper, middle, or lower class, Arab women share a similar subordination to men, which in turn becomes the basis for solidarity between women across class lines.

This solidarity among women is expressed by both Adnan and El Saadawi through narrative technique. El Saadawi's narrator, who as a professional is considered a respectable member of society, reports feeling like an "insignificant insect" compared to Firdaus who, as a prostitute, is conventionally considered at the bottom of social hierarchy (El Saadawi 1983, 3). When Firdaus finally grants the narrator an interview with her, the narrator exclaims: "I was full of a wonderful feeling, proud, elated, happy.... It was a feeling I had known only once before.... I was on my way to meet the first man I loved for the first time"(6). By likening her feelings for Firdaus to those of a lover, the narrator establishes the strength of the interpersonal link between Firdaus and herself, both examiner and subject becoming intertwined in each other's lives like lovers.[3]

Such an intertwining between narrator and narrative subject destabilizes the professional's own narrative authority.[4] Identifying El Saadawi's narrator as a "Shahrazadian character" (Malti-Douglas 1995, 44), Fedwa Malti-Douglas points out that in *The Thousand and One Nights* Shahrazad "has not created her text" but has "merely learned it and is transmitting it," adding that "it is Shahriyar who has them [the stories] written down, to be eventually copied and distributed by his male successor" (1991, 23, 28). As Malti-Douglas makes apparent, *The Thousand and One Nights* seems to identify the written text with a type of male scribal authority that supersedes the power of the female oral transmission of preexisting texts (23, 28).

Unlike *The Thousand and One Nights*, however, El Saadawi's text endows Firdaus's oral account with originality, reserving the role of transmitter to the now female scribe. In so doing, El Saadawi at once disrupts any clear identification of either Firdaus or the narrator with the figure of Shahrazad. While Shahrazad's nightly storytellings extend her life and win the love of her would-be executor, Firdaus's oral account of her life story does not save her life. On the contrary, she "even refuse[s] to sign an appeal to the President so that her sentence be commuted to imprisonment for life" (El Saadawi 1983, 1). Preferring death to a compromise in personal integrity, Firdaus tells the narrator: "I want nothing. I hope for nothing. I fear nothing. Therefore I am free. For during life it is our wants, our hopes, our fears that enslave us. The freedom I enjoy fills them with anger. They would like to discover that there is after all something which I desire, or fear, or hope for. Then they know they can enslave me once more" (101). The only form of self-assertion left open to Firdaus is in an ironic sort of triumphant negation. Transforming the murder weapon from a literal knife to a figurative truth, Firdaus insists that "to have arrived at the truth means that one no longer fears death.... And truth is like death in that it kills. When I killed I did it with truth not with a knife" (102).

Rather than signaling the end of the narrative, Firdaus's death gives El Saadawi the reason as well as the material for her own contribution, through writing, to the critique of oppressive social structures.[5] Like Shahrazad, who "consciously takes on her shoulders the burden of saving womankind from the royal serial murderer" (Malti-Douglas 1995, 107), the narrator, herself a figure who stands in for the actual writer, records Firdaus's story in order to "challenge and to overcome those forces that deprive human beings of their right to live, to love and to real freedom" (El Saadawi 1983, iv).

Significantly, the vacillating identifications of both the narrator and protagonist with the figure of Shahrazad grant Firdaus's oral delivery the authority usually reserved for written forms at the same time that they endow El Saadawi's written text with the incantatory and spellbinding aspects of the oral. For recorded within the written account is an insistence on the validity of the oral. Endowing the power of her voice to a privileged listener, Firdaus, who first "asked for pen and paper, then spent hours hunched over them without moving" so that she seemed to be "not writing anything at all," commands the writer, "Let me speak. Do not interrupt me" (El Saadawi 1983, 1, 11). As the narrator notes: "her voice continued to echo in my ears, vibrating in my head, in the cell, in the prison, in the streets, in the whole world, shaking everything, spreading fear wherever it went, the fear of the truth which kills, the power of truth, as savage, as simple, and as awesome as death...." (108). Describing writing *Woman at Point Zero* as a form of exorcism of the haunting effect of Firdaus upon her, El Saadawi remarks: "She ... vibrated within me, or sometimes lay quiet, until the day when I put her down in ink on paper and gave her life after she had died" (iii). As Barbara Harlow notices, by passing on her story to El Saadawi, Firdaus "allow[s] her individual act of challenge and defiance to become part of the public record of social opposition to the authoritarian political structures and patriarchal hierarchies of Egyptian society" (Harlow 1987, 118). El Saadawi's literary voice allows Firdaus's individual voice to be heard after death. In turn, Firdaus's struggle for independence and autonomy provides El Saadawi with the material necessary for exposing the political, economic, and social structures that ensure the continued subordination of females to males in patriarchal society.

Like *Woman at Point Zero, Sitt Marie Rose* is concerned with the relationship between female speech, narrative voice, and the death of the defiant, outspoken woman. Like El Saadawi's narrator, Adnan's narrator also discovers a kind of truth in her protagonist's assertion of self even in the face of torture and death: "When I'm right I know it.... Then I take off, believing that I'm really free of the cage. But to discover a truth is to discover a fundamental limit, a kind of inner wall to the mind, so I fall again to the ground of passing time, and discover that it's Marie Rose who's right" (Adnan 1982, 100).

Unlike *Woman at Point Zero*, however, *Sitt Marie Rose* highlights the struggles of the female narrator herself for finding a narrative voice of her own. In so doing, Adnan creates a stronger identification between her primary female narrator and protagonist than does El Saadawi. While El Saadawi's narrator occupies a somewhat privileged position within the text, Adnan's narrator occupies a subaltern position, for she must, like the protagonist Marie Rose, fight those forces that would stifle her self-expression. In the first section of *Sitt Marie Rose*, "Time I: A Million Birds," Mounir, who stands for sensitive yet privileged, upper-class, French-educated, Lebanese Christian males, wants the female narrator to write the script for a film he wants to make with her. At the same time, he doesn't want her to contribute her ideas to it. He tells her, "I want to make a film with you. But it will be my film. I just want to make it with you.... You'll write the script. I'll make the film" (Adnan 1982, 4, 7). Denied her own narrative voice, the "script-writer" becomes simply a reflection of Mounir's "modernism," part of his entourage, but not an actual contributor. Indeed, Adnan's narrator-figure first identifies herself as one of the women who provide an audience to Mounir's film of his hunting trip in Syria with his male friends: "'We women' were happy with this little bit of imperfect, colored cinema which gave, for twenty minutes, a kind of additional prestige to these men we see every day" (4). As Mounir would have it, women function either as audience or echo for men.[6]

Significantly, what is being silenced is the political edge to the narrator's voice. She wants to investigate the lives of Syrian workers in Lebanon because, to her, "This film should say something" (Adnan 1982, 7). Mounir, however, wants to concentrate on a romanticized, orientalist image of Syrian villagers; to him, the "people there are very simple, very hospitable, not at all ruined" by the modernity that he, as a Lebanese, presents to them with his "touristo-military gear" (5, 3). This desire to depict the other as a voiceless mass is explicated in the second section of the text. In "Time II: Marie Rose," Marie Rose's deaf-mute Lebanese pupils, themselves constructed as "the People" but nonetheless given a collective voice within Adnan's work, offer a definition of the subaltern within the text. Speaking of how Marie Rose takes them to the movies twice a year, they discuss an Egyptian film they saw:

> The people in the film were different. They were smiling and laughing all the time.... We have been told that to be The People is to be like [sic] in the film, lots and lots of smiling folks. When we grow up, we'll be The People too.... It's not enough just to be poor to be The People. You have to be docile and innocent. You have to be a part of things like [sic] clouds are a part of the sky. [44-45]

Unwilling to share the female narrator's interest in the problems facing Syrian workers in Lebanon, Mounir wants to impose a romanticized image upon the Syrian villagers, who become for him, "The People," a voiceless part of "the beauty of the [Syrian] desert (6). Assuming the attitude of the European orientalist, whose romanticized visions of the East and its peoples, as Edward Said has demonstrated, went hand in hand with European colonialist projects, Mounir elicits the help of his "friend Jean-Pierre from Paris" and misidentifies himself as European, not Lebanese, in relation to the Syrians. He tells the narrator: "we were the first Europeans they [the villagers] had ever seen. Excuse me, I mean Lebanese" (7,5). In the original French of *Sitt Marie Rose*, Mounir's verbal slip appears at once natural and self-condemnatory, since French, not Arabic, would be the most likely language of choice among French-educated Lebanese (whether Christian or Muslim) who, like Etel Adnan herself, were forbidden to speak Arabic in school (Adnan 1990, 7).

Mounir's attitude toward the Syrian villagers in Time I provides an opportunity for exposing the connection between denying speech to the subaltern and what Spivak terms "colonial production." More to the point, his attitude toward women in general and the narrator in particular demonstrates how "the subaltern as female is even more deeply in shadow." Women in Mounir's world are allowed a narrative voice so long as that voice remains an echo of a hegemonic vision of male orientalist power. As Adnan remarks about her own engagement with political, feminist writing in *Sitt Marie Rose*, "it is not in the literary world but in the political world that men resent women who express themselves freely" (1985, 119).

In an article that first appeared in 1978, the same year as the publication of *Sitt Marie Rose*, Yolla Polity Sharara notes, "Political questions [in Lebanon] were settled for us at the level of what is 'done' and what is 'not done,' of what was or was not suitable for a woman" (1983, 20). Refusing to be bound to such constraints, Adnan, a French-educated, Catholic-baptized, Syrian-Lebanese, rejects the sectarianism that cannot represent her. Writing in French while using Lebanese-specific Arabic terms such as "Sitt" for "Mrs." and "Bouna" for "Father," Adnan refuses allegiance to any specific group, and insists that the sectarianism of the Christian right is a specifically Arab malady. Linking in one breath, "Islamic tribes in southern Tunisia" and "Christian tribes from the Lebanese mountains," *Sitt Marie Rose* depicts the prevailing Arab mentality "from the Gulf to the Atlantic" as one that is closed in upon itself: "The scouts of the clan hunt and bring the prey back to the fold" (Adnan 1982, 101). While such a critique of the Arab world remains at the level of generalization, it does allow Adnan to present the sectarianism that erupted in Lebanon at the beginning of the civil war not as an aberration or peculiarity of the Lebanese or the Christians, but rather as part of a larger regional problem epitomized in the picture of "concentric circles" of allegiance proposed by "this hero of Arab History," Gamal Abdel Nasser, circles which for the narrator become redefined as "circles of oppression" (103). In focusing on a woman protagonist who defies the norms of what is "done" and what is "not done," Adnan articulates her generalized political critique of tribalism in particularized gendered terms.

Speaking of Lebanese women writers of the civil war, whom she calls "Beirut Decentrists," and among whom she numbers Etel Adnan, Miriam Cooke notes: "These women used discourse to undermine and expose assumptions so that their experience was not only accommodated along with that of the men but in some cases came to supplant it.... By the late 1970s, the Beirut Decentrists were using language to create a new reality. Their writings were becoming transformative, even prescriptive" (1988, 11). Of her own project Adnan comments: "Women are the theme of my novel *Sitt Marie Rose*, women within the Arab context and more particularly against the background of the Lebanese civil war (1985, 119). Indeed, what Adnan does in *Sitt Marie Rose* is what Sharara says must be done for the war in Lebanon: "To try to see in the present political situation in Lebanon an antagonism of class and of religious communities, but also an antagonism between the sexes, to try to see the war through, and starting from, the feminine universe" (Sharara 1983, 25). This "feminine universe" is depicted for us in *Sitt Marie Rose* through the interweaving of a some-times overly didactic feminine narrative voice with the events surround-ing Marie Rose's abduction and murder.

Significantly, it is the outbreak of the war in Lebanon that occasions the narrator's break from restrictive gender roles. With the disruptions of normalcy brought about by the war, the narrator feels that "the mecha-nism of time is out of order" (Adnan 1982, 15). Such a dislocation of time brings with it an end to the narrator's acquiescence to the gender, social, political, and artistic roles carved out for her in Mounir's world. After Mounir refuses to consider the plight of three Syrian workers who were killed in Lebanon, insisting instead that such a thing would be "too vio-lent, too political" and counter to his "point of view," the narrator puts an end to her artistic collaboration with him. Her final words in Time I, which ironically are lost on Mounir, are: "I think Mounir that I really can't make this film with you" (24).

Following upon the narrator's rejection of Mounir's narrative and political visions, Time II functions as a type of defiant narrative response to Mounir, whose world-view is shown to be no longer viable in the com-motion of war. The loosening of pre war conventions is highlighted through the actions of "the young couple who live downstairs making love on their verandah in the middle of the afternoon," and who "never would have been so innocent normally" (Adnan 1982, 17). In the shift from Time I to Time II, Adnan's text enacts within it a narrative move away from a male-defined, "colonialist" closed narrative to a female-centered open text. Unlike Mounir, who, in spite of his sensitivity is nonetheless "com-pletely locked into [his] own logic," so that he views the war as "clean and definitive," where "there will be a victor and a vanquished," Adnan repeat-edly shows that "in this country there were too many factions, too many currents of ideas, too many individual cases for one theory to contain" (46, 74, 33, 75). Indeed, throughout *Sitt Marie Rose*, but especially in Time II, we are presented with a narrative that is "fragmented into sections," where no one character, including the narrator, "has an exact image of the whole" (17). News reports mingle with eyewitness accounts, fictional imaginings, historical facts, didacticism, and the thoughts of deaf-mutes.[7] In the words of Elizabeth Warnock Fernea, Adnan's narrative strategy presents a "liter-ary *bricolage*," one that "uses traditional and modern literary conventions from both East and West and from oral as well as written traditions, as well as ethnography, journalism, and film" (1989, 1, 163).

The first person narrator is repeatedly displaced in this narrative, in which the narrative "I" shifts and becomes occupied by many different figures, ranging from Bouna Lias, the friar who sanctions the militiamen's actions, to the militiamen themselves, Mounir, the deaf-mutes, Marie Rose, and the narrator. Depicting its narrator as omniscient observer and involved participant, Adnan's text, in Thomas Foster's words, "simultaneously establishes its narrative authority and problematizes the position of the narrating subject" (1995, 61). As the narrator describes herself: "I saw a plant and it seemed very straight to me, and to know where it was going. I allowed myself to say: I'm like that, I climb, I raise myself, I hover above this city, this country, and the continent to which they belong.... I've surveyed the currents which cross this part of the world, following some, opposing others, dismantling the mechanism of false alliances, and smelling out traitors like garlic in cooking. I know what's going on. But in fact, I am more like a four-footed animal than the plant. I go along with my head always to the ground" (Adnan 1982, 39). Registering the impulse toward omniscience, Adnan's narrator acknowledges her limitations and figuratively brings herself back down to earth. Adnan's text thus seems to offer a direct alternative to the type of narrative exemplified by Mounir, whose inability to tolerate a multiplicity of factions and ideas in both his film and "ideal country" leads directly to his permission of Marie Rose's execution (75).

Adnan's refusal to be bound to any one narrative technique in *Sitt Marie Rose* is a textual mirroring of Marie Rose's own refusal to adhere to a tribal mentality that would confine her geographically, ideologically, and emotionally to her own community. While she acknowledges that "everyone warned [her] not to cross the line which divides the city into two enemy camps, she nonetheless insists on crossing and recrossing the line both literally and figuratively (Adnan 1982, 31). Unconventional, she refuses to be like the "women [who] stay at home more than ever" because they "consider the war like an evening of scores between men" (13). Instead, as she puts it: "I continued to fight the visible and invisible things that thwarted me" (49). A Christian living in West Beirut, she crosses the green line into East Beirut in order to teach her deaf-mute students, who recognize that their parents view them as "worthless" and "put [them] in this school" where "only Sitt Marie Rose loves [them]" (44). Refusing to succumb to a suffocating marriage, she seeks out a university education, obtains a divorce, and tries to raise her three sons in a way that breaks from the tribalism so decried throughout the text (50). She throws herself "into a sort of public life"; in Mounir's words, "First it was educational reform, then it was the typographer's strike, then women's liberation ... " (49, 35). She joins the Palestinian resistance and has a Palestinian lover with whom she finds mutual love and respect (38, 70-72). It becomes obvious that Marie Rose's politicization coincides with — indeed seems an integral part of — a personal, feminist, and sexual awakening.

Refusing to play "servile roles," Marie Rose crosses the "green line," and figuratively breakes down the "barricades, which are also called barriers, as though it were necessary both to hold back the weight of a quarter's anger as well as to keep out the enemy" (Adnan 1982, 13-14). In turn, what unleashes the militiamen's anger toward Marie Rose is not simply her political allegiances, but rather the way that her political actions are intertwined with her defiance of gender and sexual roles. She of the blue eyes, which to Mounir represent modernity and westernization, nonetheless refuses to "come back to the community" (34, 64). As the narrator would have us understand it, the men react violently to Marie Rose because, "finding themselves before a woman who can stand up to them," they "are terrified" (68). While for Fouad women and war should not mix — "I didn't position artillery on the hills of this city to get myself mixed up in some story about a woman"— for Tony, the very entry of women into politics becomes a sign of female sexual depravation: "when whores like this get mixed up in war, now that's something to get disgusted about" (37, 60). Political transgression becomes cast here as sexual transgression. Ironically, only after her rebellion does Mounir take Marie Rose seriously. In his words, "it's taken nearly a year of civil war, hundreds dead every day in Beirut, and an upsetting of the old alliance between heaven and earth, for me to conceive of a woman as a worthy partner, ally or enemy" (35). As the narrator puts it, Marie Rose "was, they admit, a worthy prey.... She was a woman, an imprudent woman, gone over to the enemy and mixing in politics, which is normally their personal hunting ground" (100). The once fashionable bird hunters become here eager predators who cannot tolerate Marie Rose's rejection of their macho world-order: "Like a bird flying alone in a seemingly untroubled sky, Marie Rose was cut down by hunters on the look-out" (103).

As Adnan sees it, the violence inflicted upon Marie Rose stems from displaced maternal love; in the narrator's words, the "exclusive love of the mother sets the cycle of violence in motion" (Adnan 1982, 67). In contrast to the men's "sick sexuality" and "mad love, where images of crushing and cries dominate," Marie Rose presents for Adnan an alternative image of the feminine and maternal (66). Alluding to her namesake, who is often symbolized by a rose, the deaf-mutes remark: "She looks like the Blessed Virgin at church, the big one, the one that stares at us during mass" (45). Unlike her namesake, however, Marie Rose is not asexual. On the contrary, she is at once maternal, sexual, and independent, as is evidenced by her love for both her own children and the deaf-mutes, by her relationship with a Palestinian doctor, and by her refusal to be bound to oppressive social and political codes.

The critique of the maternal in *Sitt Marie Rose* has been noted by such critics as Foster and Accad. To Foster, the militiamen's lesson to Marie Rose's deaf-mute pupils, which was intended to show them what happens to traitors, instead allows "the children [to] learn that their teacher's love does not offer the security of a maternal space" (1995, 71). Accad sees in Adnan's critique of possessive motherhood a failure to acknowledge "the fact that mothers are also victims of the patriarchal-tribal society" (1990, 66).

What is significant for the purposes of this essay is how Marie Rose reconfigures the maternal in Adnan's text. Addressing the ways in which women's cooperation of the war was elicited, Sharara notes: "Radio programmes were specifically directed at women from both sides. Despite references to the 'Cedar of Lebanon' [the Christian right]—or the Arab destiny of the same Lebanon—[primarily Moslem Lebanese supporters of the Palestinians] these programmes were very similar.... They exalted the spirit of sacrifice of the mothers who had borne the heroes.... "*Ommash-shahid*", the mother of the martyr, became the object of endless glorification" (1983, 28). Refusing to become the mother of martyrs, Marie Rose becomes herself a martyr.

Told to think of her children in considering her exchange for her Palestinian lover, Marie Rose remarks: "How could I tell my children that I owed my life to such a deal?" (Adnan 1982, 88). Indeed, at several crucial moments in the text, we are told that Marie Rose has three sons whom she leaves in West Beirut to come teach and love the deaf-mute children in East Beirut, that she has three sons and a Palestinian lover, and that she has three sons and espouses the Palestinian cause. The narrative's refusal to disassociate Marie Rose's maternal, sexual, and political lives makes possible an image of the maternal that neither denies sexuality and political activism for women, nor demands absolute devotion from offspring, especially sons.

Significantly, the concern with maternal love is also in El Saadaw's *Woman at Point Zero*. However, while in Adnan's text the violence inflicted upon Marie Rose is shown to stem in part from displaced maternal love, in El Saadawi's text the violence inflicted upon Firdaus is repeatedly shown to be a product of a patriarchal structure that can deflect even maternal love for its own purposes. Drawing upon specific imagery and word-order repetition that function as a refrain within the novel, El Saadawi traces Firdaus's coming of age as a movement away from the maternal loving gaze and protection to abandonment and scopic, sexual objectification. Recalling her feelings toward her mother, Firdaus remarks: "I can remember two eyes ... that alone seemed to hold me up.... I only had to look into them for the white to become whiter and the black even blacker, as though sunlight was pouring into them from some magical source" (El Saadawi 1983, 16-17). When the mother participates in Firdaus's sexual excision and takes her husband's side against her daughter, the maternal gaze loses its brightness and thereby signals the mother's participation in the subordination and oppression of women and girls in patriarchal societies. After recurring at several crucial moments in the text, the eye imagery becomes ultimately a sign of Firdaus's victimization: "In the dark I suddenly perceived two eyes, or rather felt them, moving towards me very slowly, closer and closer. They dropped their gaze with slow intent down to my shoes, rested there for a moment, then gradually started to climb up my legs, to my thighs, my belly, my breasts, my neck and finally came to a stop, fastening themselves steadily in my eyes, with the same cold intent" (41-42).

The once maternal, loving gaze becomes transformed within the course of the text into an invasive male weapon of female commodification. In this way, the text illustrates what El Saadawi insists on elsewhere, that "the oppression of women in any society is in its turn an expression of an economic structure built on land ownership, systems of inheritance and parenthood, and the patriarchal family as an in built social unit" (El Saadawi 1980, 4). Beginning with her forced marriage, where her uncle sells the not yet nineteen-year old Firdaus to an abusive and repulsive man over sixty for the price of one hundred pounds, Firdaus is passed from one sort of "pimp" to another. The process demonstrates El Saadawi's views on how "marriage customs and laws followed in ... patriarchal and class society ... have transformed woman into merchandise, which can be bought in exchange for a dowry and sold at the price of an alimony" (51). When Firdaus finally flees from her marriage, she finds herself tricked by her would-be savior, Bayoumi, who locks her up and invites other men to rape her as he does. When she manages to run away from Bayoumi, she meets Sharifa, whose name ironically means honor in Arabic, who shows her how women themselves can profit from selling their own bodies.

Significantly, El Saadawi connects Firdaus's commodification to her inability to articulate her own voice. In response to Bayoumi's question on whether she prefers oranges or tangerines, Firdaus finds herself unable to respond: "I tried to reply but my voice failed me. No one had asked me before whether I preferred oranges or tangerines.... As a matter of fact, I myself had never thought whether I preferred oranges to tangerines, or tangerines to oranges.... 'Tangerines,' I answered. But after he had bought them, I realized that I liked oranges better, but I was ashamed to say so, because the tangerines were cheaper" (El Saadawi 1983, 47). As a poor female, Firdaus had been denied freedom of choice — expressed through a loss of voice — to such an extent that she is unable to articulate her own desires.

Paradoxically, the only form that Firdaus can find for self-assertion and economic control over her body is in her active (as opposed to forced) choice of prostitution. For only when Firdaus chooses to become an independent prostitute does she attain any degree of control over her life: "How many were the years of my life that went by before my body, and my self became really mine, to do with them as I wished? ...Now I could decide on the food I wanted to eat, the house I preferred to live in, refuse the man for whom I felt an aversion no matter what the reason... " (El Saadawi 1983, 68-69). Here we notice that for Firdaus emancipation means concrete control over her own body, her own wishes — her own voice — and her immediate surroundings. But it is only after she gains control over her economic situation that Firdaus begins to control her voice, her body and her life. Ironically, only by selling her body, or her honor, as it is perceived in Arab society, can Firdaus attain dignity and power over her life.[8] For as she discovers in her attempt to gain social respectability, "as a prostitute [she] had been looked upon with more respect, and been valued more highly than all the female employees, [herself] included" (75).

In its ironic depiction of social degradation as female empowerment, El Saadawi's narrative also depicts each successive form of abuse that Firdaus experiences as an enlightenment that tears the veil of ignorance and acquiescence from her eyes. Firdaus lives in a society where, as she discovers at a young age, the "rulers [are] men," money buys power, and cultural and religious practices serve only those already in power (El Saadawi 1983, 27, 65, 12, 18). Her life experience dramatizes El Saadawi's view that even "religion ... serves the same purpose as juridical, educational, police and even psychiatric systems used to perpetuate the patriarchal family" (27). No matter how hard she tries, Firdaus cannot be free from the power of patriarchal structures over her life. Marzouk, a powerful pimp, proves to her that he has more money as well as more influence with the police and the courts of law than she, and thus more means at his disposal to dominate her (92). The only recourse left for Firdaus to resist such an assault on her independence is to kill Marzouk and thus die from a crime she herself has committed rather than from one committed against her (101). Ironically, this final act of self-assertion is depicted as a kind of reverse-rape: "everything in my hand could be moved with a natural ease, even if it were a sharp knife which I thrust into a chest and then withdrew. It would penetrate in and come out with the natural ease of air entering the lungs and then flowing out" (102). Unlike her own physical violations, however, Firdaus regards her action as different in kind from the type of physical violations to which she had been repeatedly subjected. She tells the narrator: "I am a killer, but I've committed no crime" (100).

If El Saadawi offers a critique of patriarchal co-optation of maternal love in an effort to expose the destructive powers of patriarchal hegemony as seen in their ultimate commodification of women, Adnan offers a more hopeful restatement of the maternal through Marie Rose, who "represent[s] love, new roads, the unknown, the untried" (Adnan 1982, 58). This love is itself presented as an alternative to what Adnan depicts as the Lebanese right's misguided Christianity. Attributing their actions to the legacy of French colonial influence in Lebanon, Marie Rose claims that the Christian militias act as they do "because they were taught by Jesuits who oriented them toward Paris and the quarrels of the French kings" (47). She elaborates, "The Crusade which I always thought was impossible has, in fact, taken place. But it's not really religious. It's part of a larger Crusade directed against the poor.... Jerusalem is the great absent. It is no longer in the Middle East" (52).

Counter to this misdirected Christianity, which has lost both its spiritual and political origins, Adnan offers through Marie Rose a type of love that underscores traditional understandings of charity, a sentiment the narrator finds lacking in both Christian and Muslim fighters in Lebanon: "The Churches of the Arab East are those of the catacombs, those of the Faith, of course, but also those of obscurity. They still define themselves in opposition to an imaginary paganism. ... Set against these churches is an Islam that forgets all too often that the divine mercy affirmed by the first verse of the Koran can only be expressed by human mercy" (Adnan 1982, 65). In contrast to such a lack of charity, Marie Rose accusingly tells Bouna Lias, "I know that the only true love is the love of the Stranger" (95).

This stranger is depicted in the text by the Palestinians, who for Marie Rose "represent a new beginning," an alternative to the current state of the Arab world "made up of sects and sub-sects, ghettos, communities, worked by envy, rotten, closed back on themselves like worms" (Adnan 1982, 57).[9] The proof of this alternative for Marie Rose is the fact that "mixed in the blood of the dead Palestinians is as much Lebanese blood, Lebanese who died for them, and with them" (57). And the lie to Mounir's claim to total representation of the Lebanese by his group is the fact that "half of the country, made up of as many Christians as Moslems ... are fighting for and with the Palestinians" (57).[10]

It is important to note, however, that while Adnan insists on representing the Palestinians and those who fight with and for them as an alternative to the tribalism of the Arabs, both Christian and Muslim, she nonetheless registers her awareness of the idealism of such claims and of the deeper complexity of the issues at hand. As the narrator puts it toward the end of the book: "She [Marie Rose] believed that this cause must be sacred to all, and when she suspected hypocrisy, she silenced her mistrust" (Adnan 1982, 102). Indeed, this "mistrust" is voiced and muted several times within the text. The deaf-mutes mention that just as the Christian militiamen tear apart a sheep in order to eat its liver, so too those militiamen "do the same thing with the Moslems and Palestinians" (44). At the same time, however, the deaf-mutes also reluctantly acknowledge that "they say the Moslems and Palestinians do the same thing to Christians. It's possible" (44). When the narrator comments on how "the Chabab [the young men], had to bring women back to order, in this Orient, at once nomadic and immobile," she also notes that "on the Palestinian side, they dealt with crimes similarly" (100). In such ways the text acknowledges the possible blindness of its own idealism.

Just as the Palestinians represent the possibilities for a new beginning whose success is doubted within the text, so too the deaf-mute children, who are made witnesses to Marie Rose's execution, provide a doubtful hope for the forging of a new political language in Lebanon and the Arab world, a hope that is undercut at the moment of its articulation. Positioned as speechless, the deaf-mutes are paradoxically given a collective voice within the text: "In this classroom ... there's US, the deaf-mutes" (Adnan 1982, 29). Unable to hear what is around them, uttering "sounds that make people shudder it seems," the deaf-mute children nonetheless "can forecast earthquakes" and can dance to vibrations that their bodies feel (29). Their deafness highlights their incomprehension and exclusion from the events taking place before their eyes, while their muteness reveals their inability to make their voices heard by others. Coupled with their exclusion from the events around them, their child-like prescience underscores the need "to learn the special languages that will help us communicate with others"(29). This need for a new language is emphasized by Marie Rose when, upon her abduction, she registers her recognition that with the words of the militiamen, she "was leaving the world of ordinary speech" (32).

Thomas Foster regards the collective voice of the deaf-mutes as an alternative type of "national unity that does not depend on the ideological containment of women within the horizon of motherhood" (1995, 71). If this is the case, however, Adnan's text itself points out the near impossibilities of such a harmonious unity. Even the children are made to say: "Perhaps one day speech and sound will be restored to us, we'll be able to hear and speak and say what happened. But it's not certain. Some sicknesses are incurable" (Adnan 1982, 82). Shared by many Lebanese, Adnan's skepticism about the possibilities for curing the "sickness" that is both the children's physical condition and the Lebanese society's political status at this early stage in the war exposes the international character of the war in Lebanon: "They have separated the bodies ... the minds, those who govern as well as those foreigners brought on a wind from the West, those from Iran and the Soviet Union, all, all have sown poison herbs in these peasant mentalities, in these uprooted brains, in these slum children, in their schizophrenic student logic. They have done this so that the population, turning a hundred ways at once, loses its way, and sees every mobile being as a target or a sure threat of death" (98). If Marie Rose's death and the children's response to it offer a kind of hope for Lebanon and the Arabs, Marie Rose ironically also risks becoming simply one more casualty of a tribal mentality that can be easily manipulated by outsiders.

Commenting on her decision to present the literary Marie Rose's pupils as deaf-mute, not as mentally retarded as were the pupils of the actual Marie Rose, Adnan says: "I consider that the deaf mutes represent the Arab people" (quoted in Accad 1990, 64). Such a presentation of the Arab people is both complex and problematic. For although the relationship of the narrator to the deaf-mutes is left unproblematized in the text, their treatment as subaltern, unlike Mounir's treatment of the Syrian villagers, at least recognizes both their complicated desires and their exclusion from the events around them. Attracted to the "beautiful guns they [the militiamen] have," the deaf-mutes also dislike the war "because [they] can't take part in it" (Adnan 1982, 30). At the same time, the deaf-mute children are made witness to and celebrants of Marie Rose's triumph-in-death at the hands of her captors. The deaf-mute children's bodies redefine the meaning of Marie Rose's execution as their rhythmic dance to the sound of falling bombs around them acknowledges Marie Rose's refusal to "bow before such a fantasy" as tribalism. According to the narrator, "an execution is always a celebration. It is the dance of Signs and their stabilization in Death" (105). What makes Marie Rose's death triumphant instead of sacrificial is her insistence on affirming her beliefs till the very end.[11] As Adnan says of herself, "I am accustomed to equate freedom with thinking, and I was made ready to understand political rebellion as an affirmation of the self" (1990, 14).

It is precisely in those terms that Adnan depicts Marie Rose's death. Twice within the text, Marie Rose is given a choice between a political surrender that is cast as self-denial and death. Each time she chooses to preserve her integrity. The first instance is when Mounir suggests her exchange with her Palestinian lover (Adnan 1982, 88). The second is when the friar

Bouna Lias recommends that she admit her political errors through a "religious" confession (93). Refusing both, she prefers instead "to keep [her] pride" even at the price of her life (88). Unlike the Belgian reporter mentioned in the text who was captured and released in Vietnam shortly before the war ended, Marie Rose hastens her death, not by swallowing her tongue as the reporter claims he would have done to avoid being tortured, but by refusing to be silenced, by refusing to eat her words as it were (102). Significantly, the response of Adnan's narrator to Marie Rose's fatal outspokenness is a narrative compulsion to provide a verbal critique of the oppressive social structures that sacrifice someone like Marie Rose. Envisioning the entire Arab world as a patient on an operating table, the narrator insists: "The patient should be obliged to spit out, not the mucous, but the original illness, not the blood clogging his throat but the words, the words, the swamp of words that have been waiting there for so long" (100).[12] In *Sitt Marie Rose* the price of death that the resistant woman incurs for her defiance of structures becomes the occasion for both a political critique and a narrative extension of the "silenced" voice. Significantly, Marie Rose's defiant voice is made audible in a textual temporality that allows her voice to be heard after the narrative event of her death. Furthermore, by narrating her death through the admittedly problematic narrative voice of deaf-mutes, Adnan's text asserts Marie Rose's triumph over the forces that would silence and efface her. In turn, what rescues Marie Rose's as well as the deaf-mutes' "voices" from silence and incomprehension is the narrative retelling of Marie Rose's abduction and murder. As the narrator cries out: "It must be said, said so that this civilization ... hears what its masses want to tell it, so that it can scale the final mountain" (100). The very act of narrating Marie Rose's story thus at once enables and extends Marie Rose's own voice at the same time that it empowers the voice of the writer-narrator within the text, a voice that, in a sense, resurrects the murdered defiant woman's voice from the dead.

If death is the means to silence defiant women such as Firdaus and Marie Rose, the literary narrative retelling of those women's experiences by writers like El Saadawi and Adnan ensures that the resistant voices of the murdered women not only continue to be heard after death, but that their now literary voices also become a rallying cry for effective social change. Building upon and redefining the Shahrazadian connection between the death of the sexual female figure and the compulsion to speak, both El Saadawi in *Woman at Point Zero* and Adnan in *Sitt Marie Rose*, in their different ways, contribute to a feminist tradition where one woman passes on her story — and her voice — to another who writes it in her own literary creation, a reciprocal act of support and empowerment as well as a hope for meaningful change in the future. By problematizing and frag-menting the primary narrative voices within her text, Adnan, like El Saadawi before her, encodes orality within the life-giving force of narra-tive retellings even as she extends El Saadawi's critique and makes a more intricate link between voice and feminist writing, between pacificist action and politicized writing. In the striking coincidences and important dis-tinctions between Adnan's and El Saadawi's works we find a feminism and modes of narrative expression that transcend tribalism and defy patriar-chal hegemony. Giving narrative voice to actual women who chose death over silence or co-optation, both Adnan and El Saadawi — in their own ways— manage to conceive of and represent the female subaltern as both "historical subject and agent of an oppositional discourse."

Notes

1. Adnan's novel was banned from East Beirut when it first appeared in French, whereas El Saadawi's works are frequently banned in several Arab coun-tries. However, simply because they were officially banned in certain places does not necessarily mean that these writers were not read in those same places. Peo-ple and their objects crisscrossed the "green line" dividing East and West Beirut at different times throughout the war, and El Saadawi's books appear unofficially throughout the Arab world.

2. For an anthology of Arab feminist writings in English translation, see Bad-ran and Cooke. Also see Evelyne Accad (1990) who maintains elsewhere (1993) that Arab women writers since 1965 "reflect a greater awareness of and commit-ment to the political, social, and sexual issues facing Arab women today" (233).

3. On the Arabic tradition of eroticism associated with women's bodies that goes back to the Middle Ages, see Ahmed (1989, 43). Ahmed, however, sees El Saadawi, especially in *The Hidden Face of Eve*, as identifying an alternate, though equally long tradition, which held a negative attitude toward women's bodies. Associating the professionalism of the narrator with "male standards of rational-ity" as opposed to a more feminine identified solidarity among women that she sees being developed within the text, Françoise Lionnet links the initial reaction of the narrator to Firdaus to El Saadawi's experience of excision (1995, 144). Fedwa Malti-Douglas finds echoes in the narrator's and protagonist's rejoinders to the question of the relationship between cruelty and killing and maintains that the echoing "unites them even before the narrative, with its homosexual subtext, is set in motion" (1995, 67).

4. Several critics have written on the relationship between narrator and pro-tagonist in *Woman at Point Zero*. Françoise Lionnet notes that in *Woman at Point Zero*, "A doubling occurs and functions as a metonymic displacement between author and narrator, whose voices so echo each other that it is hard for the reader to know who speaks" (1995, 144). In contrast, Mona Fayad sees the frame struc-ture as a distancing device that seems to "enclose rather than disclose female sub-jectivity" (1987, 7). My own discussion focuses on the ways in which the elasticity

of the first person narrative "I," which in the frame refers to the writer, but in the narrative itself refers to the protagonist through the writer's transcription, allows for a reconceptualization of narrative voice within the novel.

5. Finding an analogy between Firdaus's knife that kills the pimp and El Saadawi's pen, Lionnet maintains: "Saadawi's inscription of a woman's text on the masculine fabric of Egyptian culture is a form of trespass that deserves punishment because it interferes with the culturally acceptable codes of femininity" (1995, 150). Lionnet does not distinguish between different types of women's writings. It's important, however, to keep in mind that it is not the act but the type of writing that constitutes a trespassing here. See for example, El Saadawi (1993, 43) and Adnan (1985, 119–20).

6. Thomas Foster (1995, 63) makes a similar point.

7. On the didacticism in *Sitt Marie Rose*, see Accad (1990, 65).

8. For a discussion of the way family honor is tied to female chastity and especially virginity in unmarried women, see El Saadawi (1980, 25–32), Mernissi (1987, 46–64), and Hijab (1988, 89).

9. For a detailed look at the text's treatment of 'asabiya, or tribal mentality, see Foster (1995, especially 66).

10. For a critique of what she sees as Adnan's idealistic view of the Palestinian position in Lebanon, see Accad (1990, 73–75).

11. My interpretation here differs from Fayad's, who sees Marie Rose as a sacrificial victim (1987, 5).

12. For a view of speech in *Sitt Marie Rose* as "loving violence," which becomes "the medium of ultimate reconciliation," see Cassidy (1995, 290).

References

Accad, Evelyne. 1990. *Sexuality and War: Literary Masks of the Middle East.* New York: New York University Press.

_____. 1993. "Rebellion, Maturity, and the Social Context: Arab Women's Special Contribution to Literature." In *Arab Women: Old Boundaries, New Frontiers*, edited by Judith E. Tucker, 224–53. Bloomington: Indiana University Press.

Adnan, Etel. 1977. *Sitt Marie Rose.* Paris: Des Femmes.

_____. 1982. *Sitt Marie Rose.* Translated by Georgina Kleege. Sausalito: Post-Apollo.

_____. 1983a. "Outside the Tribe." Interview by Judith Pierce. *The Middle East Magazine* (September) 51–52.

_____. 1983b. "Tribal Mentality." Interview by Inez Reider. *Off Our Backs*, (August-September): 31–32.

_____. 1985. "Interview with Etel Adnan." By Hilary Kilpatrick. In *Unheard Words: Women and Literature in Africa, the Arab World, Asia, the Caribbean, and Latin America*, edited by Mineke Schipper, translated from the Dutch by Barbara Potter Fasting, 114–120. London and New York: Allison and Busby.

_____. 1990. "Growing Up to be a Woman Writer in Lebanon." In *Opening the Gates: A Century of Arab Feminist Writing*, edited by Margot Badran and Miriam Cooke, 5–20. Bloomington and Indianapolis: Indiana University Press.

Ahmed, Leila. 1989. "Arab Culture and Writing Women's Bodies." *Feminist Issues* 9, no. 1 (Spring): 41–55.

Al-Samman, Ghadah. 1977. "The Sexual Revolution and the Total Revolution." Translated by Elizabeth Warnock Fernea and Basima Qattan Bezirgan. In *Middle Eastern Muslim Women Speak*, edited by Elizabeth Warnock Fernea and Basima Qattan Bezirgan, 391–99. Austin: The University of Texas Press.

Badran, Margot, and Miriam Cooke, eds. 1990. *Opening the Gates: A Century of Arab feminist Writing*. Bloomington: Indiana University Press.

Cassidy, Madeline. 1995. "'Love is a Supreme Violence': The Deconstruction Of Gendered Space in Etel Adnan's *Sitt Marie Rose*." In *Violence, Silence, and Anger: Women's Writing as Transgression*, edited by Deirdre Lashgari, 282–90. Charlottesville: University Press of Virginia.

Cooke, Miriam. 1988. *War's Other Voices: Women Writers on the Lebanese Civil War*. Cambridge: Cambridge University Press.

El Saadawi, Nawal. 1980. *The Hidden Face of Eve: Women in the Arab World*. Boston: Beacon.

_____. 1983. *Woman at Point Zero*. Translated by Sherif Hetata. London: Zed.

_____. 1986. "Writing is Power." Interview by Rosemary Clunie. *West Africa* 3598 (August): 1735–1736.

_____. 1989. *Imra'ah 'inda nuktat al-sifer*. Beirut: Dar al-Adab.

_____. 1993. "Feminism and an Arab Humanism: An Interview with Nawal El Saadawi and Sherif Hetata." By Gaurav Desai and David Chioni Moore. *Sapina-Bulletin* 5, no. 1 (January–June): 28–51.

Fayad, Mona. 1987. *The Road to Feminism: Arab Women Writers*. Working Papers on Women in International Development, no. 158 East Lansing: Michigan State University.

Fernea, Elizabeth Warnock. 1989. "The Case of *Sitt Marie Rose*: An Ethnographic Novel from the Modern Middle East." *Studies in Literature and Anthropology* 20: 153–64.

Foster, Thomas. 1995. "Circles of Oppression, Circles of Repression: Etel Adnan's *Sitt Marie Rose*." *PMLA* 110, no. 1 (January): 59–74.

Harlow, Barbara. 1987. *Resistance Literature*. New York: Methuen.

Hijab, Nadia. 1988. *Womanpower: The Arab Debate on Women at Work*. Cambridge: Cambridge University Press.

Lionnet, Françoise. 1995. *Postcolonial Representations: Women, Literature, Identity*. Ithaca, NY: Cornell University Press.

Malti-Douglas, Fedwa. 1991. *Woman's Body, Woman's Word: Gender and Discourse in Arabo-Islamic Writing*. Princeton, NJ: Princeton University Press.

_____. 1995. *Men, Women, and God(s): Nawal El Saadawi and Arab Feminist Poetics*. Berkeley: University of California Press.

Mernissi, Fatima. 1987. *Beyond the Veil: Male-Female Dynamics in Modern Muslim Society*. Revised ed. Bloomington and Indianapolis: Indiana University Press.

Perry, Benita. 1995. "Problems in Current Theories of Colonial Discourse." In *The Post-colonial Studies Reader*, edited by Bill Ashcroft, Gareth Griffiths and Helen Tiffin, 36–44 London: Routledge.

Sharara, Yolla Polity. 1983. "Women and Politics in Lebanon." In *Third World — Second Sex*, edited by Miranda Davies, 19–29. London: Zed.

Spivak, Gayatri Chakravorty. 1988. "Can the Subaltern Speak?" In *Marxism and the Interpretation of Culture*, edited by Cary Nelson and Lawrence Grossberg, 271–313. Urbana and Chicago: University of Illinois Press.

About the Contributors

Lisa Suhair Majaj is co-editor, with Amal Amireh, of *Going Global: The Transnational Reception of Third World Women Writers* (Garland, 2000) and with Paula W. Sunderman and Therese Saliba of *Intersections: Gender, Nation and Community in Arab Women's Novels* (Syracuse University Press, forthcoming 2002). Her essays on Arab-American literature and culture have appeared in various journals and collections including *U.S. Ethnicities and Postcolonial Theory* (University of Mississippi Press, 2000) *Arabs in America* (Temple University Press, 1999), *Memory and Cultural Politics* (Northeastern University Press, 1996). She also publishes poetry and creative essays. Majaj studied at the American University of Beirut and the University of Michigan, and has held teaching and research positions at Northeastern University, Amherst College and College of the Holy Cross. She currently lives in Cyprus.

Amal Amireh is Assistant Professor of English, world literature and postcolonial theory at George Mason University. She is author of *The Factory Girl and the Seamstress: Imagining Gender and Class in Nineteenth-Century American Fiction* (Garland 2000), and is co-editor, with Lisa Suhair Majaj of *Going Global: The Transnational Reception of Third World Women Writers* (Garland 2000). Her essays on Arab women and Arabic literature have appeared in *Signs: World Literature Today*, and *Edebiyat: The Journal of Middle Eastern Literatures*. Before joining George Mason University, Amireh taught at An-Najah National University and Birzeit University, both in the West Bank/Palestine. Her current work focuses on gender, nationalism, and Islam in postcolonial literature.

John Champagne is an Associate Professor of English at Penn State Erie, the Behrend College. He is the author of *The Ethics of Marginality: A New Approach to Gay Studies* (University of Minnesota Press, 1995). His essays have appeared in such journals as *College English, College Literature, Cinema Journal, Genders,* and *Boundary 2*.

Simone Fattal was born in Damascus, Syria. She studied Philosophy and Humanities in Beirut and then in Paris at the Sorbonne. An artist, she started painting in 1969 and had several one-woman and group shows. Before the Lebanese civil war, she was an art critic for Beirut radio. In 1982, in Sausalito, California, she started the Post-Apollo Press, a press dedicated to publishing literature. She is also a sculptor and a translator. Among her translations include *Rumi & Sufism*, by Eva de Vitray-Meyerovitch, published in 1987. She has also translated short stories from Arabic. In 2000 she participated in the Ceramics Biennale show in Cairo, and also had a one-woman show in Beirut.

Sabah Ghandour teaches English language and literature at the University of Balamand, Lebanon. She received her Ph.D. in Comparative Literature from the University of California at Los Angeles. She is the author of two forewords to Elias Khoury's translated novels, *Gates of the City* and *The Journey of Little Gandhi*, both published by the University of Minnesota Press. Her articles, reviews, and translations appeared in *Mawaqif, Fusul, Emergences, Edebiyat*, the *International Journal of Middle East Studies*, and in edited books.

Mohomodou Houssouba graduated from Ecole Normale Supérieure at Bamako, Mali. He received his Ph.D. in English Studies from Illinois State University. He coordinates the MaliWatch Initiative's documentation program, which sponsors the Mali Symposium on Applied Sciences and independent research projects in public ethics. He is currently writing a novel on the Tuareg rebellions in Mali and Niger from 1990 to 1996.

Annes McCann-Baker publishes three series of books on and from the Middle East for the Center for Middle Eastern Studies at the University of Texas. As editor of the Modern Middle Eastern Literatures in Translation Series, she has been responsible for 36 titles in the three series over the last 17 years. In 1993 she traveled as a Malone Fellow for the National Committee for U.S.-Arab Relations to Syria and Kuwait to participate in the Islamic Studies Program. mcCann-Baker is a member of the American Literary Translators Association, and has presented papers regularly at the annual meetings.

Haas Mroue is a poet and travel writer. His first book of poems, *Beirut Seizures*, was published in 1993. He writes regularly for Frommer's, Fodor's and National Gepgraphic Travel Guides. His latest guide was *Frommer's Memorable Walks in Paris*, published in 2001.

Sami Ofeish is Assistant Professor of political science at the University of Balamand, Lebanon. He received his Ph.D. from the University of Southern California. His articles on lebanon's politics and culture, literature, and theater have appeared in edited books and journals.

Wen-chin Ouyang was born in Taiwan but grew up in Libya. She received a Ph.D. in Arabic literature from Columbia University. She taught Arabic language and literature at the University of Virginia before she moved to London where she is currently a Lecturer in Arabic at the School of Oriental and African Studies (University of London). Her publications include *Literary Criticism in Medieval Arabic-Islamic Culture: The Making of a Tradition* (Edinburgh: Edinburgh University Press, 1997).

Eric Sellin (Ph.D., University of Pennsylvania, 1965) is Professor of French and Francophone Literature at Tulane University in New Orleans since 1991. He has also taught French and Comparative Literature at Temple University and English, Creative Writing, and American Literature at the Universities of Pennsylvania, Bordeaux, Algiers, and Dakar. Sellin is the author of *The Dramatic Concepts of Antonin Artaud* (1965; paperback, 1975), *Reflections on the Aesthetics of Futurism, Dadaism, and Surrealism: A Prosody beyond Words* (1993), and some 200 scholarly articles and translations (many involving Francophone literature). He has guest-edited special issues of *L'Esprit Créateur, Books Abroad, Africana Journal,* and *The Literary Review*. In 1999 the Conseil International d'Etudes Francophones (CIEF) awarded Sellin a "certificat d'honneur" for his life's work on behalf of Francophone studies ("En reconnaissance de sa contribution exceptionnelle au développement des études francophones dans le monde").

Michael Sells is the Emily Judson Baugh and John Marshall Gest Professor of Comparative Religions at Haverford College. His books include *Deseret Tracings: Six Classic Arabian Odes* (Wesleyan, 1989); *Mystical Languages of Unsaying* (University of Chicago Press, 1994); *Early Islamic Mysticism* (Classics of Western Spirituality, 1996); and *The Bridge Betrayed: Religion and Genocide in Bosnia* (University of California Press, 1996); *Approaching the Qur'an: The Early Revelations* (White Cloud Press, 1999); *Stations of Desire* (Ibis Editions, 2000). The latter text includes new translations of poems from Ibn 'Arabi's *Interpreter of Desires,* Sells' commentary on the poems, and a collection of his own poetry. Sells is co-editor and contributor for *The Cambridge History of Arabic Literature, al-Andalus* (2000) and the forthcoming *The New Crusades: Constructing the Muslim Enemy* (Columbia University Press). He is the founder and president of the Community of Bosnia, a non-profit organization dedicated to supporting a peaceful, democratic, and multireligious Bosnia-Herzegovina.

Caroline Seymour-Jorn received her graduate degrees in Anthropology from the University of Chicago. She has researched the social discourse of women writers in Cairo, Egypt. Seymour-Jorn lives in Milwaukee, where she teaches Arabic and Anthoropology at the University of Wisconsin.

Fawwaz Trabulsi is a Lebanese intellectual and journalist. He has written extensively on Arab affairs and Lebanese society, politics, and culture, and has translated works by Gramsci, John Reed, and Edward Said. His books include *Guerica/Beirut, On an Incurable Hope: A Diary of the Siege of Beirut in 1982,* and *Promises of Aden: Yemenese Journeys.* He lives In Beirut, where he teaches History and Political Science at the Lebanese American University.

Pauline Homsi Vinson was born in Lebanon and has a Ph.D. in English literature from Northwestern University. She has taught at various universities both in the U.S. and abroad, including such coountries as Malaysia and the United Arab Emirates. Her interests include contemporary Arab writers, women's studies, and English Renaissance drama, especially Shakespeare.

Index